ROUTLEDGE LIBRARY EDITIONS:
ECONOMICS AND SOCIETY

Volume 6

BRITISH ECONOMIC PERFORMANCE 1880–1980

BRITISH ECONOMIC PERFORMANCE 1880–1980

Edited by
REX POPE
AND
BERNARD HOYLE

Routledge
Taylor & Francis Group
LONDON AND NEW YORK

First published in 1985 by Croom Helm Ltd.

This edition first published in 2026
by Routledge
4 Park Square, Milton Park, Abingdon, Oxon OX14 4RN

and by Routledge
605 Third Avenue, New York, NY 10158

Routledge is an imprint of the Taylor & Francis Group, an informa business

British Library Cataloguing in Publication Data
A catalogue record for this book is available from the British Library

ISBN: 978-1-032-97576-4 (Set)
ISBN: 978-1-041-13622-4 (Volume 6) (hbk)
ISBN: 978-1-041-13628-6 (Volume 6) (pbk)
ISBN: 978-1-003-67071-1 (Volume 6) (ebk)

DOI: 10.4324/9781003670711

Publisher's Note
The publisher has gone to great lengths to ensure the quality of this reprint but points out that some imperfections in the original copies may be apparent.

Disclaimer
The publisher has made every effort to trace copyright holders and would welcome correspondence from those they have been unable to trace.

British Economic Performance 1880-1980

Edited by REX POPE and BERNARD HOYLE

CROOM HELM
London • Sydney • Dover, New Hampshire

Croom Helm Ltd, Provident House, Burrell Row,
Beckenham, Kent BR3 1AT
Croom Helm Australia Pty Ltd, First Floor,
139 King Street, Sydney, Australia

British Library Cataloguing in Publication Data

British economic performance, 1880 – 1980.
1. Great Britain — Economic conditions —
19th century — Sources 2. Great Britain —
Economic conditions — 20th century — Sources
I. Pope, Rex II. Hoyle, Bernard
330.941'082 HC255

ISBN 0-7099-2061-X
ISBN 0-7099-2077-6 Pbk

Croom Helm, 51 Washington St, Dover,
New Hampshire 03820, USA

Library of Congress Cataloging in Publication Data
Main entry under title

British economic performance, 1880-1980

Bibliography: p.
Includes index.
1. Great Britain – Economic conditions – 19th century – Sources. 2. Great Britain – Economic conditions – 20th century – Sources. I. Pope, Rex. II. Hoyle, Bernard.
HC255. B812 1985 330.941'08 84-29217
ISBN 0-7099-2061-X
ISBN 0-7099-2077-6 (Pbk.)

Printed and bound in Great Britain

CONTENTS

Section D: Statistics

PREFACE

This book is designed to fill a gap in the bibliography for modern economic history. To the best of our knowledge, no other documentary collection covers British economic performance over the period selected. The primary concern in selecting extracts was to present contemporary views on economic performance or prospects. These views include observations about the contribution to achievement (or lack of it) of the policies pursued by governments.

The period 1880 – 1980 in British economic history is sometimes seen as something of a rake's progress. There has been a near-continuous and an almost obsessive concern at Britain's economic ills and, inevitably, a large proportion of the extracts reflect this. It is only with the advantage of hindsight that one can see developments in a more balanced historical or international perspective. Even that minority of documents which do adopt a more optimistic outlook appear, at times, misguided to the present-day historian or economist.

The collection was originally devised as a consequence of the commitment to increased use of historical sources in GCE A level syllabuses (see, for instance, the Inter-Board Common Core for History, 1983). It is intended, though, that this book should be of use and interest not only to A level students of History, Economic and Social History, or Economics, but also to students of these subjects in institutions of higher education and to the public at large. The inclusion of extracts incorporating statistics, together with the simple series and diagrams presented in Section D, reflects our belief in the importance of such evidence and in its educational value for students.

The target group determined the pricing and, therefore, the size of this volume. Many potentially useful and interesting sources have, in consequence, had to be omitted.

Rex Pope
Bernard Hoyle
December 1983

ACKNOWLEDGEMENTS

The editors are extremely grateful to the copyright-holders who have kindly allowed their material to be reproduced in this book. In particular, acknowledgement is due in the cases listed below. If the editors have inadvertently included copyright material without making due acknowledgement, they offer their sincere apologies.

Associated Business Press (C19); British Association for the Advancement of Science (B16, B17, B21, B22); Cambridge University Press (D4); Chapman and Hall Ltd (A10); Conservative Research Department (A12); *The Economist* (A13, A14, A15, C10, C11, C15, C17, C18); Economist Intelligence Unit Ltd (C9); Fabian Society (C3); William Heinemann Ltd (A6, A7); the Controller of Her Majesty's Stationery Office (A1, A2, A5, A8, A9, B2, B3, B4, B9, B12, B13, B14, B15, B18, C2, C4, C12, C13, C16); Her Majesty's Treasury (C20, C21); Liberal Party Organisation (A11, B10, B11); Lloyds Bank Review (C14); Macmillan Publishers Ltd (B8); Manchester University Press (B19); the Organisation for Economic Co-operation and Development (C22); Policy Studies Institute (formerly Political and Economic Planning) (B20, C5, C6); *Punch* (C8); Times Newspapers Ltd (B1, B5, B6, B7, C7); the Trustees of the Mass-Observation Archive, University of Sussex (C1).

SECTION A: 1880 – 1914

To contemporaries and many subsequent historians, British economic performance in the last quarter of the nineteenth century appeared to compare unfavourably with what had gone before. Earlier growth rates were not maintained, prices and profits were depressed, unemployment (with its attendant political dangers) was more evident. Some traditional markets were lost and powerful competitors appeared not only abroad but also in domestic trade. In particular, countries like Germany and the United States forged ahead in the adoption of new techniques and the development of science-based industries. From early in the new century, however, conditions appeared to improve. Prices were rising and the years 1907 and 1912 – 13 saw new peaks of economic performance. Old and new industries appeared to be shaking off the effects of foreign competition.

Most of the extracts presented in this section reveal this pattern of concern and later relief, seeking to explain causes and, where appropriate, remedies. *A1* and *A4* discuss the problems of agriculture and *A2*, *A5* and *A6* those of the metal trades. *A7* describes the difficulties faced by a section of the chemical industry, while *A12* purports to deal with those of the woollen and worsted cloth trade. The fact that volumes as well as values are affected is the subject of *A8* and *A9*.

The most common explanation of export problems is the presence of tariffs (e.g. *A2* and *A5*). The adoption of protective duties by Britain is proposed not only as a means of protecting home markets (*A4* and *A12*) but also as a bargaining device or, by implication, as a policy which, by increasing the size of the guaranteed home market, could make British exports more competitive (e.g. *A5*, *A6* and *A12*). Cheapness of rival foreign products is emphasised in *A1*, *A4* and *A5* but attention is also given to the needs of the market (*A5* and *A10*) and to carriage costs (*A1*, *A5* and *A6*). Entrepreneurial failings and backwardness in the adoption of new scientific processes are the main themes of *A7*.

More recently, economic historians have tended towards a more favourable view of Britain's economic performance from the 1870s to the 1890s, giving a less favourable view of the period after 1900.

They point out that the end to Britain's industrial hegemony was inevitable but that, until 1914, her economic strength remained formidable. The current account remained in surplus. Britain owned most of the world's shipping. She remained the world's major exporting nation. Her people were, on average, better off than those in the rest of Europe. There were important areas of expansion (especially in the tertiary sector) and overall indicators of economic performance show rates of growth, at least before 1900, only marginally lower than in the mid-nineteenth century. In short, it is argued that there was no 'great depression' and no 'failure of entrepreneurship'. On the other hand, the early twentieth century is seen as something of an Indian summer, disguising underlying weaknesses in Britain's long-term economic position.

Among the extracts presented in this section, several contain contemporary reactions which share something of the more favourable interpretation of developments in the late nineteenth century. *A3* argues that there is no evidence to support any attempt to redirect trade artificially. *A1* and *A9* refer to Britain's continuing predominance as an exporter of manufactures and the absence of any serious threat from increased imports. The twentieth-century extracts, though, reveal little of the new caution. *A11* restates the case for free trade. *The Economist* (in *A14* and *A15*) welcomes the booms of 1907 and 1912 with an exuberance which most historians would deem injudicious, seeing them and the conquest of competition at home and abroad as further justifications for resisting protection and imperial preference. Only in relation to railways (*A13*) is there any note of concern and their problems are seen largely as the result of interference by central and local government in the transport industries.

A1 Influences on Agriculture (1882)

Causes of Agricultural Depression

There is no question connected with this Inquiry which it is more important to determine than what are the causes to which this great and widespread distress may be attributed.

All the witnesses whom we have examined have agreed in ascribing it mainly to a succession of unfavourable seasons. One witness says 'It is really owing to the absence of sun and the presence of an extra quantity of rain . . . Nothing in fact in the last year or two has matured properly.' Mr. Squarey says 'I believe the approximate and most intense cause of the depression is the series of unfavourable seasons which we have had during the past four, and in some counties five years, and that mischief has been intensified to a great extent by the extremely low quality as well as quantity of the produce in England; whilst on the other hand the Americans have had exceptionally large crops and have been able to send us their produce at prices which have, of course, pro tanto depreciated ours . . .'

Other witnesses concur in regarding as the chief causes of depression, the deficient yield of corn, the poor quality, the low prices of both it and wool, the losses in livestock by contagious and other diseases, and the ungenial seasons, which have rendered the keeping of stock most expensive and the profit nil . . .

Although it may not be possible either to estimate with accuracy the full effect of foreign competition or to anticipate the extent of its furture development, yet it does not admit of question that the unprecedentedly large importations, chiefly from America, have, by lowering the prices of home produce, greatly increased agricultural depression. Nor does there appear to be room for doubt that English farmers must lay their account to a continuance of this competition, pursued with unabated energy and with yearly increasing enterprise.

Local Taxation

Amongst the causes which have tended to aggravate the existing agricultural depression, a prominent place is assigned by witnesses to the presence of local taxation. Although, looking to the increase of population, the amount of the poor's rates does not appear to be excessive, yet the imposition of new rates, viz., the education rate and the sanitary rate, and the increase of old rates, especially the highway rate, in consequence of the abolition of turnpikes, press very heavily upon the agricultural interest.

Railway Rates

Upon the subject of railway rates, we have to report that although the Railway and Canal Traffic Act, 1854, provides 'that no railway or canal company shall make or give any undue or reasonable preference or advantage to or in favour of any particular person or company, or any particular description of traffic to any undue or unreasonable prejudice or disadvantage in any respect whatsoever', yet evidence has been given by several witnesses in support of complaints both of unequal mileage charges and of preferential rates in favour of foreign produce. It is stated that goods can be carried from America to London, *via* Liverpool, at a cheaper rate than from Liverpool to London. Special instances of the charges referred to are found in the evidence.

In the rates for home-grown grain going to Leeds from Wakefield and Doncaster, and for foreign grain going to Leeds from Grimsby, there is a difference in favour of foreign corn of 5s per ton, the rates being 11s and 6s respectively. English wheat put on the railway at stations within six miles of Hull, though nearer to Leeds and Wakefield, would pay more than foreign corn from Hull to Leeds or Wakefield. Upon the other hand, it is alleged by the railway companies that, as American produce is consigned in large quantities from one consigner, it can be conveyed much more economically than if picked up at different stations and in small quantities. It is urged that in order for railways to compete with water carriage, preferential or very low rates are necessary. If railways did not carry at a very low rate from Hull and Glasgow to London, ships, instead of unloading at these ports, would go direct to London.

Education

There is a very general complaint amongst farmers that the present system of education operates prejudicially to the interests of agriculture. Boys, it is said, are kept at school at an age at which they might be usefully employed upon the farm, and be thus acquiring habits and tastes which would fit them for farm service. As it is, the standard of education is so fixed that not only are the first years of industrial training lost before a boy can attain it, but when he does attain it, he acquires with it a desire for what he regards as more suitable occupation, so that the class which was formerly trained into farm service is now gradually absorbed into other industries. Farmers very naturally complain of this, as in districts in which there are School Boards they have to pay for education which not only deprives them, for the present, of the labour of boys, and obliges them to pay men's wages for boys' work, but tends to drain from the land the sources of future labour.

Agricultural Education

We have received a good deal of evidence upon the subject of agricultural education in Great Britain and foreign countries, and the desirableness of encouraging scientific together with practical instruction has been urged by several witnesses.

We concur in these opinions, and, whilst we are not prepared to suggest the manner in which this instruction should be supplied, we are of the opinion that the subject is well worthy of consideration.

Compared with some foreign countries, the facilities for obtaining technical education in Great Britain are very limited, although several county schools have been established for the education of the sons of farmers. The advantage of such an institution as Cirencester College are practically limited to those who, intending to adopt the career of estate agents, to farm, or to emigrate, are able to afford the expense beyond the reach of the ordinary farmer. Some impulse has been given to scientific agricultural education by the scholarships and bursaries founded by the Royal Agricultural Society of England, and the Highland and Agricultural Society of Scotland. In addition to these, the Science and Art Department hold out considerable inducement by the conditions under which they offer half the cost of county scholarships.

from the Report of Her Majesty's Commission on Agriculture (1882): C.3309.

A2 The Depression of Trade and Industry (1886)

(The following are extracts from the evidence given to a Royal Commission by three witnesses.)

(i) *The examination of Mr Charles M. Kennedy, CB* (Head of the Commercial Department of the Foreign Office)

191 (*Chairman: Earl of Iddesleigh*) With regard to the present policy and tendency, I understand you to say that of late years there has been a reaction from the practice and policy of the year 1860 — Yes.

192 From what time should you say that reaction had dated?— That reaction took a definite form about the year 1886.

193 Could you tell us whether that was the case in all of the European countries? — In very many: Russia, Austria, and several others.

194 Subsequently have they been made in other countries? — Yes, alterations in Russia have been continued in subsequent years, and also in Austria. Then there was the commencement

of the present protectionist policy in Germany in 1879, and there have been revisions of the tariff with increase of duties to some extent in France in 1882, and in Switzerland and Greece last year . . .

196 Do you consider that the increase of duties to which you refer is entirely the result of a protectionist policy or tendency? — No, not altogether; it is partly the result of the necessity for an increase of revenue and the resource to indirect taxation for raising the increase of revenue desired.

197 How far do you consider those tariff alterations to have been prejudicial to the revenue of British trade? — They have been distinctly prejudicial to British trade in Spain and in Russia also, the difference being that in Spain the action of the Government was intended to be adverse to British trade, while in Russia it is the result of a general policy of a protectionist character which applies to all foreign trade alike, and which has tended to bring about a considerable diminution in the imports of British products. In other countries, Germany, France and Italy, it does not seem that the British trade as a whole has in the long run been seriously affected, though particular branches of commerce have suffered . . .

(ii) *Evidence from Mr Chas. Belk*, Master Cutler of Sheffield

2659 I do not think there has been any diminution in the number of hands employed in the various trades during the last 20 years, one or two excepted; but material alterations have taken place owing to the requirements changing; for instance, agricultural implements are so much more largely used than formerly, and the demand for sickles and scythes has given place to a demand for machine knives.

Foreign import duties undoubtedly press most heavily on all engaged in the export trades, and there being no part of the habitable world in which our manufacturers are not desirous of trading, the complaints are as bitter as universal of the hindrances offered by such tariffs. These tariffs are in many cases all but prohibitory, and would be entirely so were it not for the demand for special brands. Differential duties are thought to be but aggravations of this general complaint.

Foreign competition is reported to be on the increase, partly by reason of the growing attention to manufacturing by foreign nations, and partly because the longer hours and greater frugality of some of the foreign artisans reduce the cost of labour, and so the price of the finished article. This, of course, refers to competition in neutral markets, the home market of such nations being largely kept to themselves. While there are often loud complaints of our home market being invaded by foreign goods, I think the amount of this competition may very easily be exaggerated and that only in certain branches, and to a limited extent, has this sort of competition developed. I am also of the opinion that in most of our local industries we still hold our own for colonial demand. As is natural, much prominence is given to and much outcry made against foreign competition by those who suffer therefrom, while those unaffected thereby quietly pursue their trading, and so undue weight may be attached to the extent of the evil. With regard to foreign markets, the feeling is that, notwithstanding the advantages of their own producers, we could successfully compete in most of our manufactures but for the tariffs. The introduction of machinery has largely increased the productive powers of some of our staple trades . . .

(iii) *The Examination of Mr Thos. Edmund Vickers*, engaged in the crucible bar and sheet steel trade and also in the manufacture of steel for ordnance, marine and locomotive work

3412 (*Chairman*) With regard to the trade of which you have most experience in bars and sheets, and the trade generally, as far as you are acquainted with it, do you consider that there is at the present time a depression? — There is a great depression . . .

3413 . . . I mean that a number of years ago there was a very large export from Sheffield of steel in bars and sheets for the manufacture of tools of all classes. My business in this trade was chiefly with America, and is now nearly extinct.

3414 That may be a cause, but what do you mean by depression itself, because the losing of a single market does not necessarily imply depression generally? — The loss not only of America but of other markets causes depression.

3415 And have they gained nothing else in return? — No.

3416 What was the cause of your losing these markets? — The high duties against us.

3417 It was not in consequence of any change in the demand for particular classes of goods or the alteration of processes, or anything of the sort? — In this particular trade which I am speaking of, no process has been invented which we have not in England, and we can work to just as great advantage in England as in America.

3418 Then has the trade decreased both in value and in volume, or only in one respect? — The amount of trade in bar and sheet steel with America in 1864 of my firm was £83,000; last year, our whole business with America was under £1,000 in value. Again, our trade with that country in railway material amounted to nearly £100,000 in 1873 and last year it did not reach £1,000 . . .

3426 Are you able to compete with the Americans in national markets? — Certainly; I do not at all believe in American workmen being superior to English workmen, as some people choose to say, and therefore able to manufacture at lower cost.

from the Minutes of Evidence of the Royal Commission on the Depression of Trade and Industry (1886).

A3 Exports and Foreign Competition (1893)

In any question affecting the permanence or changes of our foreign trade, it is the distribution and nature of our exports that we must study. For the payment of our exports ultimately we obtain goods, not money; but immediately the dealer obtains a bill-of-exchange, which answers the same purpose as money, and with which any goods can be obtained from any country. These transactions in the mass with the mechanism of the exchanges must balance each other. The important point to notice is, that, given a market for exports, we may get exactly what we please in return.

The following table shows the present distribution of our exports.

Thus we see that India is our best customer, followed at no great distance by the United States, Germany, and Australia; and that we export about equal quantities to the whole of our possessions and to Europe.

Exports to the following countries of British and Irish produce (Stat. Abstract, 1891):

India and Ceylon		£32 million.
Australia		25 ,,
North America		7 ,,
Other British Possessions		12 ,,
Total British Possessions		£86 million
United States, America	£27 million	
Europe	84 ,,	
Central and South America	19 ,,	
China and Japan	8 ,,	
Other Foreign Countries	23 ,,	
Total Foreign Countries		161 ,,
Total Exports		£247 million

EUROPE.

Germany Holland Belgium	£35 million[a]	
France	16 ,,	
Italy	6 ,,	
Spain and Portugal	7 ,,	
Russia	5 ,,	
Sweden and Norway Denmark and Iceland	7 ,,	
Other European Countries	8 ,,	(approximately)
	£84 million	

[a]Grouped together because part of the exports to Holland and Belgium are re-exported to Germany.

Next let us notice in what way the proportions of our exports to different districts have been changing.

Exports of British and Irish Produce.

	1860.		1870.		1880.		1891.	
	Value.	Per-cent-age.	Value.	Per-cent-age.	Value.	Per-cent-age.	Value.	Per-cent-age.
	Million		Million		Million		Million	
To Europe	£45	33	£76	38	£82	37	£84	34
,, United States, America	21	16	28	14	30	13	27	11
,, British Possessions	43	32	51	26	75	34	86	35
,, Other Countries	26	19	44	22	36	16	50	20
Total	£135	100	£199	100	£223	100	£247	100

A glance at these tables shows first that the distribution of our exports is co-extensive with the world; and secondly, that, divided on the broadest lines, in spite of all changes, the percentages of exports to the same group have remained almost unchanged.

We will briefly consider the meaning of these figures. Our possessions only take one-third of our exports, and this proportion shows no signs of a rapid increase at present; nor is there any sign of decrease. Natural causes and the freedom of trade have fixed this proportion. In thirty years these exports have doubled in value, and we have the satisfaction of seeing both branches of our trade progressing with equal rapidity.

It is important to realise this when any scheme of Imperial federation is under discussion. Any customs union, or commercial arrangement with our colonies, must be an artificial fostering of our colonial relatively to our other trade. Surely the first lesson of these figures is that colonial trade is only of the same importance as European, that during the vicissitudes of thirty years their progress has been the same, and that any tampering with the one in a way which may injure the other can hardly be an advantage to the whole.

That is the first lesson of these figures; but it is, of course, a very small part of the considerations to be taken into account when dealing with our colonial empire, which we will briefly mention without discussion.

In the future are our kinsfolk abroad likely to show marked preference for dealing with England, when trade with other countries is equally or more profitable, and will the greater facilities of intercourse in trading with a nation of the same language and customs bring us colonial trade? Will it be beneficial, if other nations separate themselves into isolated groups by tariffs, to have a vast group of English countries already united, and does this question differ in any way from the general problem of Free Trade? Is it necessary to take precautions to secure a supply of food in case of war, and if so, would federation be a stronger safeguard than the present vast extent and variety of the sources of our wheat? Would federation strengthen us politically, and finally, do the colonies desire it?

The changes in the proportions are so slight that slight causes might have produced them; but they give some indication of the broad changes of the conditions of English trade.

The great proportion to British possessions in 1860 reminds us that the gold discoveries were followed by rapid colonial development.

The increment to Europe and to 'other countries' in 1870 marks the great railway boom.

The continuous proportionate decrease to the States shows the cumulative effects of their tariff, while the slight percentage fall in the case of Europe is due to the increase of their tariffs and the growth of home manufactures.

from A.L. Bowley, *England's Foreign Trade in the Nineteenth Century* (Swan, Sonneschein & Co., 1893).

A4 The Condition of Agriculture (1894)

While the returns show a considerable increase in permanent pasture, there is reason to believe that a large portion of the area so returned, is simply land which has been abandoned, and now grows only weeds and thistles. In 1887 Mr Pryor sent to the newspapers a list of 75 farms, comprising 21,472 acres, within 30 miles of London, all of which were without a tenant, and 3237 of these acres 'absolutely and wholly uncultivated.' In 1890, there was published in the *County Gentleman's Newspaper*, a list of 19 landed properties in England and Scotland, which had been sold for the aggregate price of £662,700, and which had cost the previous owners £1,404,000; 15 others, withdrawn from sale, for which the highest offers only amounted to £363,400, had cost £611,000. The *Manchester Guardian*, an out-and-out supporter of our system, stated in 1889,

> Numerous farms in Essex, Suffolk, and Kent are absolutely idle, which once maintained a happy peasantry, and yet nothing is so certain as that the soil of these counties is the best in the world for the production of wheat, peas, beans, and root and fodder crops. The average yield of wheat in Sheppey on deserted farms was 50 bushels to the acre. The American average is 13 bushels to the acre. A farm of 340 acres on Sheppey, which was bought for £16,000, is now offered for £3400. A farm of 260 acres near Chelmsford, in Essex, is offered at £7 an acre. There is no sign of national decadence so mournful or so certain as this — that the farmer's business is no longer possible in these places. The climate is suitable, the soil is fertile, the people are in want, and yet they may not stretch out their hands for the divine bounty.

The institutions are human and not divine which have brought this to pass, and they must be mended, or they will make an end of us. Forsaken husbandry was a sign of falling Rome, and it is one which ought to arouse our patriotic solicitude in England.

The returns of live stock raised in the United Kingdom have been as follows:

	1870	1880	1893
Cattle	9,235,052	9,871,153	11,207,554
Sheep	32,786,783	30,239,620	31,774,824
Pigs	3,650,730	2,863,488	3,278,030

These figures show some increase, but from the rapidity with which the imports of meat and beef are growing, there is every reason to fear that the raising of live stock will soon become as unprofitable as the cultivation of wheat. These have, on the average been, annually, as follow:

1873–77	1878–82	1883–87	1888–92	1893	
769,212	1,589,558	2,171,352	4,119,851	4,749,494	Cwts.

If there is one point on which all are agreed, free traders and protectionists alike, it is that, under no circumstances, shall the raw materials of industry be taxed. What is land, but the raw material of industry? Yet free traders, who sneer at the fiscal policy of the States, with strange inconsistency, have not a word to say against our not only taxing the land, but taxing it to an extent, far in excess of that borne by other industries, which are not taxed on their raw materials at all.

from A. Williamson, *British Industries and Foreign Competition* (Simpkin, Marshall, Hamilton, Kent & Co., 1894)

A5 Foreign Competition in the Hardware Trade (1895)

The Wolverhampton Chamber of Commerce decided to restrict the inquiry* mainly to the question of wages, hours of labour, and cost

*The inquiry was undertaken in 1895 in order to investigate foreign competition in the hardware trade.

of carriage, and in the first instance to obtain from abroad as much information bearing upon these subjects as might be possible, and then for purposes of comparison to collect corresponding statistics from manufacturers in the United Kingdom.

The inquiries of the committee extended into Germany, Belgium, and France, but as the result of these inquiries tended to show that there was no very serious competition on the part of France with the hardware industries, it was not thought necessary to publish statistics relating to that country. It is sufficient to say that, on the whole, and especially in the iron and steel trades, the wages paid in France appear to be much higher than either in Germany or Belgium.

. . . as far as the iron trade is concerned, the Belgian and German workers (*i.e.* puddlers, shinglers, rollers, and furnace men) will work for an average of 60 (in Germany) and (in Belgium) 65 hours a week, as against the average of 56 hours of an English workman.

The average wage of an overhand iron puddler in England is 7.92d per hour, in Germany, 4d to 5.4d and in Belgium 4.43d.

The average pay of a forge-mill roller of the first grade is 16.34d per hour in England, 7.2d to 8d per hour in Germany, and only 3.78d per hour in Belgium; of a sheet and plate roller of the first grade, 24d per hour in England, 8d to 9.6d per hour in Germany, and 6.64d per hour in Belgium; of a merchant bar roller of the first grade, 20d per hour in England, 7d to 8d per hour in Germany, and 5.72d per hour in Belgium. Other tables published in the report, and relating to various branches of the hardware industries, show similar differences, so that the average wages paid in England are much in excess of the average paid in similar trades abroad, and the average hours worked in England are for the most part from four to six hours per week less. Assuming that a German or Belgian workman can turn out as much work in a stated time as an English workman, the foreign manufacturer has the distinct advantage of a greater production for less money, which to English manufacturers cannot fail to be of very serious importance in any competition with their Continental opponents.

The prohibitive rates of carriage in the English Midlands in comparison with those paid in Belgium and Germany is instanced in the report as another reason for the severity of foreign competition, the average cost of carriage per 100 miles being 5s 4d per ton in Germany (in lots of 10 tons), 5s 8d per ton in Belgium, and 14s 6½d in England. Some considerable saving is effected abroad by means of forwarding agents, who collect goods of similar class from various manufacturers, and consign them in 10-ton lots at the minimum rate of a sliding scale, so that all who avail themselves of the services of a forwarding agent can, by paying a moderate commission, gain the advantage of the minimum freight. The committee, therefore, are of opinion that the severity of foreign competition is due primarily to lower rates of wages, longer hours of labour, and cheaper rates of carriage.

But they also consider that some part of it is due to the practice of foreign manufacturers producing certain leading lines in very large quantities in order to minimise the cost of production, and then exporting at reduced prices what they cannot sell at home. Under a system of protection, a German manufacturer is assured of a certain sale in his own country at remunerative prices, and can therefore afford to export any surplus stock at cost price, or possibly even at a small loss.

Foreign competitors also derive advantage, although perhaps in a minor degree, from the decimal system of weights, measures, and currency, which is universal in all Continental manufacturing countries, and which to a foreign buyer is undeniably more intelligible, and for purposes of calculation much simpler than the complicated standard system in force in this country. In former times, when England had a practical monopoly of hardware manufacturing industries, a matter of this kind was probably of little importance, but in the present days of keen competition it is one that may easily act unfavourable towards English manufacturers, and in cases where all other things were equal it certainly would do so.

Again, it is a matter of common knowledge among merchants and shippers that English manufacturers, speaking generally, are prejudiced far more than is supposed by the greater willingness of their foreign opponents to conform to the special requirements of foreign markets. A German, for example, will, as a rule, and within certain limits, make any article, whether as to size or construction, that may be asked for, whereas an English manufacturer will too often plead that he has not the necessary tools or appliances, and on that ground will refuse work which his foreign rival will be only too ready to accept.

Some advantage attaches also to foreign competitors in consequence of the specially attractive manner in which, as a rule, they are in the habit of putting up their goods, and by the more general adoption of the use of cardboard boxes for that purpose, which, for obvious reasons, are more convenient than paper parcels, and on that account are naturally preferred, and also by their practice so to regulate prices as to include the cost of packages and of delivery, not only within the limits of their own countries, but to any part of the world, the invoice value thus representing to a buyer, without further calculation, the actual cost to him of any given article as it comes into his possession.

German manufacturers, moreover, are accustomed to invoice not only in foreign languages, but also in foreign currencies, which must often tend to the diversion of business in their favour.

The committee also found in the course of their investigation that in respect of certain foreign and colonial markets, English manufacturers are often seriously affected by the lower rates of over-sea freights which are offered by Continental steamship owners, who, being practically exempt from the monopolies and combinations prevailing to a large extent among certain lines of steamships in England, are able to quote and accept rates with greater freedom, and with more regard to competition and circumstances than their English rivals.

It is obvious that on all heavy articles, at least, the question of freight is one of supreme importance to the shipper, and that even if the cost of production at the shipping port were equal, a lower charge for delivery is one that may easily turn the scale in favour of the country which is able to offer this advantage.

The committee conclude their report with a short reference to an impression which is far too prevalent, that foreign competition is applicable only to the cheaper and commoner classes of hardware. This, no doubt, was the case a few years ago, but it cannot be too strongly urged upon all who are interested that it is so no longer. With the exception of some of the higher branches of skilled labour industries in which England still holds a position of pre-eminence and superiority, a foreign workman can, and in reality does, produce just as good an article, both as construction and intrinsic merit, as an English workman. It may even be doubted whether in respect of some industries involving taste, artistic design, and adaptive skill, for which by reason of his superior technical education he is specially qualified, a foreign workman should not be classed not only as an equal, but even as something more. It is, in any case, the opinion of the committee that foreign, and more particularly German, competition in the hardware trades should be regarded as a serious and increasing force, well worthy to be opposed by the best energy, enterprise, and ability of which English manufacturers and English artisans are capable.

from *The Board of Trade Journal* (vol. XIX, no. 113, December 1895)

A6 German Advantages in the Iron and Steel Industry (1896)

I do not purpose now to discuss the general causes of German success and English failure: but in the case of special causes affecting a particular trade it is as well to allude to them by the way. In the case of Iron and Steel such special causes are in operation. Chief among them is the lower cost of production.

It must not, however, be inferred — as English people are far too ready to infer — that this means lower wages. That explanation has long been worn threadbare; it is an easy disposition of the question, and saves the manufacturer from the exercise of that searching of heart as to his own shortcomings, which is as precious in commerce as in morals; at the same time that it serves as a clinching argument against any application for better pay on the part of his servants. But it has the demerit of being founded on a great delusion and a lie. Thus, it was found by the delegates of British Iron that for loading-plates German mechanics are paid at the rate of a franc per ton, whereas the Middlesborough man gets only 5½d to 7d. An Englishman employed at certain ironworks in Germany, who had once been at Darlington and Middlesborough, and was therefore fitted to compare, discoursed the delegates thus: — 'Undoubtedly our men are better off than the men in England. We pay, generally speaking, higher wages. You have some few men who get higher wages than any men in our works; but over the whole of the men we get higher wages than you pay. That is an absolute fact.' This is emphatic; but it is fortified by the observations of such Englishmen interested in the trade as have travelled the Continent in a note-taking spirit. Further, the official statistics of wages in Germany may be cited in confirmation. These show — not only that the German worker's income averages very fairly with the English ditto's, but — that the German's wages are on a pretty steady upward grade: which explains the signs of a higher standard of living now noticeable among the German people. I am speaking more particularly of the manufacture of finished iron and steel; miners and workers in the pig-iron furnaces are not so well paid, and it may be that their wages will not bear favourable comparison with Englishmen's for similar work. It is, nevertheless, a great mistake to suppose that the cheaper pig-iron to which the Germans now have access, is inexpensive solely by reason of low wages. The better explanation is to be found in the increased productivity of the German furnaces. 'Ten or twelve years ago,' says Herr Weinlig, 'a daily turn-out of 60 to 70 tons of forge-pig iron or 50 tons of *Spiegeleisen* was considered large; but 150 to 170 tons of best quality forge-pig iron, 100 to 120 tons of *Spiegeleisen*, &c., are now quite common.' Here is a more excellent reason for the cheapening of German pig-iron. Note the progressive productivity of the English furnaces, and the argument will be complete. In '81 our annual output averaged 15,176 tons per furnace, giving an advantage over the Germans of 3,567 tons per furnace. By '93 we, too, had advanced towards perfection; but only to the extent of 21,400 tons of annual output. This leaves us 3,041 tons behind our rivals. And yet the English manufacturer goes on his fine, old crusted way and seeks to dissemble his stupor, and his narrow and dogged aloofness from improved methods, in the miserable excuse of 'German cheap labour.'

There are other reasons for German cheap production. They don't waste their material in the prodigal fashion which obtains this side of the North Sea. When the British Iron delegates visited a certain plate mill, they found that the arrangements involved 15 per cent. less waste — 'practically no waste' was one delegate's description. He significantly added: — 'It would be absolutely impossible to produce sheets in such a quantity, and of such an appearance, with the appliances we have at our disposal.' Another commissioner remarked: — 'As a practical man I must admit that I never saw anything like it, and could not have believed it possible unless I had seen it with my own eyes.' This Practical Man admitted also that 'there is a danger to the Midland District unless we can, by some means, increase our output, develop our machinery, and bring our sheets to greater perfection.' The Practical Man is right: there *is* a considerable 'danger.' He would have been justified in the use of a stronger word. Another cause of comparative cheapness of production is the lower railway rate which iron has to pay. Railway rates are a fluctuating quantity just now, both in this country and on the Continent; but analyses show them to be very much lower in Germany, as well as Belgium and Sweden, than they are in England. The figures are hopelessly complicated for purposes of comparison; but there is little danger of exaggeration in saying that on the Continent they do not pay for railway carriage half what is charged in England. It is worth noting that German railways are especially moderate in their rates to shipping ports. Account must also be taken of the Dephosphorizing inventions already referred to, which came into use early in the Eighties. Between '78 and '80 the Germans had to buy ore for pig-iron at prices ranging from 22s for common forge to 38s 6d for Bessemer; but the ore cost of pig of qualities suitable for making wrought iron or basic Bessemer steel is probably at the present time not more than from 15s to 20s per ton. Then, as regards the two export trades, the staunchest Free-Trader cannot afford to overlook the advantages of the German Protective System. English iron and steel, on entering Germany, are handicapped with a duty varying in amount, but reaching to over half-a-crown a hundredweight for tin plates. This makes it very difficult for us to compete with home-made metals. It likewise enables the German to raise his prices to his compatriots, and screw such a profit from them that he can afford a big reduction on his export prices, so that he cuts at his English rival in two directions. The duty makes our goods too dear to sell in Germany, at the same time that it makes German goods so cheap in the world-market that we are being undersold therein and ousted therefrom. The cheap export manufacture also enables the Germans to keep their works fully employed; and this means a great saving in standing charges. Moreover, to pass from cheaper production and distribution, the method of conducting business in many English houses is as rigid as their own cast iron, which makes it difficult for the English patriot to keep patience with the English manufacturer. Here is an excerpt from the correspondence columns of a trade journal*:

> Sir, — Some time ago I had occasion to place an order for thin wrought-iron sheets. In answer to my enquiry one firm wrote: 'We regret the specification would not suit us'; another, 'We regret it does not suit us to quote for black sheets at present'; and other makers in the same strain.
>
> Last month I required some steel sheets, and received almost identical replies.
>
> My friends are now putting down a plant abroad for rolling their own — meanwhile the sheets they require are
>
> MADE IN GERMANY.

Brussels, December 9.

**Ironmonger*, 14th December, '95.

Surely this letter 'speaks for itself'?

from E.E. Williams, *Made In Germany* (Heinemann, 1896). Reprinted by permission of William Heinemann Ltd

A7 Alkali (1896)

The industries technically known as Heavy Chemicals group themselves largely round Alkali and its products. Down to late years, Alkali was a peculiarly English industry. We manufactured not alone for ourselves but for the world at large, as may be gathered from the fact that in '73 our Alkali Export was worth near three millions sterling. How we have fared since that year is told by the following table:

'73.	'83.	'93.	'94.	'95.
£	£	£	£	£
2,929,006	2,124,962	1,857,928	1,630,948	1,560,140

Here we are confronted with the damning fact that, whereas fresh uses and (owing to the growth of manufactures abroad) fresh markets for Alkali Products are continually being found, the export of the greatest Alkali Trader in the world was last year of little more than half its value in the early Seventies. Nor do the latest years show any signs of recuperation. The decline since '91 has been continuous; and that it had no connection with any 'general depression' is shown by the failure of the '95 Revival to help it one whit.

Down to some five years ago, the trade was in the hands of a number of different firms, all struggling along under the adverse influences of competition and the Middleman. In '90 about forty of these houses — as a last hope of salvation — combined themselves into a huge concern, with eight millions capital, under the name of the United Alkali Company. Internecine competition was stopped, the Middleman was abolished, and better times were confidently announced. The Company, in the first two years of its existence, managed to pay a dividend on all its shares; then it ceased to pay on the ordinary until '95, when a dividend of one per cent. was declared; but already in '96 it has had to close more than one works. Its utter failure to stay the ebb of a national industry is shown by the steady fall in its lifetime in a national export. That it is in low water is not due to foreign competition alone; for the rivalry of Brunner, Mond, and Company,* with other firms, among which may soon be reckoned the new Castner-Kellner Company (already building works in England), is largely responsible. Largely too, is foreign competition: Sweden, among other countries, is competing heavily with England. The electrolytic processes in use there are damaging the United Alkali Company's trade in Chlorate of Potash, which is used in the Swedish match factories; and — what is worse— Swedish Chlorate of Potash found its way last year to the English market. The Tyne, too, is in no better case than the Mersey. It is exactly a century since the Leblanc Process began to be worked at Newcastle. In 1799 the make of Soda-Crystals was about 10 tons; in 1830 it was over 3,000 tons; in '62 it was 51,000 tons; and in '82 it was 104,000. The weight of Salt decomposed in '82 was 188,000 tons; but in '93 it was only 90,963. Again, in '30 there were four Alkali Works on Tyneside; in '73 there were twenty-four; now there are five.

I have mentioned Sweden as one formidable competitor. Another is Switzerland. But I need not travel beyond the familiar field. That our neighbour, the German, is more than equal to the task of crowding us out of the market, may be gathered from the statement (in the German Catalogue of the Chicago Exhibition) that, whereas Germany as late as '77 produced about 42,000 tons of Soda a year, her annual output is now considerably over 195,000. In the ten years from '85 to '94 her export of Soda-Ash grew from 11,981 to 33,556 tons. In the same period her import diminished in like proportion. Our own export of Alkali to Germany has dropped from 134,300 tons in '93 to 112,198 in '95; our export of bleaching materials from 7,740 tons in '90 to 2,330 in '95. This growing inability of ours to sell in Europe is owing in no small measure to the high Protective Duties in which our Alkalis are mulcted (on Caustic Soda they reach 2s 0½d per cwt.); so that reports from Her Majesty's Consuls in Germany are rich in references to the prosperity of the Heavy Chemicals Trade. From Stettin, for example, you learn† that the Union Chemical Manufacturing Company's 'production was not

*The fact that Brunner, Mond, and Company, the one really successful firm in England, is practically an international concern, puts it in a separate category from the genuine local English industry. The ownership of certain patents, with certain other causes, sets this house beyond the reach of foreign competition; but it is a deadly rival to other English Alkali Works.

†*Foreign Office*, Annual Series, No. 1652.

equal to the demand'; that 'it was necessary to erect two new acid-producing apparatus'; and that the Company has declared a dividend of 10 per cent. There is no question here of an insidious advance. The matter is, simply, that our trade has gone to the devil, while the Germans are piling up fortunes.

from E.E. Williams, *Made In Germany* (Heinemann, 1896). Reprinted by permission of William Heinemann Ltd

A8 Cotton Exports (1896)

Taking first into consideration . . . the export trade of the United Kingdom . . . it appears that the most important customer of British cotton yarn and piece goods in Africa and the East has always been British India, the amount of yarn imported from the United Kingdom in 1895 having been 41,070,600 lbs., of a value of £1,627,360, as against the rather smaller amount in 1894 of 39,996,600 lbs. which, however, was valued at £1,643,254. This decline in the value of yarn did not commence last year, the amount for the two preceding years being in each case smaller, but the value higher than in 1895. In 1889 the figures were 45,354,300 lbs. of a value of £2,250,292, so that in the last seven years the export trade of British cotton yarn to British India has not only decreased in amount by over 4½ million lbs., but the value of the article itself has declined also. With regard to cotton piece goods, the quantity exported to British India in 1895 was 1,718,224,000 yards of a value of £12,608,045, as against 2,276,227,700 yards valued at £17,994,094 in 1894, and 2,001,153,400 yards of a value of £17,399,475 in 1889.

Of the countries under consideration Japan is the next most important buyer of cotton yarn from the United Kingdom, the value of this article imported into Japan in 1895 having been £858,516 as against £662,846 in 1894; in 1893 the value was £811,350, and in 1892, £839,474. The diminution in value is not noticeable in this case, the 21,266,000 lbs. imported in 1895 having been valued at a higher figure than the 23,384,900 lbs. received in 1892. With regard, however, to cotton piece goods, Japan stands lower down the list, the value of the exports to China in 1895 having reached the large amount of £3,684,323, those to Egypt having been valued at £1,437,386, and to Java £1,253,131, while Japan in the same year received but £909,868 worth of the same description of goods. The remaining principal customers in Africa and the East for British cotton yarns in 1895 were Hong Kong, Egypt, Straits Settlements, and China, and for cotton piece goods Hong Kong, West Africa, Cape Colony, Morocco, Tunis, and the Philippine Islands (including Ladrones), in the order of their importance.

The German export trade in cotton yarns and piece goods with the countries under review is still insignificant; the value of yarns exported to British India (which in the German trade accounts is made to include French and Portuguese Possessions) in 1894 (the latest year for which the returns are available) having been 223,000 marks (£11,100), and in many cases (notably Japan) the value has not reached 1,000 marks (£50). In piece goods (cotton cloths) the value of the German exports to British India (including, as in the case of the yarns, French, and Portuguese Possessions) in 1894 reached 704,000 marks (£35,200), and to Cape Colony (including other British Possessions of South Africa) 572,000 marks (£28,600). The values of German exports to other countries in the list hardly call for comment, except, perhaps, may be noticed the commencement of a trade with Japan, the exports to which country (*nil* in 1888 and 1889) were valued at 58,000 marks (£2,900) in 1894.

from *The Board of Trade Journal* (vol. XXI, no. 121, August 1896)

A9 Exports and Imports of Manufactured Goods (1897)

. . . comparing 1883 with 1895 there was a decrease in the value of our exports of manufactured articles from 215 to 196 million pounds. There have been intermediate fluctuations, however, at one time—as in 1885 and 1886 — to a lower level than that of 1895, and at another — as in 1889 and 1890 — to a higher level than that of 1883, and coupling the fact that the value of our exports of manufactured articles in 1895 was 11 million pounds larger than in 1894 with the fact of the general increase in our export trade which has been in progress this year it would seem that we are once again on the ascending scale. The greater portion of the decline between 1883 and 1895, will be seen to have been occasioned by the fall in the value of the exports of textile and metal goods. The fall in the former class is practically largely due to a decline in the value of the raw material previously imported contained in the articles exported.

That in the latter class is also largely due to a reduction in prices. But nevertheless the superficial aspect of the facts is not so satisfactory as it was a few years ago although there are signs of improvement.

At the same time . . . the import of articles called manufactured into the United Kingdom in the same period has enormously increased, viz. from £53,000,000 in 1883 to £76,000,000 in 1895. Moreover, the increase in this case has been virtually continuous throughout the whole period. The bulk of this increase is under the heads of leather, and silk and woollen goods. The first named is a raw material, while our woollen industry, with which imported woollens might compete, has developed largely of late years . . . the figures undoubtedly afford an indication of advance in manufacturing abroad, though they do not justify the inference that our home manufacturing is being displaced.

On the whole, however, the conclusion from this part of the investigation is that we still preponderate greatly as a country manufacturing for export. Neither of our rivals exports manufactures to the same extent, although Germany has undoubtedly made some gains, and both Germany and the United States have developed in capacity to manufacture not only for their home markets, but to some extent for export also. Still our exports consist more largely of manufactured goods in proportion to our wholesale exports than do those of Germany, and . . . measuring per head of population we are as an exporting country far ahead of Germany or any other of our competitors.

from the Board of Trade Memorandum on the Comparative Statistics of Population Industry and Commerce in the United Kingdom and Some Leading Foreign Countries (1897): C.3322.

A10 Marketing (1897)

One of the causes of success in foreign competition may be said to be the greater attention paid abroad to the art of *exactly suiting the foreign customer's pocket, taste, and convenience*, an art in which foreign nations pre-eminently excel. The vital importance of pleasing the customer in these essential points has been often too much ignored and neglected at home; and our neglect has been profitably turned to account by others to our present detriment. Two other causes have, no doubt, also contributed largely to the remarkable advance of foreign trade. The first is the superior technical education often to be found abroad; and the second is the superior commercial acquirements, especially in command of languages, enjoyed by the foreigner. There are many other minor causes, but the foregoing three are the chief ones in the opinion of competent persons, and what the Englishman must see to is, that he is not behind his Continental competitor in these essential points.

The next thing to consider is how the foreigner carries out his fundamental maxim of exactly suiting his customer's pocket, taste, and convenience; for that he is most successful in doing so is an absolute certainty. Quite apart from all considerations of the many forms of State-aid given in Germany and other countries, which result in cheapening production, the facilities accorded by foreigners to trade are many, and, as a rule, more advantageous than ours. It may be taken as an axiom of modern trade that *the goods must seek the customer*; for the customer will no longer seek the goods, as in bygone days. In former times, England was practically the only export market for many articles of manufacture (staple industries such as iron, steel, cotton, and woollen goods, etc.), and often had a monopoly of the foreign market; but now that the industrial products of Germany (especially), the United States, France, and Belgium have so rapidly developed, there are several export markets of similar articles.

In former days foreign customers, naturally, turned to England for certain commodities; now they can buy equally well in other countries, and often *do* because of the peculiar and greater suitability of the article they require, or because of the better facilities offered them there. Moreover, the goods of those countries seek the foreign purchaser pertinaciously by every conceivable device; British goods apparently do not do so to an equal extent.

The customer, instead of having to seek British firms to give his orders, now has the goods of some of these other countries brought daily and cleverly to his immediate notice by adroit commercial travellers (speaking his own language fluently), by personal solicitation of foreign firms or their agents, or by the extensive catalogues (in the language he understands) which give him every particular of the article he wants *in the weights, measures, and currency of his own country*. What English firms carry commercial enterprise to this extent? Some, doubtless, do; but others do not. But these things must be now done and many others, unless we are willing to give up without a struggle a part of our well-earned commercial and industrial supremacy. Such surrender must not and cannot be, and British merchants and manufacturers who do not employ such methods, will surely realise the changes that have to be made by them when dealing with foreign trade and foreign competition.

Now as regards suiting the customer's 'pocket,' no doubt British manufactured goods are often the best in the world and worth their price; but often it is not the best that the foreigner wants, but merely a similar article that will answer the purpose for which it is required at a cheaper price. He cannot afford *the best*, but wants an inferior quality which will look as well and do as well, and for which *he can pay*. He would, in many cases, rather pay less and purchase more often, than expend a larger sum on the best article which would last him twice as long. The ready money or payment at short credit for the best may not be forthcoming, whereas sufficient for the cheaper article is. Great Britain sells the former; other nations the latter. Naturally the latter is often chosen; and, probably, the many sales of a cheaper article yield a far better profit than the fewer sales of an expensive one. Though dearer to the buyer in the long run, it suits his immediate convenience far better. Then again, foreign firms appear to grant easier and longer credits. 'Terms cash' are often not possible and are never palatable to foreign purchasers, especially among those of small standing and capital. Some middlemen are in the position of having to re-sell the article bought from the manufacturer before they are able to pay its value to the latter.

'Suiting the customer's taste' is a most essential requisite of successful trade. The great and minute attention paid abroad to the particular form, design, quality, 'showiness,' colour, look, or peculiarity of the article exported, in order to *exactly* suit the customer's perhaps fastidious taste, is deserving of closer attention on the part of the English manufacturer and exporter. That taste may be barbarous, inexplicable, and unreasonable, but the mere fact of satisfying it (in whatever trivial form it may be) supplies a want and pleases the buyer; and those who are practicable and sharp enough to adapt their goods exactly to the customer's fantastic wishes are, naturally, those who get many orders. I imagine that this is one of the prime causes of the transfer of part of what was once British trade to other foreign countries. Competition is now so keen in the industrial race that our manufacturers and exporters cannot afford to neglect the smallest detail which may facilitate foreign orders. Our once absolute industrial supremacy is fast losing ground, and will go faster still if English trade continues to despise the many small devices and expedients resorted to by the foreigner in order to undersell us by more exactly suiting foreign taste and its many requirements. The foreigner *always* tries to do his best to supply just what his customer wants; if he has not the exact thing he will make it. The Englishman does not always do his best to suit the buyer in his peculiarities, but is inclined to say, 'This is the best article of its kind; take it or leave it, but it is the cheapest in the long run,' — so runs the text throughout consular reports. He does not exert himself half enough to insinuate his goods with his customer, or to entice orders out of him as the foreigner does. If he cannot supply the exact thing wanted, he will, perhaps, not make it.

The third point, that of 'suiting the customer's convenience,' is one that cannot be too much urged as a means of promoting foreign trade. Some of the excellent practical ways of doing so in vogue among other nations will be here mentioned. The foreigner does everything in his power to save his customer trouble. He quotes him a fixed price for goods delivered duty free practically at his own door (at the quay of a port, or in any particular town abroad), which includes freight, shipping charges, packing, etc., up to that point. He states that price (or the catalogues do) in the language of the country where the sale is effected, and in the currency of that country, instead of in that of the export market — an inestimable advantage. A purchaser abroad is thereby enabled to see at a glance what the article ordered and delivered at his own door will cost him, and can exactly calculate if he can buy cheaper elsewhere, and what profit he could make if for re-sale.

A usual practice with us is merely to give in English the cost of the article at the home manufactory, and in English money, an almost exactly opposite system, which leaves the buyer to discover for himself, *if he can* (a work he will often not take the trouble to do), what the cost of that article will be when it reaches him, after paying freight, shipping, packing, and other charges, etc., and what the cost in £sd is equivalent to in his own currency. These all involve nice calculations, which some would-be purchasers may not be capable of performing, and which, in any case, require considerable labour and inquiry. And why should he make any effort to do so when the foreign commercial traveller or the foreign catalogue, which he *can* read and perfectly understands, does all those calculations, and saves him all trouble in the matter? Moreover, they both go even further, and give him in his own language a description of the article, its weight in kilos, or in terms he understands (instead of in lbs. and tons, for instance, which he does *not* understand), its measurement when packed, and cost of packing, insurance, etc. This is intensely practical, and deserves the success in which it has resulted. Lastly, the question of commercial travellers is one that has been much neglected as a means of extending our trade. Their name is legion; but few are English. In comparison with foreign nations, we have absurdly few. Their advantages are manifest, bringing, as they do, not only full details as to price, etc., but also actual samples of the manufactured goods themselves. What customer would not rather buy from those nations which actually produce to them a sample of the article they have to sell, rather than from a mere catalogue's description, with its meagre supply of information, and in a language often not understood?

It was and may be still the practice of many English firms to refuse small orders from abroad for quite little sums (even if offered to their agents or commercial travellers), and they never solicited them. They forgot that a small beginning often has important consequences, resulting in large profits. Foreigners do not, and did not, disdain them; they even sought them. They know that a small order, if satisfactorily executed, often leads to larger ones. This is but another instance of the attention paid by them to small things in trade. But it is just attention to trifles in commerce that so often leads to consequences of appalling magnitude, such as Germany's gradual rise in the industrial world and foreign commerce which is due, not so much to any great changes, improvements, or alterations, but to a mass of small variations, innovations, and modifications in her methods of dealing with industrial and commercial questions . . .

There is much reason to fear that British enterprise in commercial matters is not now by any means what it should be in many parts of the world; and it is far too often testified to by diplomatic and consular reports, to which but little attention is paid. Much valuable information and hints for the manufacturer have in the past been collected and published by our Foreign Office; but how little use has, unfortunately, been made at home of the continual advice and warnings which have emanated from her Majesty's representatives at all times and from all countries! As recently as July, 1895, Lord Cromer called attention to the unfavourable results for English firms and mercantile houses in competition for contracts and tenders even in Egypt — where one would imagine our opportunities to be great and quite exceptional — and to the increasing tendency of foreign enterprise to beat them in the open market. This is but one instance of the many on record. Markets for some commodities are lost through the reluctance of our merchants to make sacrifices at first in order to establish the reputation of their wares with the foreign public. The standing of good English makers is often recognised; but, unfortunately for us, business is now so much influenced by cheapness and facility of payment — two points in which our trade rivals appear to succeed better than we do — that once buyers go to other countries and find things are cheaper and good enough for their purpose, they are reluctant to change back to British goods. Complaints, too, are heard that the former are always exactly what have been ordered, while our manufacturers do not always supply 'repeat' orders of identically the same commodity, but sent something similar, which, however, is not what was wanted by the customer. He, therefore, sometimes gives up English goods, even if he has tried them. One curious point is mentioned here that occurred in California. English exporters lost almost entirely the San Francisco market through their selling there to wholesale and retail people at a like price. The former, consequently, gave up buying direct from England or English agents, and now go to New York importers. The fact that British goods go to San Francisco *via* New York, and through the hands of American importers there, and over 3,400 miles of railway rather than direct by sea from the exporters of Great Britain, shows that there must be something wrong in some details of our trading system.

From every corner of the world comes the universal cry, 'Don't send us English catalogues.' Consuls are tired of pointing out the uselessness of this procedure; their consulates are inundated with them, and they are unintelligible to the natives to whom they are intended to appeal. A few now turn up in foreign languages, but every one sent abroad should be in the language of the country it is sent to; and exporters should take steps and a great deal of trouble to distribute them to all foreign firms by post or by their commercial travellers and agents. Consuls assert that our catalogues are far behind those of the United States and Germany in every way, and need some of the radical improvements pointed out above.

from W.S.H. Gaskell, *Our Trade in the World in Relation to Foreign Competition, 1885 – 1895* (Chapman and Hall Ltd, 1897).

A11 Are Our Trades Being *Ruined* by Free Trade? (1903)

This is constantly asserted by Protectionists.

Let us examine the facts.

There is a continual change going on in all Trades.

Stage coaches gave place to railways and the drivers of stage coaches were thrown out of work.

Sailing ships have largely been replaced by steamers.

Rush candles, which were once a common light, are scarcely seen now.

Gas and electric light take their place. No doubt the makers of rush candles lost their occupation.

Hand weaving has become machine weaving. There has, therefore, been a displacement of labour.

The sickle and the scythe have been succeeded by the mowing machine.

These changes have nothing to do with Protection or Free Trade, except that under a system of Free Trade such changes are more gradual and natural than under a system of Protection.

It is, therefore, incorrect to think that because a trade is in a bad condition, this must necessarily be due to Free Trade.

Here are a few facts showing how the country has gained under Free Trade — that is, by receiving goods (food, raw material, partly-manufactured and fully-manufactured goods) without taxing them.

The Corn Laws were repealed in 1846 — the Act came into full effect in 1849.

After this taxes were gradually taken off other goods, until practically all goods entered our ports free in 1861.

Let us look at the progress of the nation under Free Trade:

	1861.	1902.	
Population	28·9	41·9	millions.
Paupers	36	23	per 1,000 population.
Goods Exported	£125	£283	millions.
Goods Imported	£217	£528	millions.
Income Tax — Yield per 1d.	£1,162	£2,580	thousands.
Deposits in Savings Banks	£41·5	£197·1	millions.
British Shipping	4·8	10·0	million tons.

Government Return No. 340, August 12th, 1903.

Protectionists say that certain trades have been ruined by foreign competition. This is not so. Where new appliances and energy have been used the result has been otherwise.

The Sugar Trade.

This trade — the refining of sugar — has felt foreign competition more than any other trade, owing to foreign Governments having given bounties on the export of sugar. Many of the smaller works with old fashioned machinery closed, but there is evidence to show that up-to-date works have done well and even increased their output.

On March 7th, 1903, Henry Tate and Sons, Ltd., Sugar Refiners, issued a prospectus asking for debentures. They showed profits:

	£		£
1896	91,012	1900	100,263
1897	148,390	1901	215,274
1898	104,307	1902	97,582
1899	62,161		

Not bad for a 'RUINED' trade!

Owing to cheap sugar — the result of foreign bounties — the confectionery, biscuit, and other industries have been created employing over 100,000 people.

Iron and Steel Trade.

The Protectionists say this is 'ruined.' The Profits of this trade returned for income-tax were:

	£		£
1898	2,556,392	1901	5,380,418
1899	3,007,591	1902	6,600,263
1900	3,211,984		

Statistical Abstract, Cd. 1727.

Persons employed—

1861	129,507
1891	202,406
1901	216,022

Government Return, Cd. 1761.

Not bad progress for a 'RUINED' trade!

Tinplate Trade.

The Protectionists say this is a 'ruined' trade.

Exports	1881–1890	65,869,180	cwts.
,,	1891–1900	71,175,980	,,
		5,306,800	Gain.

Note the McKinley tariff, which was said to have 'ruined' the trade, came into force in July 1891. In spite of this 'ruin' the trade has increased. (From Mr. Charles Lancaster — Hughes and Lancaster, the well-known tinplate exporters — in *Liverpool Daily Post*, October 15th, 1903.)

Number of Tinplate Mills Working.

Average 1895–6	Average 1898–1901	Average 1902
318	358	397

Government Return, Cd. 1761.

Boot Trade.

This trade suffered from an American invasion. It altered its methods, and the invasion is coming to an end.

Dozen Pairs of Boots.

(10 months in each year)	1901	1902	1903
Imports	260,387	205,289	202,821
Exports	544,390	610,364	661,520

Government Return 26 – IX.

Imports decreasing! Exports increasing!

Hosiery Trade.

	1898	1902
Exports	£1,118,160	£1,410,509

Government Return, Cd. 1582.

Trade Increasing!

Brass Trade.

Exports	£471,234	£613,441

Government Return, Cd. 1582.

Trade Increasing!
But all 'decaying' trades, according to the Protectionists!

Silk Trade.

Since 1898 the exports of silk Broad Stuffs and unenumerated silks, also manufactures of silk and other materials, have LARGELY increased, but exports of silk handkerchiefs, scarfs, and shawls have decreased. Is this not due to changes of fashion! Lyons in France, the 'protected' home of the silk trade, is complaining of bad times!

Cotton and Wool Trades.

These are being 'ruined,' according to Protectionists.

Consumption in the United Kingdom.

	Average 1885–9	Average 1890–4	Average 1895–9
Raw Cotton (in million cwts.)	13·1	14·2	15·0
Raw Wool (in million lbs.)	416	475	523

Government Return, Cd. 1761.

There is no cause for alarm in these figures!

Glass Trade.

The Brussels correspondent of *The Times* writes on October 13th, 1903: 'The glass industry of Belgium is still in a very depressed condition.'

Note that owing to Belgium having a special glass sand conveniently situated, she is the great glass-maker of the world!

Exports from United Kingdom:

	1898	1902
Plate glass	£96,498	£108,112
Flint, Plain, Cut, &c.	£211,352	£248,454
Bottles	£364,653	£171,162
Other glass	£212,529	£270,202

Government Return, Cd. 1582.

Trade Increasing!

Wire Trade.

	1898	1902
Exports (Iron and Steel)	44,123 tons. £772,604	55,046 tons. £1,042,869

Government Return, Cd. 1582.

Trade Increasing!

Earthenware and Glass Trades.

	1861	1881	1901
Persons employed	53,611	68,226	92,556

Government Return, Cd. 1761.

Milling Trade.

Mr. George Seatree (of the well-known firm of millers, Messrs. G. Seatree and Sons, Liverpool) writing to *Milling*, October 24th, 1903, says 'that never in its history was the milling trade of the country doing better (speculative booms excepted).'

Watch Trade.

	1898	1902
Clocks, Watches, and parts thereof – Exports	£80,037	£101,567

Government Return, Cd. 1582.

Trade Increasing!

Jewellery Trade.

(Not specified separately prior to 1900.)

	1900	1902
Exports	£178,204	£182,820

Government Return, Cd. 1582.

Trade Increasing!

Earthenware Trade.

	1898	1902
Earthenware, Chinaware, Parian, and Porcelain – Exports	£1,650;728	£1,731,731

Government Return, Cd. 1582.

Trade Increasing!

In some of these trades the imports are also increasing — much to the benefit of this country — although to the alarm of a few Protectionists. This is due mainly to two causes — that some articles included in the above trades are, for local and special reasons, made more easily in certain foreign countries, and that the consumption of most articles has so enormously increased in this country that it has been impossible in every instance to find sufficient skilled workers in certain trades to keep pace with the demand. It is not every man who is a brass fitter or tinplate worker. Even if an individual trade has, in a very rare instance, been damaged by free imports.

The PEOPLE have certainly GAINED by Cheap Food, Cheap Clothing, and Increased Wages following on Prosperity.

from the Liberal Party Leaflet, no. 1973 (1903)

A12 Our Woollen and Worsted Industry (1903)

Unfair competition and Its Results

The British Woollen and Worsted Industry is being seriously damaged by the defenceless position in which it is placed by our system of Free Imports. The Census Returns show a marked decrease since 1851 in the number of persons employed in England and Wales in the manufacture of woollens and worsteds, when the total was 255,750.

This deplorable reduction in the numbers employed is to a considerable extent the result of the enormous increase in our imports of these goods. Foreign countries are pouring into England, in fast increasing quantities, the finished articles of the trade. The value of these imports in 1861 (the first year after *the last toll on foreign imports had been removed by Mr. Gladstone*) was £987,731. In 1902 it had risen to £10,641,564 — *an increase of 977 per cent.*!

Our exports of British woollen and worsted manufactures increased steadily from 1851 (when they were valued at £8,377,183) to 1872, when they reached their highest value, viz.: — £32,383,273. From that year down to 1902, with some few exceptions, there has been a downward tendency, the value in the latter year being stated at £15,261,359.

The following figures will be of interest:

Year.	Employed in Woollen and Worsted industry in England and Wales	Imports of Foreign Woollen and Worsted Manufactures.	Exports of British Woollen and Worsted Manufactures.
	No.	£	£
1861	230,029	987,731	11,118,692
1871	246,645	4,637,625	27,182,385
1881	240,006	5,985,863	18,128,756
1891	258,356	9,669,179	18,446,640
1901	236,106	9,577,680	14,237,368
1902	—[a]	10,641,564	15,261,359

[a] Figures only available in census years.

Presented shortly, the figures already given show the following depressing results since 1871:

Decrease in British workpeople employed. 1871 – 1901	Increase in Imports of Foreign Manufactures. 1871 – 1902	Decrease in Exports of British Manufactures. 1871 – 1902
No.	£	£
10,539	6,003,939	11,921,026

Vide Statistical Abstracts and Census Reports.

For the decrease in British exports the hostile duties imposed by foreigners on British woollen and worsted manufactures are responsible. As examples it may be pointed out that they range, in Russia from 220 per cent. to 76 per cent. *ad valorem*, and in the United States of America from 159 per cent. to 93 per cent. *ad valorem*.

Of the direct influence of Foreign tariff duties on our trade the case of the United States forms a striking example. In 1889 we sent there woollen and worsted manufactures to the value of £5,189,250. In 1890 the McKinley Tariff came into force. Our exports in 1891 fell to £3,178,093!!

Yet Great Britain has deprived herself of the weapons to combat these tariffs, and continues to feed her competitors with raw material, while they not only encroach on her Home market, but cripple and undersell her in foreign markets.

The Unionist Government are alive to the evils of our 'free Importing' system. They ask 'the people of this country to give to the Government of this country . . . that freedom of negotiation of which we have been deprived' in order that these damaging inequalities may be removed.

from the Conservative National Union Leaflet, no. 259 (1903)

A13 The Railway Position (1907)

The abnormally low prices prevailing amongst railway stocks at the present time is the subject of general comment. That the state of the money market generally is largely responsible for this condition of things is no doubt true, but there are other considerations of a more serious, because less temporary, nature, which are unquestionably exercising a direct influence on the present value of railway stocks, and to which it is well that attention should be directed.

Some interesting figures have lately been published bearing upon the increase in the aggregate working expenses of the twelve principal English railway companies during the last ten years. Between 1896 and 1906 the total revenue of these companies increased from about 68½ millions to nearly 88 millions, or about 28 per cent., the growth being a steady one from year to year all through the period. But, unfortunately, the working expenditure increased between the same years in a still greater ratio. In 1896 the total working expenses of these companies amounted to about 38 millions, while ten years later they were about 54 millions, the increase in this case being 42 per cent. To put the matter in another way, and dealing with the half-years separately, we find that in the June half-year of 1896 the percentage of working expenses to gross receipts in the case of the twelve companies referred to was 55.6 per cent., while in the first half of 1906 it was 62.2 per cent. Similarly, in the December half-years of 1896 and 1906 the corresponding figures were 53.8 per cent. and 59.4 per cent. respectively. To complete the picture, we require to see what additional capital the twelve companies have had to spend in order to enable them to earn the increased revenue. Here again we find the very heavy increase of 128 millions, or 19½ per cent.

The obvious inference to be drawn from the fact that the working expenses are increasing in greater ratio than the receipts is, that the travelling public and the railway *employés* are getting an undue proportion of advantage as compared with the shareholders, and this is again proved by the fact that the average dividend paid on the ordinary stock of the twelve companies in question has declined nearly 1 per cent. between the years 1896 and 1906. During the decade referred to the travelling facilities to the public have been very greatly increased, while the tendency of both passenger fares and goods rates has been in a downward direction. The services of high-speed passenger trains have been largely augmented; dining, luncheon, and sleeping cars are much more general than formerly; steam heating of trains is now almost universal, and the rolling-stock generally has been improved in various ways. All these things involve expense, and are not always sources of increased revenue. Then, the conditions of service of railway *employés* have been very much improved. In some grades wages have been increased, and in others hours of duty have been shortened, while, at the same time, many old-age pension and other benefit funds have been commenced, to which the companies contribute. That the policy of having a contented staff is a wise one nobody will for a moment doubt, but the cost involved is a factor that must not be lost sight of.

An effort is at present being made by the Amalgamated Society of Railway Servants to force from the companies still further concessions in the way of higher wages and shorter hours, but this action need not give rise to any apprehension on the part of those who are financially interested in the lines. The demands are extremely ill-timed, and have no real grievances as their basis. The great majority of railway men are sufficiently wise to see that their interests are much safer in the hands of the companies that employ them than in those of paid agitators, and this is proved by the fact that after years of strenuous canvassing the society has only succeeded in enrolling as members about 12 per cent. of the railway *employés* of the country.

The acquaintance of investors with figures such as those quoted above in regard to the increased cost of working is, of course, calculated to depress the price of stocks, but there can be no doubt that another important cause of nervousness at the present time arises from the unfortunate attitude assumed by the Government towards the railway interest. The recent tendency of the Board of Trade appears to be too much inclined to ignore the fact that railway companies are commercial concerns, having dividends to earn. It is true that they exist for the benefit of the public and of the trade of the country, but it is also true that they exist to make a return on the money invested in them, and it should not be overlooked that an undue amount of legislative interference to the detriment of the railways is liable to place a check upon the investment of money in such undertakings, and this would inevitably put a stop to their expansion and seriously curtail their usefulness.

There is, for instance, the threatened legislation in regard to workmen's trains. The railway companies are at present running a large proportion of their workmen's trains at an actual loss, and if any of the demands made by the Parliamentary Committee of the Trade Union Congress at their recent interview with the Board of Trade are conceded, the result will be that the railway companies' losses will be largely increased. It is well known that railway companies can only exist by specific Act of Parliament, and that they are subject to all manner of restrictions and obligations in regard not only to their construction and methods of working, but also as to the charges they are allowed to make for the conveyance of both passengers and merchandise. At the time of the inception of railways in this country the means of transit were such that the railways constituted a monopoly, and it was considered by Parliament to be necessary for the protection of the public that their powers should be limited in various ways. The conditions prevailing to-day are totally different, and, so far, at any rate, as local traffic is concerned, the monopoly has entirely ceased to exist. Electric trams worked by the municipalities and supported out of the rates, and motor omnibuses running at high speed over the public roads without contributing anything towards their cost or upkeep, have brought about a complete change in the situation, and while the advantages which railway companies at one time enjoyed through having a partial monopoly of the local carrying business have entirely disappeared, the obligations attaching to the privilege still remain. Some legislation on the subject is undoubtedly necessary, but instead of its being in the direction asked for by the Trades Union Congress, it is to be hoped that the Government will see the equity of providing some means of recouping the railway companies for the loss they are required to sustain in meeting obligations imposed upon them under conditions which are non-existent to-day.

from *The Economist* (11 May 1907)

A14 The Foreign Trade Record (1907)

Mr Gladstone, in one of his exuberant periods, declared that our trade was 'advancing by leaps and bounds,' and the phrase would be perfectly justified if applied to the condition of our foreign commerce at the present moment. The buoyancy, moreover, is not a momentary or casual phase, but has been steadily growing for the past four years, the period being, rather curiously, coincident with that in which the Tariff Reformers have been engaged in prosecuting their campaign for the resuscitation of our 'dead or dying' industries.

The returns published this week show that the growth in our foreign trade during the month of April was larger than in any month of the remarkable period of expansion we have referred to.

Exports of British produce and manufactures for the month of April are valued at £34,416,866, as compared with £27,032,306 in April, 1906, the increase of £7,384,560 being equal to 27.3 per cent. For the four months the aggregate value of our exports is returned at £136,283,852 as compared with £118,229,402, thus showing an increase of £18,054,450, equal to 15.2 per cent. In Section I. and II. of the classification, comprising food and raw materials, the only item calling for notice is coal, and this shows an increase of £803,608 for the month and of £2,212,256 for the four months. The average price obtained is higher than last year, the increase in quantity for the four months being 11.2 per cent., while in value it is 23.2 per cent.

Our exports of iron and steel goods show increases of £1,024,303 and £3,310,529 for the month and four months respectively. In the longer period pig-iron shows an excess in value over last year of £1,143,441, chiefly on account of larger shipments to the United States. Good increases are shown in galvanised sheets, tinned plates, and other descriptions, the larger quantities going mainly to India, Germany, and Japan. To an increase of £1,300,000 in other metals for the four months the main contributions are £600,000 in copper, of which larger quantities were sent to the Netherlands, Australia, and 'other countries'; and £207,000 in tin, our exports of which to all the principal countries are considerably larger than for the corresponding period last year. Exports of machinery show an increase of £466,183 for April, and are £1,280,290 ahead for the four months, while new ships sent out as exports show an increase of more than 100 per cent. for the month, and of £1,216,071, or 67 per cent., for the four months.

Cotton exports, as well as imports, make the biggest individual contribution to the aggregate increase, the gain for the month amounting to £1,681,091, and for the four months to £3,497,095. In cotton yarn there is an increase for the four months of £600,000, Germany having been our best customer for this material. The larger demand for cotton piece goods emanates mainly from Turkey, Egypt, China, and India. Germany also takes the bulk of our exports of woollen yarn, and is responsible for £100,000 out of a total increase of £250,000. Woollen goods show an increase for April, but a slight falling off for the four months, the United States having taken only £325,094 worth, as compared with £450,333 worth last year. On the other hand, America has taken more jute and linen goods, Germany, as in other textiles, taking larger quantities of yarn; and France has reciprocated our purchases of silk goods by taking more of the same material from us. Apparel shows a small increase, though South Africa, which is the principal market for these goods, has taken less than last year. An increase of £880,000 in chemicals occurs, mainly on account of increased shipments of chemical manure, soda compounds, and sulphate of copper.

The Direction of Trade

Appended to the Trade and Navigation Returns for the month of April are the valuable tables showing the extent of our trade with each of the principal foreign countries and British possessions during the three months ended March 31, 1907, as compared with the corresponding period in the two preceding years. The monthly returns have shown the total increase in our imports and exports, and these tables show that out of an expansion of £16,940,000 in the value of our imports, £6,410,000 was in imports from British possessions and £10,530,000 in the value of commodities received from foreign countries. Out of a total increase of £10,670,000 in our exports for the quarter, £2,270,000 occurred in shipments to countries under the British flag and £8,400,000 in exports to foreign countries. The details are subjoined:

Quarter Ended March 31st

	1907	1906	1905
Imports from –	£	£	£
British possessions	41,363,000	34,953,000	33,739,000
Foreign countries	129,829,000	119,299,000	105,831,000
	171,192,000	154,252,000	139,570,000
Exports to –			
British possessions	32,192,000	29,922,000	27,829,000
Foreign countries	69,675,000	61,275,000	50,501,000
	101,867,000	91,197,000	78,330,000

In reviewing these figures, it is almost impossible to avoid reference to the discussion on Preference that has taken place at the Imperial Conference. It appears that the increase in our imports from the colonies in the first quarter of this year, as compared with the same period last year, was equal to 18.3 per cent., while we took from foreign countries an excess equal to only 8.8 per cent. On the export side, the expansion in our trade with British possessions was equal to only 7.6 per cent., while foreign countries exceeded their last year's takings by as much as 13.7 per cent.

In the quarter under notice the United States was for once our best foreign customer, the value of our exports thither amounting to £8,682,160, against £8,525,577 sent to Germany, who is usually first. The increases amounted to £1,801,000 and £835,000 respectively. America's increased takings were chiefly in pig-iron, while Germany took much larger quantities of cotton, woollen, and linen yarn. In spite of the unfavourable economic conditions in Russia, we sent there goods to the value of £1,928,384, as compared with £1,509,970 in the corresponding period a year ago. France and other European countries took in each case slightly more of our products than last year, Italy being foremost with an increase of £400,000. Substantial increases were recorded in the exports to Turkey, Egypt, China, and Japan. A good export trade also took place with the principal South American Republics, the order of importance being Argentina, Brazil, Chile, Uruguay.

from *The Economist* (11 May 1907)

A15 The Foreign Trade Record (1913)

The foreign trade returns for December issued by the Board of Trade on Tuesday complete the figures of a wonderful record year. The month's statistics show an increase of nearly three millions in British exports compared with December, 1911, of nine millions in imports, and of more than half-a-million in re-exports, making the total turnover for the month 124¾ millions, compared with 112¼ millions a year ago. The import figure is 3 millions larger than has ever been recorded before in a single month, while the export figure has only been exceeded in the immediately preceding months. The returns for the last three Decembers and for the last three years are as follows:

Foreign Trade in December

	Imports £	Exports £	Re-exports £
1910	69,109,461	37,424,110	9,876,619
1911	64,937,887	38,571,879	8,679,849
1912	74,068,698	41,459,038	9,241,907

Foreign Trade for the Whole Year

	Imports £	Exports £	Re-exports £
1910	678,257,024	430,384,772	103,761,045
1911	680,157,527	454,119,298	102,759,134
1912	744,896,514	487,434,002	111,837,905

The December figures are, on the whole, very similar to those of the last few months, and do not call for a detailed discussion, the one significant feature being that raw cotton accounts for nearly 4½ millions of the increase on the import side. A highly satisfactory feature of the boom of the last two years has been the absence of excessive one-sided development such as occurred in the case of shipbuilding in the 1898 – 1900 boom or of the cotton trade in 1906 – 7. For some time past the iron and steel trades have been making the pace, but latterly cotton has once more forged ahead, and the exceptionally heavy purchases of raw cotton at enhanced prices during December are a sign of the tremendous activity which prevails in Lancashire. These are the figures for the last two Decembers:

	Centals	£	Average Value per Cental £ s d
December, 1911	3,408,326	9,403,429	2 15 0
December, 1912	4,539,242	13,783,767	3 1 0

Other noteworthy changes are an increase in imports of wheat and flour at rather lower prices, a big decline in the value of sugar imported owing to the fall in price, increases in exports of coal, cotton goods, woollen goods, and electrical goods, and a very large increase in iron and steel manufactures.

To all except those who are anxiously waiting for bad times in the hope of inducing the country to alter a fiscal policy which has served it well for 70 years and brought exceptional prosperity during the last decade, the figures for 1912 must prove highly satisfactory. Imports are 64 millions more than last year, exports are up by 33 millions, and re-exports by 9 millions, so that the turnover has increased by 106 millions, or nearly 10 per cent. In the whole list of changes there are only six items which fail to show increases —three on the import and three on the export side. Of these the decline in meat imports is significant of an important economic change, for a considerable increase in the frozen meat trade has been more than offset by the rapid disappearance of the importation of live animals for food from North America. The figures for beef are the most significant:

	1910 £	1911 £	1912 £
Live cattle for food	4,027,918	3,776,404	982,958
Beef, fresh, frozen and chilled	11,745,146	11,134,482	13,692,059

The first of these two classes comes almost entirely from the United States, the second from the Argentine and Australasia. It is evident that the American home market is rapidly taking all available home supplies of meat. To this statement, however, bacon and ham still remains an important exception. Sugar and new ships — a very unimportant item — are the other two classes with decreases on the import side. Iron ore, oils and oil seeds, and silk manufactures show declines on the export side. Some conception of the rest of the return may be gleaned from the following statement of increases in the cases of the chief articles of trade:

Increases in 1912 Compared with 1911.

Imports	£	Exports	£
Grain and flour	+ 12,746,268	Iron and steel	+ 4,898,626
Raw cotton	+ 9,083,446	Coal	+ 4,137,420
Jute, flax, hemp, &c.	+ 3,967,054	Food other than grain and meat	+ 2,464,572
Non-dutiable food and drink	+ 3,678,390	Machinery	+ 2,201,094
Copper, tin, zinc, lead, &c.	+ 3,618,654	Cotton goods	+ 2,164,560
Rubber	+ 3,247,739	Apparel	+ 1,892,758
Hides and skins	+ 2,613,386	Electrical goods	+ 1,550,503
Wood and timber	+ 2,489,144	Hemp, jute, and flax manufactures	+ 1,376,487
Oils, oil seeds, &c.	+ 2,397,031	Ships	+ 1,358,784
Iron and steel and manufactures thereof	+ 1,837,008	Metal goods other than iron and steel	+ 1,276,613

Leather	+ 1,871,295	Chemicals	+ 1,019,621
Cutlery, hardware	+ 1,717,532		
Chemicals, &c.	+ 1,150,501		
Tobacco	+ 1,088,933		
Machinery	+ 1,052,082		

Many of the items on the import side are swollen by the higher prices of materials, due to the keen industrial demand all over the world; a full examination requires that allowance should be made in this respect before we can ascertain the real increase in the volume of trade . . .

But a first survey of the figures shows that the rise of prices has affected imports much more than exports, while even in the former case the increase is due much more to the expanding volume of trade than to rising prices. The increase in the quantity of British exports cannot be less than 6 or 7 per cent. as compared with 1911. Some particular items of manufacture may be quoted in illustration:

	1911	1912	Increase per Cent.
Iron & steel manufac.	4,515,905 tons	4,814,005 tons	6.6
Machinery	683,651 tons	707,094 tons	3.4
Cotton yarn	224 million lbs.	244 million lbs.	8.9
Cotton piece goods	6,653 million yds.	6,912 million yds.	3.9
Boots and shoes	1,152,000 pairs	1,392,989 pairs	20.8
Motor cars	5,271	6,461	22.6
Motor cycles	7,350	13,024	77.2

And when all allowance has been made for rising prices, the figures show a wonderful expansion in foreign trade compared with ten years ago. The beginning of the Tariff Reform agitation, in fact, marks an important turning point in our overseas commerce. For the preceding three decades the value of our trade has shown no increase, and, though this was largely due to thc fact that prices were falling, even the volume of foreign trade had not increased at anything like the same pace as in the period 1850 to 1874. But, as we have said, 1903 marks a turning point. From that date trade started to increase rapidly, and has never looked back. At the end of the nineteenth century foreign competition with Great Britain reached its most acute stage, alike in the home and neutral markets. English business men seemed to be wedded to traditional and conservative methods, both in manufacturing and in marketing. Our markets seemed to be inundated with goods 'made in Germany'; American bicycles and boots were to be seen everywhere. But with the new century our manufacturers and merchants woke up to the situation; the Tariff Reform agitation forcefully called attention to the condition of affairs; men of business began to look into German and American methods, technical education was improved, the Board of Trade developed its Commercial Intelligence Department, and this revival, stimulated by foreign competition, and working with all the advantages of cheap production, achieved the following stupendous results:

	Imports £	Exports £	Re-exports £	Total £
1903	542,600,000	290,800,000	69,574,000	902,974,000
1904	551,039,000	300,711,000	70,304,000	922,054,000
1905	565,279,000	330,023,000	77,779,000	973,081,000
1906	607,888,500	375,575,000	85,102,000	1,068,565,000
1907	645,808,000	426,035,000	91,942,000	1,163,785,000
1908	593,141,000	377,220,000	79,666,000	1,050,027,000
1909	624,705,000	378,180,000	91,345,000	1,094,230,000
1910	678,257,000	430,385,000	103,761,000	1,212,403,000
1911	680,158,000	454,119,000	102,759,000	1,237,036,000
1912	744,897,000	487,434,000	111,838,000	1,344,169,000
Inc. in 10 yrs	40%	69%	60%	49%

The American bicycle was driven off the market, the American boot has lost its hold, the British clock has recaptured its market, the motor trade has grown up and is pushing its sales abroad. The great staple trades are more prosperous than ever before. To a large extent these results are attributable to the rising cost of production abroad, thanks to American and German tariffs; but in some measure this extraordinary triumph of Free-trade may be attributed to an expansion of business intelligence in reply to Mr Chamberlain's raging, tearing propaganda.

from *The Economist* (11 January 1913)

Section B: 1914 – 40

The First World War disrupted traditional economic arrangements and trading patterns. Government intervention, albeit piecemeal, eventually affected a large area of the economy. The effect of the war on international trade, and on the world productive capacity of heavy industries such as shipbuilding or iron and steel manufacture, was an important element in Britain's postwar difficulties.

After the war, a short-lived boom was followed by the deep slump of 1920 – 2. Thereafter, although the middle and late 1920s saw some improvement, the traditional staple industries failed to regain much of their export trade. In consequence, in economic terms Britain appeared to fare worse than other industrial nations. The slump of 1929 – 32, by contrast, did not affect Britain overall as badly as it did, say, Germany or the United States. In addition, Britain's recovery, at least until 1937, was more marked, better sustained and more firmly based than that of other major industrial countries although regional experience varied widely.

During the period itself, and for many years afterwards, the constantly high levels of unemployment and the evident idle capacity led many to a deeply pessimistic assessment of Britain's economic performance. More recently, attention has focused on the major expanding sectors of the period (including the motor industry, chemicals, electrical engineering, housebuilding and retailing) and on the overall growth record. The latter, in fact, compared quite favourably with what had gone before (1901 – 14) and with the contemporary experience of other countries.

B2 deals with the effect of war on the production of metals and sulphuric acid, while *B3* is something of a eulogy on the wartime achievement of the railways. These contrast with *B1* which reflects the problems of coal production, especially those resulting from poor industrial relations. *B9* and *B4* demonstrate another consequence of the war, the attention given to scientific research for industrial purposes and that given to industries where, hitherto, there had been heavy dependence on the Germans. The extracts from *The Times* of 1920 – 1 reveal certain problems: the limited extent of trade recovery in 1919 (*B5*); contemporary fears at the effects of spiralling inflation and wage costs and of continuing high levels of government expenditure (*B6*); and anticipation of difficulties to come when the record shipbuilding achievement of 1920 is contrasted with the collapse in freight rates and the laying-up of vessels due to excess world carrying capacity (*B7*).

The problems of the export industries in the 1920s and the early 1930s are dealt with in *B10–B14* and *B20*. All see the return to gold at prewar parity as an important contributor to the difficulties faced, particularly in view of the increased competitiveness of world markets. Keynes, in *B8*, considers the likely consequences of this measure, particularly for employment. Excess world capacity in iron and steel manufacture is emphasised in *B10* and the need for more modern plant and new working practices in *B10*, *B12* and *B20*. Technical efficiency as a major influence is, however, rejected in *B14* but this source, along with *B10* and *B13*, does identify tariffs, and their increasingly sophisticated application, as a cause of difficulty. Comparative wage costs are seen as a problem for British producers in *B12*, *B13* and *B14* but are rejected, so far as the coalmining industry is concerned, in *B20*. The roles of poor entrepreneurship and poor industrial relations are concerns of *B11*, while *B20* also comments on the consequences of the latter.

The remaining extracts in this section deal with the period of economic recovery after 1932. *B22* shows that, while exports did increase, the main success of the motor industry was in domestic markets. *B21* seeks to explain how and why the housebuilding boom of the 1930s developed. *B16* outlines the effect of government subsidies on the production of wheat and sugar beet. In *B17* it is suggested that achievement in engineering was patchy, with performance varying widely from sector to sector. *B15* reveals that, in spite of an improved political climate and a preferential tariff, British producers still faced difficulties in the important Indian market. Finally, *B18* and *B19* demonstrate the continuing problems in particular regions. While the abandonment of gold helped Lancashire after 1931 (*B19*), exports of neither cotton piece goods nor textile machinery expanded even to the limited extent of Britain's overall export trade. *B18* indicates a contrast in the rate of recovery between North-east England (where by the mid-1930s shipbuilding, although still below historic levels of production, was picking up) and South Wales (heavily dependent on sales of steam coal, for which demand remained acutely depressed).

B1 Coal Output and Lost Time (1916)

If the output of coal depended on yesterday's conference and on those who attended it, a substantial increase might confidently be expected. It was a fine meeting, attended by representatives of the whole mining industry, from Kent to the North of Scotland, and it was animated by a fine spirit. There was no jarring word, and the resolution pledging owners and men to do everything in their power to increase the output by cooperation was carried without a dissentient. But results do not depend on resolutions passed at Westminster; they depend on the men in the colliery villages scattered over our varied and extensive coalfields. This is essentially a question for the miners, the men who get coal, as some of the speakers said; and we have had abundant experience since the war began that it is one thing to have the consent and approval of trade union leaders to a course of action, and quite another to get the men whom they represent to carry it out. We do not for a moment question the sincerity of the leaders. On the contrary, we are convinced that they are in deep earnest, and we have repeatedly borne witness to their efforts to carry out their pledges to the Government. But they have very little power, and often have to contend with hostile influences. Nothing can be done with organized labour without their assistance, but the battle has by no means been won when it has been secured.

The leaders know that very well themselves, and for that reason they appeal, sometimes in almost passionate terms, to employers to help them by doing their part and sticking loyally to the terms of the pledge. Employers who do not — and there have been far too many cases since the war began — incur a very heavy responsibility. They justify the suspicion which has become second nature among the mass of the men, play into the hands of the fomenters of trouble, and frustrate all the efforts of sober and well-meaning leaders. An essential condition for the success of the present effort to increase output is that there shall be nothing of the kind in the collieries. The owners do not get coal, but they have a part to play, and reference is made to it in the terms of yesterday's resolution. The words 'if every facility is afforded for regularity of work' are an allusion to the complaint that some of the diminished output is not due to the miners, but is caused by failure on the part of the colliery management to clear away coal that has been got. This is analogous to the complaint of delay through bad management in munition works. Such delay is usually due to the abnormal conditions under which work is carried on, and is unavoidable. But there are defects of management too, and it is most important in the present crisis that mine managers should avoid giving any ground for the complaint. MR. ADAM NIMMO, President of the Mining Association, who spoke on behalf of the owners at yesterday's conference, gave an undertaking to that effect, which was very well received.

But when all is said and done, the results will depend on the pitmen. We must hope they will respond, but we cannot be sure of it; nor can anyone. The main facts of the case were clearly stated yesterday by MR. ASQUITH. Coal is always a vital product, but it is more so than ever now. The Navy, the transport service, the merchant fleet, the munition industries of all kinds, and our Allies, France and Italy, all depend upon it. And in addition we need a supply, on which MR. ASQUITH laid particular stress, for export to neutral countries to pay for our purchases from them. But the output has been falling. It fell off by 22 million tons in 1914, and by an additional 12 millions in 1915. The reason is the withdrawal of men from the mining industry by enlistment. Some 235,000 miners have joined the Army, and though their places have been to some extent filled by newcomers, they has been a net reduction of 153,000, or 14 per cent., and the newcomers are of inferior material. The subject has been very fully investigated by the Coal Organization Committee, which is a joint body of owners and mining trade unionists, presided over by the Chief Inspector of Mines, SIR RICHARD REDMAYNE. They have come to the conclusion that an additional 15 million tons, which would meet our requirements, could be raised if the time lost by what is awkwardly called 'absenteeism' were made good. The total time lost is about 10 per cent., and it is calculated that nearly half of this is due to avoidable causes, or, in other words, to deliberate absence from work. It is, however, very unevenly distributed. Some districts have a far better record than others. The worst appear to be Staffordshire and South Wales, where lost time has recently shown a progressive increase. This is the problem which yesterday's conference was called to consider. It is only part of the whole question of our coal supply, of which a serious domestic deficiency, with high retail prices, is threatened this winter. But the main thing is to increase the output, and we must confine ourselves to that point for the present. The policy put before the meeting, and adopted, is that of inducing the men by moral suasion to work more regularly. Great satisfaction was expressed that the alternative policy of suspending the Eight

Hours Act has not been adopted by the Government. It has been advocated in various quarters, but is strongly opposed by the men, and is, we believe, not favoured by many owners. It would certainly cause great dislocation of existing arrangements, and if the end can be attained without it so much the better. At any rate, the other policy is to have a trial. MR. SMILLIE, who made a very strong speech for the men, was perfectly straightforward about it. He said that the deficient output could be made good by more regular attendance, and it was the duty of those present at the meeting to see that it was done. That they will try we have no doubt, but whether they will succeed or not depends on the measures taken. In some districts a very successful system has already been introduced. There is a joint committee of owners and unionists, and regular offenders are fined. If they refuse to pay the fine their exemption certificate is taken away. This is a perfectly legitimate proceeding, because, as MR. SMILLIE said yesterday, miners are exempted in order to get coal; if they do not get it they have no right to exemption. If this system is applied elsewhere it will probably be equally successful; but without some lever trade union leaders can do little.

from *The Times* (26 October 1916)

B2 Metals and Sulphuric Acid (1917)

Iron and Steel.

The primary task of the Ministry in relation to Iron and Steel has been to increase domestic production by bringing into operation every available blast furnace, by hastening the construction of new furnaces now building — of which there is a considerable number — by increasing the utilisation of domestic ores for the production of pig iron suitable for steel manufacture, and by the extension of steel works for the treatment of such material on an increased scale. The heavy demands for ship plates arising from the new shipbuilding programme necessitate, in addition, a considerable development of rolling mill capacity.

This country has in the past been dependent to a considerable extent on the importation of non-phosphoric ores, employed for the production of acid steel, and, although no diminution of supply is expected from this source, yet the large increase which it is hoped to achieve on the basis of domestic phosphoric ores raises new problems in as much as it necessitates the substitution to a considerable extent of basic lined steel furnaces for those of the acid type with consequent adjustments in metallurgical treatment, supply of refractory metal and the like. Already a considerable number of blast furnaces have been brought into operation under this new plan, while others have been changed over to the production of basic iron. A number of steel furnaces have also been altered to basic linings.

Iron Ore. — During the past year there has been a steady increase in the output of phosphoric ores from home sources, and the total output for the year exceeded that for 1916 by 1,600,000 tons. A much larger increase is anticipated for 1918. In the case of hematite ores, there was a serious falling off in output, in consequence of the strike in August, 1917, but during 1918 it is hoped to raise the output of hematite ore by approximately half a million tons for the year.

Pig Iron. — From new blast furnaces and extensions to plant an ultimate increase of pig iron production is anticipated which will increase the output by one-fifth.

Munitions.

Ingot Steel. — As the outcome of these developments it is estimated that, by the end of 1918, the national capacity for steel production will have been increased by more than 50 per cent.

Steel Allocation. — The current home production of steel is distributed with the utmost care among the various requirements of the army, the navy and the shipyards, leaving for other miscellaneous war and civilian needs only 11 per cent. of the total supply. There is in addition the steel received from America all of which is devoted to war purposes.

High Speed Steel.

The output of High Speed Steel, which before the War was 6,500 tons per annum, has been increased to approximately 15,000 tons per annum. Prior to 1914, tungsten, which is required for the manufacture of high speed tool steel, was not produced in this country. The wolfram ore from which it was manufactured was obtained from the Colonies, but was treated in Germany and tungsten could only be procured from Germany. It is now being produced in sufficient quantities in this country, both for our own requirements and for the substantial contribution to the needs of allied nations.

Non-Ferrous Metals.

A special department of the Ministry was established in March, 1917, to assist in increasing the output of non-ferrous minerals within the United Kingdom. This Department has already laid the foundation for many developments, not only of immediate importance but likely to produce a permanent revival of mining activities in many parts of the country. A few examples may be given:

> A sulphur mine in Wales is being developed, from which it is expected to obtain a large supply of iron pyrites containing 38 per cent. sulphur at a profitable cost. A deposit of coprolites in Cambridgeshire has been proved, which will yield 57 per cent. of tribasic phosphate of lime.
>
> With regard to tin, zinc, lead and wolfram, steps are being taken to stimulate production in a number of mining areas and progress is being made in spite of scarcity and cost of labour and materials. A systematic examination is being conducted into the economic condition of the metalliferous mining industry of the United Kingdom. When complete this will afford the necessary information on which to base a policy for future development.

Sulphuric Acid.

The supply of sulphuric acid is of great importance, not only for the manufacture of explosives, but in industry generally. In May, 1917, the Ministry took over the control of manufacture, use and distribution of sulphuric acid, and established a complete system of control both over dealing and prices. It has also been necessary to control the repair and construction of all sulphuric acid plant. A vigorous policy of manufacturing development has been pursued by the Ministry during the past year in regard to the construction of new acid plants, both at Government and at private works. During 1917, additional manufacturing capacity has been completed, or is nearing completion, which will give a large increase in manufacturing capacity (omitting concentrated acid which is produced from chamber acid).

from the War Cabinet Report for the Year 1917 (1917): d 9005

B3 Railways (1917)

In spite of the decrease in imports, the volume of goods traffic on the railways in 1917 considerably exceeded that of any previous period. A number of the imports cut off were replaced by increased home production, notably foodstuffs, timber and iron ore. The United Kingdom has throughout the war been the point of origin or the *entrepôt* of practically all supplies for our own Armies and a good proportion of the supplies for the armies of the Allies. All of this has needed conveyance over our railways and handling at our railway termini, and, gigantic as these supplies were in the previous year, they further increased during 1917 by millions of tons. Goods carried by the canals had since 1914 fallen by 5,000,000 tons per annum, all of which had gone to swell the traffic on the railways. The coastal trade of the country prior to the war found continuous employment for 4,000 steamers and sailing vessels. The huge tonnage of raw material and other merchandise previously carried by this fleet has now mainly to depend on our railways for conveyance. The intensifying of the submarine campaign at the end of 1916 and throughout 1917, in conjunction with the withdrawal of vessels from long voyages, and their concentration on Atlantic routes, made another addition to the difficulties of the railways by throwing on to the west coast ports a greater quantity of imported goods than their equipment and facilities were designed for.

Energetic action was taken to solve these difficulties. To meet the reductions in engine power, a careful analysis was made of the passenger train services of each railway. Trains running over parallel routes at the same hours were cut out, and on main routes and branch lines every train that could be dispensed with without seriously inconveniencing the public was taken off. As a result, the number of passenger trains run was reduced by nearly one-third, with a proportionate release of engine power for more necessary work in connection with the carriage of essential goods traffic. To obtain more effective use of the wagon capacity of the country, a pooling of the open goods wagons of all the railway companies was brought into operation. By this system wagons previously returned empty were reloaded at or close to the point of discharge. Thus the number of wagons running empty was greatly reduced, the train mileage correspondingly cut down, and the rolling stock available for the conveyance of goods very largely increased. To check the fall in canal traffic and its transference to the railways, the principal canals of the Kingdom were placed under Government control and active steps taken to restore them to the pre-war level as carriers.

Particular attention was given to coal, which in normal times constituted about one-third of the railway traffic of the Kingdom. In conjunction with the Coal Controller, a careful enquiry was made into the whole coal movement of the country and the geographical position of each coalfield in relation to the markets it supplied. It was found that quantities of coal were being sent to consuming centres which could be equally well supplied from coalfields less distant, demanding a shorter, and, in many instances a much shorter, railway journey. A scheme was drafted which provided that each area in the country was precluded from obtaining its coal supply except from the coalfield nearest it. The carrying out of this arrangement is estimated to have effected a saving of about 700,000,000 ton miles per annum, with a resultant reduction in the number of locomotives and trucks absorbed in carrying the coal traffic of the country and a corresponding relief to the pressure on the railways.

These several schemes of reorganisation of passenger service, of rolling stock and of the general operations have been supported by the unremitting efforts of every section of railway employees to meet all demands and ensure that the railways of the country should do everything possible to assist in the nation's efforts. To do so has demanded work under continuous pressure, often with long overtime, but in 1917, as throughout the war, this has been cheerfully endured. As a result, we have succeeded in carrying a greater traffic than at any previous period, and this has been done with a reduced number of locomotives, goods and mineral wagons, and over railways which have suffered from three years of insufficient maintenance and renewal.

Not only have the British railways, weighted down under these conditions, succeeded in carrying on all the railway traffic of the war and of the civil population, but they have been able to render immense help in personnel, permanent way and rolling stock to the armies both of ourselves and of our Allies. From the railway companies' own stock 18,000 wagons have been sent to France and other countries, whilst in the railway shops 2,000 twenty-ton covered vans have been constructed for use in France. We have supplied rails and sleepers for over 200 miles of permanent way and have sent abroad nearly 600 locomotives to France, Egypt, Salonica, Mesopotamia and Serbia in addition to constructing 20 complete trains for ambulance work on the various fronts. Side by side with this, the railway shops of the country have, during 1917, manufactured munitions to the value of five and a half million sterling, this being more than was done in the whole period from the outbreak of war until the end of 1916. Most important of all, more than 33,000 railwaymen have, since the 1st January, 1917, been transferred to military service and are either in the fighting forces or giving valuable service in the carrying on of military transport work.

from the War Cabinet Report for the year 1917 (1917): d 9005

B4 The Position of the Electrical Trades (1918)

Section I — Electricity Generation and Transmission

13. As the production of generating and distributing plant forms the chief part of electrical manufacturing it has been necessary to consider whether present methods of generation and distribution are adequate, and if not how they can be improved. The witnesses examined on these points concur in the opinion

(*a*) that it is of vital importance to every industry to have a free circulation of cheap and efficient power supply.

(*b*) that owing to obstacles caused by the present administrative methods, which they unanimously condemn, the supply has till now been deficient, with consequent serious loss to the nation.

(*c*) that the removal of these obstacles will be followed by a widespread extension in the use of electricity and a greatly increased demand for every kind of electrical plant.

14. The home demand alone for electrical machinery and apparatus should already have been sufficient to employ a manufacturing industry with at least three times the present output.

15. There is, therefore, urgent need to place electrical energy at the disposal of all manufacturers and at the lowest possible price, which can best be done by the employment of large units in large central generating stations with suitable interconnection between the various areas of supply. This will involve the subordination or discontinuance of the smaller and uneconomical power stations, and as already stated, if full advantage is taken of the modern applications of electricity the annual saving in fuel alone would be not less than 50 million tons.

16. The obstacles complained of arise partly from the prevailing official atmosphere and partly from legislative enactments. In this

country the attitude towards electrical progress has been far too restrictive, in contrast with the widespread official and public encouragement of the use of electrical energy abroad.

17. The existing procedure is complicated and responsibility divided.

18. At present all new or extension orders authorising electric supply must be sanctioned by the Board of Trade and afterwards confirmed by Parliament. All administrative matters affecting electrical undertakers generally are determined by the Board of Trade.

19. The Regulations of the Board of Trade are directed primarily to secure the safety of the public, and secondarily to ensure a proper and sufficient supply of electricity.

20. In the case of Municipal Authorities, loans for extensions or for new projects have to be submitted to and sanctioned by the Local Government Board, or in the case of the County of London, by the London County Council. These Authorities confine themselves mainly to a consideration of the financial position of the local authority, and the financial record of the undertaking, or to questions affecting lands, and have little regard to the efficiency or suitability of the projected expenditure. In Scotland and in Ireland the procedure, though differing in detail, is substantially the same.

21. In all cases, whether the undertaking be municipal or private, local considerations, owing to the possible exercise of parliamentary pressure, may become the determining factor in the action of the authorities.

22. In the past, lack of foresight in the granting of authority for the supply of electricity has allowed even adjacent undertakings to establish works differing, not only in type of plant and mains, but also in pressures and frequencies, with the result that linking-up and interchange of power is now extraordinarily difficult and costly. The mischievous effect of that policy has been brought into prominence by the attempt now being made to comply with the circular issued in 1916 by the Board of Trade urging undertakers to link up with one another in the national interests so as to reduce the consumption of coal and economise on labour.

23. As a result of this circular a Joint Committee has been appointed by the Incorporated Municipal Electrical Association and the Incorporated Association of Electrical Power Companies to consider the question of linking-up in all its aspects. This Joint Committee has issued a constructive memorandum setting out the

present position of the public supply of electricity, including the following significant paragraph:

> Sufficient time has elapsed and sufficient experience is available to show the defects of the original legislation. Experience has shown that the comparatively small areas of the companies and local authorities working under Provisional Orders are, in many cases, insufficient to enable advantage to be taken of modern improvements in plant. It is also evident that liability to compulsory purchase imposed upon the undertakings of companies working under Provisional Orders, has restricted enterprise and retarded the development of electric supply. Since some of the companies operate in very important districts, immediate measures should be adopted to deal with this difficulty.

24. In case where provision for compulsory purchase has been inserted, in the supposed interest of the public, it is impossible for the undertakings, as the time of purchase approaches, to keep abreast of technical progress or to expend fresh capital to the best advantage. The liability to purchase at short recurring intervals on terms which may not return the original outlay dictates a hand-to-mouth policy as hurtful to the public as to the undertaker. In this case there is no necessary inconsistency between the interests of the public and of the individual, and it should be the aim of the State to secure to the nation the full benefit of scientific progress. Attention is also called to the anomalous inequalities of tenure as between municipalities, Parliamentary companies and companies working under Provisional Orders . . .

Section III — Manufacturing

38. The term 'electrical manufactures' is generally understood to include boilers, turbines or engines and the electrical generators which they drive, and the mains, instruments and apparatus connected with the distribution and consumption of electrical energy.

39. The Committee has considered the relative position of electrical manufacturing in Great Britain and in competing countries, the different conditions under which the industry has been developed in each country and the remedial measures recommended.

40. The manufacturing of electrical machinery and apparatus in Great Britain has been, with few exceptions, far from prosperous. Most of the companies have sustained serious losses, necessitating

the writing down of capital. Tables have been put in evidence showing that thirty-two electrical firms, with an aggregate initial paid-up capital of just over £15,000,000, have been obliged to write off no less than £3,125,000. The tables further show that few of such companies have ever earned a satisfactory return on their capital. The notable exception has been cable making, which has been consistently successful in maintaining its lead, both in the quality of its manufactures and in financial results, and has thus been able to hold its own in the world's markets.

41. Even allowing for mistakes inevitable at the inception of an industry, and for the rapid advance of electrical science, involving changes in types of machinery, the Committee is convinced that the results would not have been so generally unfavourable but for the hampering conditions peculiar to this country, some of which are described in Section I.

42. On the other hand the German electrical manufacturing industry has been very prosperous. The approximate annual value before the war of the total products of electrical plant, mains and appliances in Great Britain and Germany respectively are set out in the following table:

	Great Britain.	Germany.
	£	£
Total electrical products	22,500,000	60,000,000
Exports	7,500,000	15,000,000
Imports	2,933,000	631,000
Consumption of *home-made* machinery	15,000,000	45,000,000

The approximate annual value of home-made electrical machinery used in Germany before the war per 100 people was about £70, which contrasted with a consumption in this country of only £33.

43. It must be noted that of the £22,500,000 manufactured in this country, a large proportion has been produced by concerns under foreign control, and in the case of British exports a proportion is known to consist of foreign manufactures reshipped as British goods.

44. Reference has already been made in Section I. to the legislative obstacles to the full development of the trade, but there was another important factor, namely, that in the initial stages foreign countries possessed a pioneering advantage in the fact that their general industrial progress had not then reached so high a degree of development as had Great Britain in the application of steam

engineering. Great Britain, on the other hand, had undoubtedly attained great prosperity and technical efficiency in her use of steam plant, and there was therefore less inducement for her manufacturers to adopt electrical driving.

45. On the Continent, however, the introduction of the use of electricity coincided with the advance in manufacturing industries, and there was every inducement to employ the new agent especially as it did not involve the scrapping of power plant still in good condition.

46. Many of the greatest electrical inventions originated in Great Britain, and there is little doubt that, as in the case of steam, our lead would have been maintained had the prevailing conditions been equally favourable, particularly as this country already possessed ample skilled labour on account of its existing engineering development.

47. Another factor retarding electrical progress in Great Britain has been the strength of the gas interests and the influence they exerted to stifle competition.

48. Again, foreign governments, appreciating the importance of conserving their home markets as a basis for the development of overseas trade, imposed protective duties, and exerted influence on State Departments to purchase native goods . . .

58. . . . The Committee is convinced that under properly organised combination or association the cost of production will be materially reduced, and that there is no reason to fear that enhanced prices will be charged to the consumer, as a result of such combination.

59. If electrical factories, which are unquestionably necessary on national considerations, are to be maintained in a state of efficiency, steps must be taken at the earliest possible moment to deal with the problem. A sound and permanent industry can be established not only to supply the home market, but to secure a much greater proportion of the overseas trade of the world. This can be done either by amalgamation among the companies engaged in the industry or by the development of the practice of association for common purposes. In whichever direction action be taken, the Committee is convinced of the need for reform. Only by the creation of strong combinations will it be possible for Great Britain to compete with the great foreign corporations, which not only manufacture, but undertake comprehensive contracts, make powerful

financial alliances, and thus exert in every direction greater influence than is possible in the case of any individual firm.

60. An important advantage resulting from such combination would be the extension of standardisation, which the Committee considers is of the highest importance from a national as well as from an international point of view. It is to be hoped that the Government will do its utmost in future to accept recognised standard plant, as its example in the past, in calling for modifications, has had a pernicious influence on other buyers. During the war makers' standards have perforce been accepted, and have been found to satisfy all practical requirements.

from the Report of the Departmental Committee of the Board of Trade to Consider the Position of the Electrical Trades After the War (1918): Cd 9072

B5 Britain's Trade Balance (1920)

The usual preliminary records of overseas trade for 1919 show very considerable increases in both imports and exports. The total value of the year's trade reached £2,594,000,000, the highest on record.

Measured by value only, exclusive of bullion and coin, imports were valued at £1,632,000,000 against £1,316,000,000 in 1918 and £1,064,000,000 in 1917; British exports reached the total of £798,000,000, against £501,000,000 in 1918 and £527,000,000 in 1917, and re-exports at £164,000,000, against £31,000,000 in 1918 and £70,000,000 in 1917. Thus there is an increase of 315¾ million pounds in imports and 430 millions in total exports. It is satisfactory to note that imports advanced by 23.9 per cent. while the total exports rose by no less than 80.8 per cent.

Advanced prices, however, account for some part of the increase. In order to measure more truly the actual volume of our trading in 1919 compared with the preceding year, as affected by difference of prices, it will be convenient to take the published index figures based upon the average prices of the chief articles of commerce. Taking the average basis of these figures for 1901–5 as 100, the index for 1918 is 274.1 and for 1919 284.0. Applying these proportions we find that if the prices of 1918 had been the same in 1919 the total value of imports would be reduced from £1,632,000,000 to £1,575,000,000 and the total value of exports from £962,000,000 to £893,000,000. From this it will be seen that of the volume of trade in

1919 as compared with 1918, imports advanced by 19.6 per cent. and exports by 67.9 per cent. Compared in the same manner with the year 1913, the last complete pre-war year, when the index was 121.7, we see that imports are reduced by 13 per cent. and the total exports by 53.5 per cent.

Imports

Food, & c. — The total quantities of grain and flour imported amounted to 145,207,000 cwts, against 136,403,000 cwts in 1918 and 174,456,000 cwts in 1917. The declared values were £175,000,000 in 1917, £154,168,000 in 1918 and £154,753,000 in 1919. The quantity of wheat rose from 58,000,000 cwts in 1918 to 71,432,000 cwts in 1919. We received 7 million cwts more from the United States, 13 million cwts more from Australia and 2 million cwts more from Canada. Barley advanced by 11½ million cwts in quantity and £12,410,000 in value, the United States sent more by 6¾ million cwts, and Canada more by 4 million cwts. Rice declined by 5½ million cwts, India being responsible for the shortage. Our supplies of meat were valued at £175,448,000 against £173,679,000 in 1918. There was a shrinkage in fresh beef of over a million cwts; on the other hand imports of mutton rose by 2 million cwts in quantity and £8,684,000 in value; nearly one half the year's supply came from New Zealand. Butter and cheese remained about level.

Raw Materials

Raw materials and articles mainly unmanufactured show an increase in value of £187,962,000; wood and timber account for £43,152,000, raw cotton for £40,486,000, wool for £65,180,000; oils, fats & c. for £14,803,000 and hides for £10,760,000. Turning to quantities, we see that hewn and sawn wood advanced by four million loads, raw cotton by 4½ million centals and sheep's wool by 629 million lbs. 'Other textile materials' fell in value by £2,550,000, the shortage being in flax and raw silk. Petroleum declined in quantity by 601¼ million gallons, probably due to reduced government imports. Rubber rose in quantity by 1,281,000 centals and in value by £12,232,000.

British Exports

The recovery in our export trade has been very marked. In 1917 exports were valued at £517,079,000, in 1918, notwithstanding rising prices, the value fell to £501,419,000 and has now risen to

£798,373,000. Of the increase of £296,954,000 over the 1918 figures articles wholly or mainly manufactured account for £225,081,000 or 75.8 per cent. of the whole increase. Raw materials are higher by £60,264,000 and food, drink and tobacco by £21,353,000, whilst miscellaneous and unclassified articles (including parcel post) fell by £9,743,000. Doubtless the removal of restrictions on shipping is responsible for the decline in parcel post. Coal, coke and manufactured fuel rose in quantity by 4,292,000 tons and in value by £39,831,000, and bunker coal increased by 3,265,000 tons; oil, seeds, fats & c. rose by £11,445,000.

In manufactured articles it is gratifying to note increased values in every section of the returns. Textile manufactures altogether account for an increase of £120,950,000, the advances being cotton manufactures £60,797,000, woollen and worsted goods £48,424,000, silk manufactures £1,591,000 and other textile manufactures £10,138,000. Cotton yarn advanced in quantity by 60,954,000 lb and by £12,522,000 in value, whilst cotton piece goods fell in quantity by 170,496,000 yards, but increased in value by £40,440,000; woollen tissues rose in quantity by 53,600,000 yards and worsted tissues by 2,480,000 yards, jute and linen yarns and piece goods also advanced considerably in quantity. Iron and steel manufactures are higher by £26,611,000, other metal manufactures by £6,266,000, machinery by £16,618,000 and miscellaneous articles not specified by £17,842,000.

Re-exports

Recovery of our entrepot trade is shown by the value of our re-exports, which rose from 31 millions in 1918 to 164¼ millions in 1919, raw materials advanced by £76,080,000, food by £38,884,000 and manufactured goods by £18,329,000.

During the year vessels entered with cargoes to the extent of 29,555,952 tons against 23,233,664 tons in 1918 and 23,228,546 tons in 1917. The clearances outwards for the same years were 34,552,730 tons in 1919, 22,737,331 tons in 1918 and 26,075,824 tons in 1917.

The revealed adverse balance of trade for the year was £669,207,000, as compared with £783,787,000 in 1918 and £467,407,000 in 1917. The later months of the past year encourage the hope that the coming year will show a reduction in this balance against us.

from *The Times Annual Financial and Commercial Review*
(23 January 1920)

B6 Wages and Public Expenditure (1920)

The Federation of British Industries has issued a statement, which we summarise today, upon the future of wages and prices. The Federation has nothing very new to say upon an issue which which has already been worn threadbare, but it sets forth a series of points which were worth reiteration. It holds that, unless means for decreasing the present cost of production are found at once, we shall see in many instances the disappearance even of that minimum of profit without which many industries cannot be carried on at all. Though the Federation does not say so, there are many examples throughout the country of businesses which have reached the stage described. The situation is held to be a result of three causes. The first is the extreme shortage of capital, due not only to destruction during the war, but also to 'the expenditure by the Government of the savings of the people'. The second is the reduction in the quantity of commodities available for consumption. The third is that, while commodities are scarcer, the Government have artificially increased the supply of money which furnishes the purchasing power of the people. Other factors are at work including the depreciation of plant, the reduced efficiency of labour, and the shortening of working hours; but the Federation finds that extremely potent causes are the methods of Government finance, and the extremely heavy expenditure of the Government, which makes it impossible to reduce the supply of money. Either the supply of goods and services must be increased, without additions to credit or currency, or the purchasing power of the people must be reduced; but in regard to the latter point, it is also contended, quite rightly, that deflation must be very gradual. The Federation points out that 'ca' canny' methods reduce the purchasing power of the present rates of wages, which is a truism not sufficiently understood by industrial workers. If one group of workers secure a special advance of wages, they do so at the expense of the rest of the community; while if there is a general increase all round, nobody is any better off. Another important and very obvious contention is that while payments made to capital are for the most part put into the development of industry, payments made to labour are used to satisfy present needs. No redistribution of the existing supplies of wealth can obviate the dangers of the existing economic situation. The Federation says very bluntly: — 'The working classes cannot expect any immediate improvement in their standard of living; They have, indeed, some reason to fear a reduction of it.'

The urgency of increased output is pressed even though factories are going on short time and unemployment is increasing; for the Federation believes that the present condition of trade is 'the direct and inevitable result' of attempts to secure 'a higher share of the nation's wealth' by increased money wages 'without any result to work done.' Higher wages will not increase purchasing power unless output also expands. The costs of production are so high that the public are refusing to buy. What is perhaps even more relevant is the Federation's argument that 'the profits of industry are carrying a deadly burden of taxation,' and that 'the State is relying on profit to provide money needed to meet current expenditure.' In reality the State is relying on sources of supply which it is itself slowly destroying. The requisite profits are no longer being made in many industries, which are being taxed out of existence. Meanwhile, provision must be made for the growing prevalence of unemployment, and no one quite knows how the problem is to be solved during the trying winter which we are now entering.

We have recorded the views of the Federation at some length because, although in several respects they need qualification, they contain statements of principle which cannot be repeated too often. It will take time, much patient exposition, and perhaps some painful experiences, to make industrial workers understand that a combination of higher wages and less work can only bring about economic disaster. We need not despair of the situation. Bad though it is, the bulk of British workers are plentifully endowed with common sense, and there are signs that elementary economic truths are making headway among them. On the other hand, there is no indication of improvement among the factors relating to State expenditure, which furnish the other half of the case drawn up by the Federation. We see no trace of any effort on the part of the Government to effect that rigorous reduction of State expenditure which must be an imperative prelude to the revival of industry and the lessening of unemployment. In a very few days Parliament will reassemble after the Recess. During the holiday period, the last flickering symptoms of an extremely artificial 'boom' have vanished, and the 'slump' is upon us. What account will Ministers give of their stewardship? Have they looked ahead and noted the black clouds which are gathering, and have they taken any steps to reduce their financial commitments and their swollen Estimates? So far as can be gathered, they have done nothing at all to initiate the era of economy which is now essential. They still take refuge in the foolish plea that they are not spending so much as in the period of a war which ended nearly two years ago. In certain instances, and notably in Mesopotania and the Middle East, as well as in Ireland, their expenditure has grown in excess of their original estimates, through causes for which they must bear the responsibility. They are still busily engaged in finding new outlets for spending 'the savings of the people', and in no single respect can they point to any large measure inspired by a desire to save. Unless they develop a new spirit and seek a new way of financial life, the autumn Session is bound to be for the Government a period of deserved retribution.

The paramount question of State expenditure lies at the root of social discontent, of the decline of industry, and of the many social evils by which we are beset. While the Government refuse to take a broad and comprehensive view of their outgoings, while the matter of spending every Minister is allowed to be a law unto himself, while there is no attempt to bring State outlay into closer relation with our greatly diminished resources, the condition of the kingdom is bound to drift from bad to worse. The Government ought to have placed themselves in a position to meet the House of Commons on Monday week with a sweeping list of economies in the current Budget. In point of fact, they will be compelled to submit an alarming array of Supplementary Estimates. They will, further, have to admit that the excess profits duty, on which they have leaned so heavily, is drying up, and that industry is drying up with it; and they will be filled with the secret consciousness that they have placed too much dependence upon the sale of war assets, and have entered upon programmes for which no provision can be made when that limited and temporary source of revenue is no longer available. While national expenditure is far in excess of the capacity of the nation to pay, the sudden increase of local rates has placed new and almost intolerable burdens upon the bulk of the community. In the past, we have been proud to call ourselves a business people. Can the Government claim to have any business instinct whatever, when they are unable to tell the country the total amount raised and expended by or through local governing bodies for several years past? Local expenditure is now a heavy and increasing part of the total annual outlay of the State. When the House of Commons votes the Budget, it ought to be in a position to know, not only how much is to be raised and spent under the Budget heads, but also what the total of local expenditure is likely to be. We shall probably hear a great deal about the rise in rates during the coming Session, for if the House of

Commons shows any disposition to shirk the issue, the ratepayers will soon call their members to account. If the Government think that because the outcry for economy has died down the tax-ridden public have been lulled into acquiescence, they will quickly be undeceived.

from *The Times*, (7 October 1920)

B7 Shipbuilding and Shipping (1921)

Shipbuilding returns of Lloyd's Register, now issued for the past quarter, show that during that period there were launched in the United Kingdom 153 steamships, representing 543,000 tons, the total tonnage launched being the highest recorded for any quarter. By adding this total to those for the previous three quarters which we have already published, we find that the output of new steam tonnage in the United Kingdom last year was approximately 1,992,000 tons. This aggregate is the largest ever launched in this country. It exceeds the production for 1919 by 372,000 tons, and that of 1913, which has hitherto marked the highest point of shipbuilding in the United Kingdom, by 72,000 tons. Yet, unfortunately, the announcement of a large increase in construction can give little satisfaction to the shipping industry. In the later years of the war the 1913 output was constantly named as the annual production at which the country ought to aim, but, when the need for it was great, it was never achieved. Even twelve months ago the news of so much additional tonnage would have been welcomed by many owners. Since then the industry has undergone a radical change. The monthly time charter rate for cargo steamers — a good index to the state of the freight market — is now just one-third of the rate ruling a year ago; many voyage freights have fallen to a similar or still greater extent; owners are ready to sell new steamers at about half the prices they paid for them, and buyers are reluctant; and cargo tonnage, in the absence of satisfactory employment, is being laid up in port.

In such depressing conditions there may be some comfort for those whose business it is to manage shipping that the tonnage now under construction in the United Kingdom, amounting to 3,709,000 tons, shows a decline on the figure of the previous quarter, although only by 22,000 tons. Still, the Register suggests that this may prove to be the beginning of a decline as rapid as the increase which has taken place since 1918. Apart from the building of certain special classes of ships, such as oil tank vessels, for which there may be some assurance of employment, and of passenger liners for the maintenance of regular services, it is difficult to see how orders for new tonnage at current high prices can be expected. When trade revives, and if costs can be put on a lower level, there may be a resumption of contracting. In the meantime, the outlook for the British shipbuilding industry is far from brilliant. In the United States the great war effort has died down. There are now building in United States yards only 1,310,000 tons gross of vessels of all descriptions, as compared with 4,185,000 tons at the end of March 1919, a reduction of nearly 69 per cent.

from *The Times*, (11 January 1921)

B8 Credit Restriction and the Bank of England (1925)

The object of credit restriction . . . is to withdraw from employers the financial means to employ labour at the existing level of prices and wages. The policy can only attain its end by intensifying unemployment without limit, until the workers are ready to accept the necessary reduction of money wages under the pressure of hard facts.

This is the so-called 'sound' policy, which is demanded as a result of the rash act of pegging sterling at a gold value, which it did not — measured in its purchasing power over British labour — possess as yet. It is a policy, nevertheless, from which any humane or judicious person must shrink. So far as I can judge, the Governor of the Bank of England shrinks from it. But what is he to do, swimming, with his boat burnt, between the devil and the deep sea? At present, it appears, he compromises. He applies the 'sound' policy half-heartedly; he avoids calling things by their right names; and he hopes — this is his best chance — that something will turn up.

The Bank of England works with so much secrecy and so much concealment of important statistics that it is never easy to state with precision what it is doing. The credit restriction already in force has been effected in several ways which are partly independent. First, there is the embargo on new issues which probably retards the normal rate of the circulation of money; then in March the bank rate was raised; more recently market rate was worked up nearer to bank rate; lastly — and far the more important of all — the Bank has manoeuvred its assets and liabilities in such a way as to reduce the amount of cash available to the Clearing Banks as a basis for credit. This last is the essential instrument of credit restriction. Failing direct information, the best reflection of the amount of this restriction is to be found in the deposits of the Clearing Banks. The tendency of these to fall indicates some significant degree of restriction. Owing, however, to seasonal fluctuations and to the artificial character of the end-June returns, it is not yet possible to estimate with accuracy how much restriction has taken place in the last three months. So far as one can judge, the amount of direct restriction is not yet considerable. But no one can say how much more restriction may become necessary if we continue on our present lines.

Nevertheless, even these limited measures are responsible, in my opinion, for an important part of the recent intensification of unemployment. Credit restriction is an incredibly powerful instrument, and even a little of it goes a long way — especially in circumstances where the opposite course is called for. The policy of deliberately intensifying unemployment with a view to forcing wage reductions is already partly in force, and the tragedy of our situation lies in the fact that, from the misguided standpoint which has been officially adopted, this course is theoretically justifiable. No section of labour will readily accept lower wages merely in response to sentimental speeches, however genuine, by Mr Baldwin. We are depending for the reduction of wages on the pressure of unemployment and of strikes and lock-outs; and in order to make sure of this result we are deliberately intensifying the unemployment.

The Bank of England is *compelled* to curtail credit by all the rules of the gold standard game. It is acting conscientiously and 'soundly' in doing so. But this does not alter the fact that to keep a tight hold on credit — and no one will deny that the Bank is doing that — necessarily involves intensifying unemployment in the present circumstances of this country. What we need to restore prosperity today is an easy credit policy. We want to encourage business men to enter on new enterprises, not, as we are doing, to discourage them. Deflation does not reduce wages 'automatically'. It reduces them by causing unemployment. The proper object of dear money is to check an incipient boom. Woe to those whose faith leads them to use it to aggravate a depression!

from J. M. Keynes, *The Economic Consequences of Mr. Churchill* (Macmillan, 1925)

B9 Scientific Research in Industry (1927)

Organisation. — The Government sought in the first place to promote industrial research by a scheme for the establishment of co-operative research associations. Parliament placed a fund of a million sterling at the disposal of the Department of Scientific and Industrial Research, and it was decided, after consultation with manufacturers, that the fund should be expended in the form of contributions towards the income raised by voluntary co-operative associations, to be formed in the various industries, for the purpose of research . . .

Results. — Almost all the inquiries that have been made show that the work of research associations has had a definite educational value. Under their influence private laboratories are known to have been set up in the works of numerous members who previously exercised no scientific control over their output, and members of the Councils of research associations have spoken of the increased interest they have taken in the technical side of their business owing to the stimulus they have received from their association.

It may be asked what benefits have actually been derived by industries and the general public from the work of research associations. A few examples of tangible benefits with a definite money value are given below. But for the most part the results of the work of research associations are reflected in a general all round improvement in technique, due to the adoption of scientific methods of control over technical operations and the more extensive use of scientific apparatus and instruments. A good instance of a research that has resulted in measurable financial gain is the work on the heating of buried cables carried out for the British Electrical and Allied Industries Research Association at the National Physical Laboratory. With the aid of the data that have now been obtained engineers are enabled to utilise existing cables to greater advantage, and to effect large economies in future extensions. The Director of the Cable Makers' Association estimates that as the result of the work of the Research Association the supply industry will at once be able to effect a saving of from £250,000 to £300,000 by the more advantageous use of existing cables, and to purchase new cables with a full knowledge of their true current-carrying capacity. Other investigations carried out by the Research Association on overhead lines, switchgear, insulators, turbines, condensers, etc., have produced results leading to considerable economies and improvements in practice. Altogether it has been estimated that the annual value to the supply industry of the work of the Electrical Research Association would be over £1,000,000 if the whole of the industry secured the full benefit of the work; it is known that at least one-third of this value has already accrued.

The work of the Scientific Instrument Research Association has led to the adoption by the makers of optical instruments (especially of photographic lenses) of the interferometer for measuring the aberrations of lenses. An immediate result was the placing of orders for the instrument to the extent of £3,000. A further result will, it is anticipated, be an all round improvement in the efficiency of the optical industry of this country. The Association has also given attention to materials such as abrasives and polishing powders used in the polishing of glass surfaces. One firm estimates that the use of the 'S.I.R.A.' abrasive has effected a saving of between £500 and £750 per annum; a second firm estimates that it has resulted in a saving in labour of 10 per cent. in the glass grinding department. Other firms have similarly expressed their appreciation of the value of the abrasive and of the economies effected by its use.

The joint research upon die castings in which research associations and Government Department are co-operating, although by no means complete, has already yielded results of industrial value. One manufacturer of aluminium alloy casting is stated to have utilised some of the results with a consequent saving of £100 a month.

In the cast iron trade the Research Association has been able to advise its members as regards cupola practice with considerable practical results. In one instance the changes suggested led to the melting of ten tons of metal per ton of coke consumed in place of eight tons; for a foundry with an output of 100 tons a week the corresponding saving would be approximately £250 per annum.

In the textile industries a modification of the wool scouring process suggested by the Woollen and Worsted Research Association led to an actual saving to one firm of at least £2,000 per annum and of at least £1,000 per annum to another. A pure strain of flax giving a notable increase of yield of fibre (25 per cent.) has been produced by the Linen Research Association and several tons of seed were subsequently handed over to another organisation by whom it is being further 'bulked' and placed on sale.

The Portland Cement Research Association devoted a great deal of attention to the operation of rotary kilns with a view to reducing working costs; one firm stated that largely due to 'more scientific management' in which the Research Association had been of very great assistance, it was saving fuel to the value of over £25,000 per annum, while a second firm found that the adoption of improvements suggested by the results of research had led to a saving of from 300 to 400 tons of coal a year.

It would be possible to quote examples of the benefits conferred by the research associations on British industry in much greater number and detail.

General Conclusions. — To sum up, it may be said that the opinions expressed by the scientific experts who have inspected the individual associations, and a survey of the scheme as a whole, lead to certain general conclusions. The scheme has enabled a number of industries to realise the potential value of scientific research and to secure results which are finding their way into industrial practice. Although the results are as yet neither great in volume nor revolutionary in character, they are of importance and are realised to be so. Now that most of the associations have passed through the preliminary stages of organisation and have acquired experience and knowledge of the basic scientific facts underlying their respective industrial operations, more numerous results of direct and practical importance may be expected to accrue.

The scheme is suitable for adoption in this country in industries which include manufacturing units of such small size as to be quite unable to maintain scientific staffs of their own. It has further had a most stimulating effect in fostering an interest in the scientific aspects of technical operations and it has led to the wider adoption of scientific methods of control. Those intimate with the work of the associations and responsible for their management have freely testified to their utility in this direction and to their influence on the future well-being of the industries concerned.

The scheme has made it possible to undertake important scientific work of a fundamental character, which no single firm could be expected to finance; it has further facilitated investigations preparatory to standardisation, and work upon other questions of general importance to an industry such, for example, as moisture standards in textile goods.

Owing largely to the unfortunate economic circumstances

experienced during the greater part of the post-war period no research association, save that founded by the cotton industry, has yet succeeded in acquiring sufficient financial support to embark upon an adequate scale of operations or to furnish undeniable proof of shortly becoming self supporting. The future of research associations must, however, rest with the industries concerned since the State cannot be expected to support indefinitely organisations instituted primarily for the benefit of the industries themselves.

from the Balfour Committee on Industry and Trade, *A Survey of Industries: Part I — Factors in Commercial and Industrial Efficiency* (1927)

B10 The Export Trade in Iron and Steel (1928)

The depression of our iron and steel industry and our inability to market abroad as large a quantity of iron and steel manufactures as before the War are also partly the result of a growth in the iron and steel industry in foreign countries. In this case, however, the situation is materially different from that of coal or cotton. It is pre-eminently a case of lop-sided productive capacity in which potential supply has greatly outrun demand. Largely as the result of the artificial stimulus given to this industry by the demand for munitions, the world's capacity for production is greater than ever before, while the steady growth of consumption which marked the pre-war period has not been maintained. Stagnant consumption outside the U.S.A., coupled with an excessive capacity for production, is mainly responsible for the fact that steel prices have recently been less than 20 per cent. above pre-war level, whereas prices in general have been 50 per cent. higher. The production figures for the world are shown in the following table:

Table 1: World Production of Steel (In millions of metric tons)

	1909-13 (pre-war boundaries)	1913 (post-war boundaries)	1924.	1925.	1926.	1927[a]
Great Britain	6.7	7.8	8.3	7.5	3.7	9.2
Germany	14.5	12.2	9.8	12.2	12.3	16.3
France	3.9	7.0	6.9	7.4	8.4	8.2
Rest of Europe	11.3	16.4	12.6	14.5	16.3	17.8
Total Europe	36.4	43.4	37.6	41.6	40.7	51.5
North America	28.5	32.9	39.2	46.9	49.9	46.0
Rest of the World	.3	.3	2.0	2.3	2.6	2.8
Total World	65.2	76.6	78.8	90.8	93.2	100.3

[a]Provisional figures

Compiled from League of Nations Memorandum on the Iron and Steel Industry and *The Economist.*

The consumption of iron and steel depends in a considerable degree on the rate of capital investment in new industrial plant, railways, ships, etc. The paucity of capital since the War is responsible for a diminished demand for the products of the iron and steel industry, except in America, and the preceding table shows that the demand is only now recovering. Our industry has been handicapped in a special degree in the last few years by the very heavy depression in our shipbuilding industry, which is the chief consumer of British iron and steel, and in 1926 by the prolonged coal dispute.

The facts that we have excellent coking coal near the seaboard and that we are excellently placed to import the world's best ores at low rates of freight are permanent influences in favour of this country as a steel producer. But we cannot maintain a large steel industry except on an export basis, for nearly half our present output is directly exported, while of the remainder almost a half is worked up in manufactures which we sell abroad.

Our plant is not, as a whole, so up-to-date as that of Germany and Lorraine. Thus, General Sir Herbert Lawrence, the Chairman of Vickers Ltd., recently declared (according to *The Times* of November 2, 1927) 'that it was a matter common knowledge . . . that there was a very large percentage of the steel and engineering businesses which for one reason or another are ill-adapted for modern production.' Moreover, the extensions made during the War were not located with an eye to foreign trade or post-war competition, but were designed to make the best use of our then existing resources. The industry, therefore, is in need of concentration and a better balancing of plant available for smelting pig-iron and making steel respectively. It has to be remembered that we have to do an export business which must necessarily be of a rather miscellaneous character and cannot effectively be turned out by giant plants such as those of Luxemburg and the United States. Such plants can only be effectively employed in producing a standard product for an immense market. But even for miscellaneous export business, orders should be as concentrated as possible if the cheapest production is to be achieved. It is universally admitted that if our national advantages are to be exploited successfully, our industry must take measures to concentrate output in the plants best fitted for production.

In the meantime, with currency fluctuations to contend against, the British steel industry has failed to maintain its hold upon foreign trade. In the following table the British export figures would look considerably better but for the large reduction in our export of pig-iron, which was an important item before the War, but is now reduced to small proportions:

Table 2: Iron and Steel — Imports and Exports (*In million of metric tons*)

	1913.	1923.	1924.	1925.
Imports				
United Kingdom[a]	2.27	1.34	2.47	2.76
Germany	.31[b]	1.76	1.29	1.20
France[c]	.17	.39	.26	.17
Belgium[d]	.89	.56	.57	.54
United States	.26	.59	.51	.78
Exports				
United Kingdom[a]	5.05	4.39	3.92	3.79
Germany	6.31[b]	1.33	1.56	3.26
France[c]	.63	2.29	2.94	3.88
Belgium[d]	1.58	2.53	3.31	3.11
United States	2.96	1.98	1.74	1.71

[a] 1913 including Ireland; 1923-5 excluding Irish Free State.

[b] Pre-war territory, including Luxemburg.

[c] The Official Trade Statistics of France include the Saar in 1925. In the above table the figures for 1923 and 1924 have also been adjusted in accordance with available figures for the iron and steel trade of France and Germany with the Saar in order to make them directly comparable with the figures for 1925.

[d] 1913 Belgium alone; 1923 and thereafter, the Belgo-Luxemburg Customs Union.

Extracted from League of Nations Memorandum on the Iron and Steel Industry, Geneva, 1927, p. 66.

This Table shows clearly the increase of British imports and the decline of British exports of iron and steel, the gain in French and Belgian exports, largely at the expense of those of Germany, and the decline of exports from the United States. The value of our exports of iron and steel, however, still greatly exceeds that of our imports, owing to our exports being chiefly highly manufactured goods, whereas our imports are mainly semi-products.

from the Liberal Party, the *Liberal Industrial Inquiry, Britain's Industrial Future* (Ernest Benn Ltd, 1928)

B11 The Troubles of the Basic Industries: External Forces and Internal Efficiency (1928)

It is, therefore, a vital question how far the troubles of the basic industries are due to remediable causes and how far they are due to changes — whether of an enduring or of a temporary character — which lie outside the control of those running these industries.

We think that there is in some cases a certain amount of remediable inefficiency within the industries themselves. In certain sections of the coal, textile, and steel industries those upon whom responsibility lies seem to outside observers to have proved themselves unequal to dealing with the new problems which confront them. For example, a failure year after year to deal with the problem of surplus capacity and a continued acquiescence in the wastes of working many plants partially instead of securing the economies of concentration does not seem creditable to the powers of initiative and adaptation of those controlling them. Though there are striking exceptions, coal-owners as a class are becoming a proverbial type of conservative obstinacy in the face of changing facts. Even in these cases, however, the inefficiency often lies not in the technical equipment and management of the individual enterprise, but in the policy and statesmanship of the industry as a whole in the face of changing circumstances. This is probably in some degree a natural consequence of diminished vitality in industries which were in their prime and in the forefront of progress two or three generations ago. Then the leaders of these industries were nearly all pioneers; now few of them have reached their present position by their own unaided abilities, but partly at least because they are the sons of their fathers or the grandsons of their grandfathers. Furthermore, the problems of surplus capacity in the face of stagnant or declining demand are of an essentially different character from those of a period of rapid and continuous expansion.

This is not intended as a criticism of individuals. But the changes which are being made by our competitors, notably in Germany and America, warn us that the organisation of business must develop on new lines, that the relations of great stock enterprises — run by salaried officials — to the public and to their workers must be put on a satisfactory footing, and that new vitality must be breathed into the system of private enterprise.

Moreover, throughout industry our competing strength has been undermined by industrial strife. A belligerent policy by labour organisations has in the past often been the only means by which they could obtain the wages which subsequent experience proved that the industry could pay, and this experience has had the unfortunate effect of instilling into the minds of many workers the false doctrine that the interests of owners, managers, and workers are fundamentally opposed. Until this idea of the class war is eliminated we cannot expect British industry to regain its full potential efficiency. Efficient business organisation and management and the effective co-operation of the partners in industry are the foundations of economic prosperity, and the solution of these twin problems is the main theme of this report.

Nevertheless, when full allowance has been made for such factors, we think that there remain substantial depressing influences of a different kind. Some of these industries are no longer of the same relative importance in the world's economy that they used to be, and are in distress not only in this country but everywhere. Some of them have inevitably lost the precarious monopoly which this country used to enjoy, and find their former customers, often behind tariff walls, making the goods for themselves. Some of them could operate effectively on a suitable scale, but, as the result of abnormal stimulus received during the War or afterwards, are trying to maintain an inflated equipment of plant and workers. In some of them there are branches which formerly yielded a large return per head of the labour employed and were therefore relatively high-wage occupations, but owing to subsequent developments it has become possible to carry them on with less-skilled and lower-paid labour. Unless this tendency is reversed by new inventions or methods, where the advantages of skill and experience can make themselves felt, such processes of production must inevitably tend in course of time to become the business of nations which do not aim at so high a standard of life as ours. Whilst, therefore, we should do everything possible to extend our foreign markets, we think that it would be unsafe to take it for granted that our troubles will be solved by the recovery of these industries to their former pre-eminence.

from the Liberal Party, the *Liberal Industrial Inquiry, Britain's Industrial Future* (Ernest Benn Ltd, 1928)

B12 Increased Foreign Competition in the Cotton Industry (1930)

Increase of Foreign Competition.

17. The manufacturing countries which have made the greatest inroads into Lancashire's export trade are those in the Far East, namely, India, Japan and, to a less extent, China. The development of home manufacture in these countries had begun long before the war, but it received an enormous impetus during the war years when British manufacturers were so handicapped that to a large extent they lost their hold on markets in which they were formerly supreme. The advantage which their rivals thus secured has been maintained and extended since the war.

18. The Indian cotton industry has replaced a large part of the piece-goods formerly imported from Great Britain with goods of a coarser grade, produced in India, at a price at which Lancashire, under present conditions, is unable to compete. The Indian manufacturer has been materially assisted by Customs duties.

19. Japan has largely ousted Great Britain from the China market. Japanese manufacturers have also developed a substantial export trade to India and are now extending it from the Far East to the other main importing countries. China also has greatly increased its production of factory-made cotton goods. Two or three mills only in that country are controlled by British capital and over forty by Japanese capital.

20. The expanding industry in the United States has been directed, for the most part, to supply the huge home market, but there are signs that, with its mass production methods, it may become a strong competitor abroad in the future. In the United States the old established factories of the North are suffering as Lancashire suffers, and the trade is passing to new factories in the Southern States equipped with modern expensive machinery, some of which is run continuously, and staffed with cheaper labour than in the North. In certain classes of goods, the Italian cotton trade is also making striking headway.

21. The effect of this widespread increase in foreign competition is well illustrated in the [figures], showing the quantities of cotton piece-goods exported from the United Kingdom to various groups of countries in recent years, with the corresponding figures for 1918. In every case the figures show a decline in trade as compared with 1913. The most serious losses are seen in exports to British India, which, in 1929, showed a fall of nearly 60 per cent.,

and to China and Japan, which show a fall of over 70 per cent.

22. As it is obvious what trade Lancashire has lost, so it is almost equally obvious how it has been lost. Its successful rivals produce and market cheap staple lines in bulk. Often they use cotton which is good enough for them and their customers but has not been thought good enough by Lancashire. The operatives in India, China and Japan work for long hours at low pay. In the United States especially, expensive automatic machinery, with a high production-capacity to the weaver, is run for many more hours in the week than are the ordinary looms in this country.

23. Lancashire must choose. She can lose her trade, she can reduce her standard of wage and living, or, perhaps, she can keep her trade and her wage standard by reducing costs and improving methods. Her rivals produce for stock, use cheaper cotton and control sales and orders. It is for the trade, employers and employed in co-operation, to decide how salvation can be found in any or all of those changes. Other manufacturing countries do not start with the advantages or the handicaps that Lancashire possesses. Their employers and their operatives have not the technical skill which has been bred into Lancashire through generations and in which her employers and men have outdistanced all competitors. They have not developed the network of merchant firms which have served Lancashire so well in the past, nor have they developed a futures market. By not hedging their cotton they made large gains when cotton prices were rising, but in the recent period of falling prices, some of the Japanese trading firms are stated, on this account, to have suffered severe losses. As a set-off against these handicaps, they are free from the adhesions of custom and practice and prejudice well founded in the past and difficult to shake off when conditions change. It was by her readiness to adopt new ideas and practices that Lancashire gained her trade 100 years ago and beat her well-established rivals of India, who clung to old ideas. Now times have changed, and once more the trade passes to the manufacturer, the operative and the merchant, who give the world what it wants at the price it can afford to pay.

24. Lancashire has always justly prided herself on the excellence, both as to quality and design, of the cotton goods which she produces. In these respects, she retains to-day her pre-eminent position. Unfortunately, however, the bulk of the consumers of exported cotton goods, many of whom are agriculturists, are persons whose purchasing power was always low and has, in many

cases, been reduced still further since the war. Price is for consumers of this class the essential factor, and the success of Lancashire's competitors, and, in particular, the success of Japan, has been due to their being able to manufacture cotton goods and market them at prices substantially less than those of competing goods made in Lancashire. The Japanese product may not be as good as that of Lancashire, but it is sufficiently good to satisfy the requirements of the markets in which it is sold. To cheapen manufacture by long runs of the same design, Japan has linked marketing to production and established a rational control over her industry. The Japanese industry has been handicapped by higher capital costs, but it has had a lower wage level, double-shifts, longer hours worked by labour, proximity to markets, monetary conditions favourable to export and lower social charges upon industry. Similar advantages are, or have been, enjoyed by a number of other competing countries.

25. After making all allowances for the disadvantages which have their causes outside the cotton industry and are shared by the Lancashire cotton industry with other British export trades, we are satisfied, from the evidence laid before us, that the British cotton industry has failed to adapt its organisation and methods to changed conditions and so has failed, and is failing, to secure that cheapness of production and efficiency in marketing which alone sells staple goods in the East to-day. . .

Indian Cotton.

40. For the manufacture of the cheap cloths with which they have so largely ousted British goods in the Eastern markets, the Japanese have made extensive use of the short-stapled Indian cotton; but only an insignificant fraction (about 5 per cent. of last year's exports) of the Indian crop is absorbed by Lancashire. This cotton has been substantially cheaper than the longer-stapled American cotton, partly because Lancashire has not bought it. In this way Lancashire has allowed Japan to start with an initial advantage in the price of raw material which she increases at every stage of manufacture and distribution. In present circumstances the Lancashire cotton industry cannot afford to use for the manufacture of cheap goods higher quality cotton than that successfully used by her foreign rivals.

41. One of the secrets of the success of the Japanese in the use of this cotton appears to lie in their skill in mixing different growths of cotton. We are assured that Lancashire has the skill to make equally

good cloth out of such mixtures if her spinners, manufacturers and operatives are prepared to co-operate to that end.

Improvements in the Spinning Processes.

42. According to the evidence received, the use of short-stapled cotton would be facilitated by the substitution of ring spindles for the mules now generally used in Lancashire. This change would also probably be required for the production of yarn suitable for weaving on automatic looms, although some success, it is claimed, has been attained in the weaving of mule-spun yarns of such looms. Further, the use of short-stapled cotton to produce coarser counts of yarn would upset the existing balance between the processes preparatory to spinning and the spinning itself. Some witnesses expressed the view that to feed the same number of spindles, the cardroom machinery would have to be extended, or else double shifts worked in these processes. They added that before spinners could adapt their mills to the use of short-stapled cotton, they would require to be assured of the existence of adequate arrangements for weaving the yarn so produced and for marketing the cloth when made.

43. At the present time, owing to the competition of the large numbers of spinning mills, much yarn is produced by mills of qualities and counts other than those for which their machinery is best adapted. This practice is uneconomic, but is a natural result of the present conditions by which small independent mills compete with one another for a reduced volume of business.

44. Foreign cotton industries are making increased use of high draft spinning machinery and the practicability of extending its use in Lancashire should, in our view, be carefully considered. Again, in preparing the yarn for weaving, high speed winding machinery is said to offer considerable economies, but it has not as yet to any considerable extent been adopted in Lancashire.

Automatic and Semi-automatic Looms.

45. Another very important question is the introduction of automatic looms for the weaving of those standard cloths in which Lancashire has been largely driven out of the market. These looms do not, as a rule, give a greater output per loom, but each weaver can mind a very much larger number than in the case of the ordinary power loom, and thus an important saving in wage costs is possible, concurrently with an improvement in the remuneration of the

individual weaver. For some cloths, at any rate, it has been suggested that it may be sufficient to add attachments to the ordinary loom containing some only of the features of the automatic loom and costing proportionately less. The initial cost of automatic looms is high, and we received important evidence that automatic looms could not be worked economically on a single shift per day, and that double shifts would be necessary for their effective use.

46. Such far-reaching mechanical changes involve serious considerations of cost and of policy vital alike to organised operatives and employers.

from the Economic Advisory Council, Report of the Committee on the Cotton Industry (1930): Cmd 3615

B13 The Causes of Industrial Depression (1930)

(The following are extracts from the evidence given to the Macmillan Committee on Finance and Industry by Sir Roland Nugent and Mr R. G. Glenday of the Federation of British Industries.)

3175 *Chairman [Lord Macmillan]*: I should like to put one or two questions, not so much on economic theories, but treating you as representatives of industry. What exactly has happened; how is industry actually hit at the present moment? — *Sir Roland Nugent*: It has not got orders, or it is not getting orders at prices at which it can profitably produce.

3176 You cannot compete; is that it? — Partly. It is difficult to answer in general terms. In particular cases, and in a good many cases there is no doubt that while there is an order going somebody else can do it cheaper.

3177 *Mr Brand*: Somebody in another country? — Yes. At the same time there is not the volume of orders. We know that in the coal trade. There is not enough demand for coal in the whole world. It is the same to a very large extent in the steel trade.

3178 *Chairman* The volume of orders available for industry has diminished? — Yes.

3179 And for those that are available the terms are not such as to enable you to accept them and make a profit. I want to get it in terms of industry at the moment in plain form? — I would say that much the more important cause is that the volume of orders available for the whole world is not enough. In other words, the whole trade of the world is not expanding as it should; consequently, that means an intensive competition for what orders there are, and in that intensive competition, not in all trades but in some, our costs are tending to be too high.

3180 *Mr Brand*: Why are our costs tending to be too high? — Largely, I should say because our costs were automatically raised by the return to the gold standard, and the general machinery of industry has not been sufficiently powerful to force these costs down, whether they are wage costs or other costs.

3181 *Chairman*: Then it is a question of the costs of production in this country being too high? — To some extent, but I would say very largely too high not through the fault of industry itself.

3182 First of all, one of the contributory causes of the comparatively high cost of production here, in your view, is the time and method of the return to the gold standard — the jolt then given to industry? — Yes.

3183 I rather gathered that that 10 per cent. had been to some extent taken up in the years that have intervened since 1925? — It has certainly been taken up to some extent, but it is extraordinarily difficult to say how much. In some trades it seems to have been taken up completely, and in those trades you would find that British firms can compete successfully.

3184 *Mr Bevin*: Would you agree that prior to the 1924 jump, or jolt as it is now described, the various industries, through their negotiating machinery for wage alterations and the introduction of payment by results, had tightened up to meet the position as it was then, as far as they humanly could? — I think, broadly speaking, that would be correct. We had in my opinion very, very nearly got readjustment.

3185 And, therefore, when this ten per cent. was put on, industry was given a task that it ought to have been given at least another five years to do? — Yes. I do not think I would dissent from that.

3186 This is for new machinery and new changes? — The whole thing, increase of efficiency, rationalisation, if you like to use the word — the whole bag of tricks.

3187 Legitimately, with industrial relations on the most perfect footing, it would have taken us five years to stand another ten per cent. even if industry had been running fairly well? — I should say so. Of course, against that you might have had a world rise in prices, which would have made your task much less difficult.

3188 *Professor Gregory*: Has the Federation of British Industries considered the question of devaluing the currency? — I think at the time Lord Bradbury's Committee was sitting there was a discussion at our own Committee, but if I recollect rightly we communicated with the Treasury and we were told that it was one of the things that was already ruled out of consideration.

3189 *Chairman*: I would like to follow up the 1925 consequences, in justice to the step then taken. I gather from you that if all the other countries had played the game we should not have had the jolt? — We should not have had anything like the jolt; and if you had had a rise in world prices following our return to gold, it would have 'cushioned' the jolt still further.

3190 And the anticipation at that time was that that would result? — I think it was the view generally held in this country at the time that the international price level would rise.

3191 So it is apparently due to disappointment of what was to happen, or what was likely to happen at that time? — I think that would be a fair way to put it.

3192 If what had been anticipated had been realised, probably we would not have had the disaster so soon? — No. Of course, one comes at this point to the difficulty as to whether what we did was not one of the causes of the expected rise in world prices failing to materialise.

3193 *Mr Bevin*: May I interpose? Assuming you had had a rise of prices and assuming that the jolt had not been so hard, do you think that the fact that you returned to the pre-War parity would have made the cycle shorter, or that for at least another 10 or 15 years, let us say, the cycle of depression would not have recurred? — I think that is beyond my knowledge. I could not really say.

3194 You have not looked at that in relation to the fact that the agricultural areas of the world have been so largely stagnating as a result of the War — Canada, Russia and so on? —

It is difficult to say. Of course, you still had a very badly shaken up world then, and it might be that even if world prices had risen we should have gone through a baddish time. It could not have been as bad a time as we have actually had.

3195 *Chairman*: Taking the situation as we find it with its disadvantages, I gather from you that to some extent, at any rate, the consequences of 1925 have been taken up? — Well, they must have been taken up to some extent. It is very difficult to say how much.

3196 Is that by increased efficiency? — Entirely, as far as they have been taken up. *Mr Glenday*: I must add with regard to that, it is rather a difficult point, this point of increased efficiency, because in every industry you have an enormous range of efficiency, and it is quite possible you may in a sense increase your average efficiency by putting certain firms out of employment. That is, of course, one way in which it works.

3197 *Mr Bevin*: Is not the cost of this increased efficiency now being borne by industry through the present method of raising money for the unemployed, so that in fact the increased efficiency is not showing the same result that it normally would? For instance, the fact that when you had increased efficiency before the War with the ordinary normal market — take the skilled trades at any rate, engineers, boilermakers and all the rest of them — their range of unemployment was never anything more than 3 per cent. to 6 per cent. at the most? — Yes.

3198 The fact that you have been obtaining increased efficiency, rationalisation, at this moment, has put up their range of unemployment to 20 per cent.? — Yes.

3199 Therefore, is not the fact that you are trying to pay for that unemployment by contributions from the workmen and the employers nullifying to some extent the effect of decreased costs at the other end? — *Sir Roland Nugent*: To some extent.

3200 If you want to get the full benefit of increased efficiency in the cost of production it is necessary, is it not, to transfer the whole cost of unemployment to income tax or some form of tax which comes out of profit? — *Mr Glenday*: That does not seem to bring it any nearer. *Sir Roland Nugent*: It is on the whole community even if it is not on the individual firm.

3201 Then, de-rating does not help you? — Only indirectly. It helps you to this extent. You are taking a direct charge on the individual firm and making it an indirect charge through placing it on the community. To that extent the industrialist is benefiting.

3202 *Mr Frater Taylor*: Surely Mr Bevin's suggestion would meet you in regard to exports since it would reduce costs? *Mr Bevin*: I do not know that it is a suggestion. I am trying to analyse the matter. — De-rating, to take a concrete example, removes something which comes directly on your cost and puts it as a charge on the whole community, some of which comes back to you.

3203 *Chairman:* It is a re-distribution of the burden? — Yes, you are shifting the point of impact of the burden.

3204 A sum has to be raised somehow or other for the purpose of providing for local government. If it is not raised from industry by valuation of industrial assets it has to be raised from some other source, but the country still has to pay? — Yes.

3205 On the other hand, inasmuch as industry has to produce money for all classes in the country, it might be worth while lightening the burden on industry in order ultimately to make things better for everybody? — Yes.

3206 *Mr Bevin*: Do you mean this: that at present the cost of unemployment which is caused by endeavouring to get increased efficiency falls, as the result of that particular form of taxation, directly on the producing trades? — Yes.

3207 And, therefore, it is not borne equally over the whole community, is it — No.

3208 *Sir Walter Raine*: Can you tell us how far you think the raising of foreign tariffs is responsible for the present situation in comparison with 1924 and 1925? — It is scarcely attributable to it. Since 1925 I do not suppose the difference is very big but since pre-War I think you have two factors: First of all, that the average tariff country is far more expert in applying its tariffs than it used to be. Their technical efficiency in applying a tariff is infinitely more than it was pre-War. Then again, you have the fact that instead of their finance being free trade, it is now in most countries national, so the financial and tariff weapons back each other up instead of mitigating each other. Compared with pre-War I think that there is no doubt that the tariffs, plus the financial policies in other countries, are very seriously impeding our trade.

3209 Do you think that tariffs were even more responsible than the changes in the international money market? — It is very difficult to say. I should say not myself. It is very much a matter of opinion. I personally should say the change in the international money market is the bigger influence of the two. That would not, probably, be the opinion held by the bulk of the Federation's members, however.

3210 I am not asking the question from any political standpoint — I should think the ordinary industrialist who is trying to get his goods abroad would put his weight on the tariffs, which are the immediate and obvious difficulty he encounters. I am only expressing a personal opinion when I say that I think the less superficially obvious influence of 'national' monetary policies has actually been the more serious obstacle.

3211 *Professor Gregory*: The rise in the ad valorem equivalent of post-War tariffs is rather less than people think? — I suppose in one way or other I have seen as much of tariffs as most men since the War, and it strikes me that is it not that foreign countries have so seriously raised their tariffs, as that they have made their tariffs so much more effective; they have very much more elaborate schedules, very careful adjustment of their Treaties so that a concession given to one country only gets to that country and is not passed on by that country to other nations and so on.

3212 I suppose that you would agree that there is this justification for the view of the ordinary businessman, that the fall in prices has, in fact, accentuated the difficulties? — Of course it has.

3213 *Chairman*: It is also an important point that tariffs are not now clumsily applied but discriminatingly applied? — They are really beautiful instruments. Take the French tariff and treaty system. It is a pure intellectual pleasure to watch them manipulate it. It is an extremely fine art.

3214 An art which we do not appreciate? — Unfortunately not.

3215 Of course, if you have an artistic system of tariffs to surmount to get your goods into foreign markets, one of the methods of surmounting the barrier is to lower cost of production? — Yes, but, of course, if the other people mean to keep you out they very soon adjust their tariffs and they get you down to the point where flesh and blood will not stand it.

3216 *Mr Keynes*: Does that not make you a little sceptical about the chances of recovering the pre-War ratio of exports to imports? — Yes. My own feelings have always been that, whilst we should have, I hope, a very substantial and important volume of export trade, 20 years hence we should find the home market relatively more important than it was in 1914. That, I am afraid, we have got to face.

3217 *Professor Gregory*: If you could get over the difficulty of costs, the world is such an enormous place compared to Great Britain and you could still hope to spread your exports over a bigger area? — One might have something similar to what was accomplished by the D'Abernon Mission to the Argentine, a deliberate bargain with a foreign market to give you such and such benefit if you will take a definite quantity of their goods. Probably one would find development of that kind profitable.

3218 *Chairman*: Large scale commercial travelling? — Yes, large scale commercial travelling, plus what amounts to higher commercial diplomacy, a certain amount of bargaining.

from Minutes of Evidence to the Macmillan Committee on Finance and Industry, 20 March 1930 (1931)

B14 Costs of Production and Foreign Competition (1931)

121. On the question of the relative costs of production here and abroad we require to examine the position in some detail. An adverse change in our effective costs of production compared with those elsewhere might be due to any of the following causes:

(i) Our technical efficiency of production might be declining, or increasing less rapidly, than that of our foreign competitors. It is extremely difficult to obtain a satisfactory statistical test of this. Doubtless our technical efficiency is not what it might be — but that is usually so; nor is a falling short of the highest a peculiarly British characteristic. It is true also that several of Great Britain's most important traditional industries are not amongst those which have been showing, of late years, the most rapid technical progress, and that we may have been somewhat slow, partly for reasons arising out of the War, in applying ourselves on an adequate scale to some of the newer industries.

On the whole, however, we incline to the view that the shortcomings of this country in technical efficiency as distinct from organisation may not have been so great or have played so large a part in producing our present difficulties as is sometimes supposed. This view is based on an examination of the relevant statistics relating to the year 1929; we take this year rather than 1930, partly because detailed statistics for 1930 are not yet available, but chiefly because for purposes of comparison with foreign countries the figures for 1930 are much confused by the effects of the world depression, an influence which has to be excluded for the purposes of the statistical test which we are trying to make.

In 1929 our exports of manufactured goods, though declining, were still greater than those of any other country in the world. At the same time our real wages, whilst comparing unfavourably with those in the United States (which country, however, is unable to compete with us in world markets in our principal staple exports such as coal or textiles and many iron and steel products) were much higher than those paid by any of our chief European competitors, as shown in the following table (for January, 1930) based on hourly time-rates of wages:

Great Britain	100
Holland	87
Germany	77
France	58
Italy	43

If we could retain so substantial an export trade in spite of so great a disparity of wage-rates, it would seem unlikely that our technical efficiency can have been much inferior to that of our competitors.

The figures for the increase in output per head per hour . . . confirm this conclusion. Those figures suggest that hourly output per head in 1929 may have been quite 10 per cent. greater than in 1924 and 33 per cent. greater than in 1907. To take particular industries, the output per worker increased between 1924 and 1929 by 27 per cent. in the case of coal, 20 per cent. in iron and steel, and 15 per cent. in engineering and shipbuilding, though the extreme depression in the volume of sales caused a decline in textiles. Indeed, it could scarcely have been possible for British employers to have paid in 1929 real wages 10 per cent. higher than in 1924 for hours 10 per cent. less than before the War, if they had not been making great technical progress, or if they had been falling seriously behind their competitors in technical efficiency.

122.(ii) Access to our established markets may be made much more difficult by reason of increases of tariffs in those markets, or analogous measures, and our relative costs may require to be reduced if we are to be in the same position as before relative to competitors working under the protection of the tariffs. It is well known that this factor has played an important part, particularly in the case of textiles . . .

123. (iii) An adverse change in our position may take place owing to a change in the relative values of the national moneys in which the costs of production are paid without a corresponding change in the amounts of these costs expressed in terms of the national moneys.

It is here that we find the major part of the explanation of the adverse change in our costs of production compared with those elsewhere. The process of raising the gold-value of sterling, which culminated in the return to the gold standard at the pre-war parity, necessarily involved an increase in our costs of production in terms of gold unless these costs were being reduced pari passu in terms of sterling, which has not been the case.

Furthermore, the difficulties which this brought on our manufacturers were seriously aggravated by the fact that shortly afterwards several of our most serious competitors, in particular France, Belgium and Germany, suffered changes in the gold-value of their national moneys of precisely the opposite kind. That is to say, the rates at which they stabilised their currencies in terms of gold had the effect of decreasing their gold-costs of production, except in so far as these costs expressed in the national currency were tending to rise, which was only partially the case. It is difficult, or impossible, to obtain an exact statistical measurement of the competitive handicap which the relative over-valuation of sterling and under-valuation of certain other countries have imposed on our exporting manufacturers. But it is certainly substantial.

124. We must, therefore, attribute the difficulties of those of our industries which are either substantially dependent on exports or which are exposed to the competition of foreign imports largely

to the fact that sterling costs did not prove adjustable to the change in the value of sterling necessary as a consequence of the return to gold at the pre-war parity; and still more so to the heavy fall in world prices which has since occurred.

125. This lack of adjustment has not, however, been a phenomenon working uniformly in all types of industry. The industries which have to sell their products at world prices in the face of foreign competition have in fact made substantial reductions in cost of production; indeed wage rates are low in comparison with other occupations. But the export industries require the services of transport and other occupations in which wage rates have been substantially improved as compared with the pre-war level and must therefore carry in their costs of production some part of the increase in the more sheltered industries. In these circumstances the export industries are driven, if they are to be successful in competition, to force their own costs yet lower in so far as the position is not met by increased efficiency in the transport and other occupations above mentioned. At the same time the cost of living is in part held high in relation to wholesale prices by the very fact that costs in the home services have been maintained, and the burden on the wage-earner in the export industries is thus intensified.

from the Report of the Macmillan Committee on Finance and Industry (1931): Cmd 3897

B15 British India's Trade with the UK (1935)

Maintenance of Imports from the United Kingdom

It is satisfactory to record that imports from the United Kingdom were remarkably well maintained in face of a combination of adverse factors. The actual decline was from Rs. 48¾ crores to Rs. 47½ crores, notwithstanding a fall of nearly Rs. 3½ crores in the imports of United Kingdom cotton piece-goods, while the percentage share of total imports rose from 37 to over 41. This improvement in the United Kingdom position may, to some extent, be attributed to the beneficial effects of the Ottawa Preferences over a wide range of miscellaneous but highly competitive trades.

The political sky is clearer than it has been for many years, and the racial feelings which were the aftermath of the boycott campaign have been replaced by a growing recognition of the value of the

British connection. The realisation of the favourable results to India of the Ottawa Trade Agreements and the visits to India of delegations from the United Kingdom cotton and steel industries have materially contributed to this better feeling, which finds its outstanding manifestation in the Clare Lees-Mody pact between the cotton industries of the two countries.

This first essay in industrial co-operation will, it is hoped, shortly be followed by a similar *rapprochement* between the British and Indian iron and steel industries. The industrialists in both countries are at last realising that the interests of all parties can best be served by substituting a progressive spirit of co-operation and mutual understanding for the old attitude of suspicion and distrust. The stimulus which this movement may be expected to exercise on the import trade is incalculable. As the late Finance Member stated in his Budget speech 'there is, on the whole, a more optimistic feeling in the main business centres than was the case last year.'

On the other hand, there are many obstacles in the path of a material increase in the volume of imports, and in the near future, at least, United Kingdom industries will have to rely on the combined effects of preferential duties and industrial co-operation to enable them to secure, at the expense of other overseas competitors, a greater share of a limited market. The benefits of the preferential duties may be expected to increase as purchasing power revives. The advantages to be derived from complementary agreements between industries in India and the United Kingdom, operating within the framework of the Indian tariff, should be equally marked.

Such industrial co-operation would not only regulate and improve Indian market conditions for both parties without detriment to the consumer, but would ensure that the United Kingdom industry concerned would enjoy an increased share of the market's requirements surplus to Indian production. Further benefits would be obtained from the co-operation of the United Kingdom organisations, with their technical experience and knowledge of world-wide conditions, and Indian industries, with their knowledge of local conditions, in research work with the object of stimulating the consumption of their products by creating fresh outlets and uses for them and by joint effort to develop backward sections of the market and promote entirely new consumptive demand.

Foreign Competition

Japanese Competition.— After the remarkable increase of Japanese imports by 50 per cent. in 1932 – 33, the year of the fall in the yen exchange, the reduction by 20 per cent. from Rs 20 crores to Rs. 16 crores last year came as an anti-climax. It must be attributed in the main to the increased import duties on foreign piece-goods imposed by the Government of India with the specific object of protecting certain Indian industries against Japanese competition, which threatened them with extinction. In June, 1933, the Government of India, by notification under Section 3 (5) of the Indian Tariff Act raised the duties on piece-goods of non-British origin from 50 per cent. to 75 per cent., and these duties remained in force until, in accordance with the terms of the Indo-Japanese Agreement, they were lowered to 50 per cent. in January 1934. This checked to some extent the influx of such great quantities of Japanese cotton piece-goods. From December 23, 1933, by virtue of the Indian Tariff (Amendment) Act, minimum specific duties were imposed on a number of articles of non-British origin, which included boots and shoes, certain chemicals, cotton and woollen hosiery, woollen fabrics, paints, soap, certain items of electrical and domestic porcelain and earthenware, certain items of glassware, hardened fish and whale oil, cast-iron pipes, and umbrellas. These duties were pitched at rates which were intended to restore Japanese prices to the level existing before the depreciation of the yen, and there is little doubt that they have checked to some extent the import from Japan of these items, although Japanese prices have not been increased to the extent that was anticipated. Japanese competition is becoming acute in a constantly widening range of items. The onslaught on the woollen trade is of very recent growth, but in spite of the specific minimum duty of 18 annas per lb., shipment are increasing from month to month and Japanese cloths are rapidly displacing some of the best-known Bradford and Continental qualities. Similarly, in chemicals, the threat to the position of existing suppliers is becoming more serious and is likely to continue.

Competition by the United States. — The effects of an adverse rate of exchange, coupled with the general reduction in imports, caused a contraction in the imports from the United States from Rs. 15 crores in 1930 – 31 to Rs. 13 crores in 1931 – 32, Rs. 11 crores in 1932 – 33, and Rs. 7 crores in the year under review. The fall in the external value of the dollar to the old par rate in May-June-July, 1933, and its subsequent further decline to 5.46 to the pound in November, 1933, gave a stimulus to United States exports in the latter half of the fiscal year, which is reflected in the import returns during recent months. Now that the dollar has for some time been comparatively stable round about 5.05 to the pound, this competition is becoming keener. Up to the end of 1933, the position was complicated by several factors, but this temporary phase, however, has now passed, and the last few months have witnessed a revival of United States competition, notably in respect of motor vehicles, tyres, machinery, hardware and tools, instruments and apparatus and chemicals.

German Competition. — Germany has suffered severely from the competition of Japanese goods, which are invading all the bazaar trades that were formerly the preserve of the Hamburg shipping merchant. She has also been affected to a much lesser extent by keener competition from United Kingdom goods aided by the preferential duties. Thus, her trade in hardware declined from Rs. 108 lakhs to Rs. 86 lakhs, yellow metal sheets from Rs. 72 lakhs to Rs. 47 lakhs, iron and steel from Rs. 42 lakhs to Rs. 37 lakhs, chemicals from Rs. 40 lakhs to Rs. 34 lakhs, instruments and appliances from Rs. 65 lakhs to Rs. 56 lakhs, rubber manufactures from Rs. 15 lakhs to Rs. 9 lakhs, and woollen goods from Rs. 24 lakhs to Rs. 16 lakhs. The effects of the differential duties on textiles of non-British origin have reduced imports from Germany in almost every item. On the other hand, arrivals of machinery rose from Rs. 98 lakhs to Rs. 132 lakhs owing to the boom in sugar machinery, while imports of German dyestuffs remained constant at Rs. 136 lakhs as a result of a firmly entrenched position and price agreements. Notwithstanding Germany's adherence to the gold standard, the desperate efforts of German exporters to retain their overseas markets prompt them to quote rates for export which cannot possibly be related to the true costs of production, and with which United Kingdom shipping merchants, even with the advantages of the depreciation in sterling and the preferential duties, find it difficult to compete.

from *The Board of Trade Journal* (3 January 1935). Reprinted by permission of the Controller of Her Majesty's Stationery Office

B16 Wheat and Sugar Beet (1935)

Wheat

Wheat prices continued to fall after the cereal year 1929/30, and following the financial crisis in September, 1931, a Bill was introduced by the National Government to provide a quota system for home-grown wheat of millable quality, which would secure to producers a certain market at a certain figure, subject to a statutory maximum which was introduced to prevent the expansion of wheat growing to undesirable lengths. Under the name of the Wheat Act, the Bill became law in May, 1932 . . .

The fund from which these deficiency payments were to be made was to be accumulated by a levy on all flour delivered for consumption in the United Kingdom, and lest there should be an undue expansion of wheat production, under the influence of the standard price, the Act provided that the full deficiency payment should not be made on more than 27,000,000 hundredweight a year. In any year in which production exceeded this amount, the deficiency payment, consequently, would be reduced *pro rata*.

The wheat crop of 1932 was the first to be affected by the Act, and it was estimated at 19,800,000 hundredweight. So satisfactory was the standard price by contrast with farmers' prices for unsubsidized products, that the wheat acreage expanded rapidly and the yield of millable wheat passed the maximum almost immediately. On the 1933 harvest, only 27/29ths of the full deficiency payment was received by growers.

The wheat policy of the British Government has been much criticized. Farmers for the most part hailed it with acclaim, and the price of imported wheat, which forms some four-fifths of the total supply, has ruled so low that consumers have hardly realized the tax placed upon them to meet the deficiency payments. On the other hand, there are those who maintain that the adoption of a wheat policy in this country is a mistake, and that state-aid should be given, rather, to commodities which bulk larger in the farmers' sales, in the production of which this country is subject to overseas competition less fierce than that which it must always encounter from the prairie wheat growers. And the wisdom of intensifying the production of a commodity with which the world is already glutted is doubted by many. It is probable, however, that the Wheat Act took no account of these things, and that it represents no more than a decision by the Government of the day to find a way of helping a much depressed branch of home agriculture.

The acreage under wheat, which was just 1,200,000 acres in 1931, rose to just 1,760,000 acres in 1934, an increase of 46 per cent in three years . . .

Sugar beet

Nothing is more remarkable in the recent history of British Agriculture than the position attained by sugar beet. Prior to 1925, the acreage under this crop was so small as to have no place in the annual Agricultural Statistics. In 1934, the crop was estimated to cover nearly 400,000 acres, and the sugar produced from it amounts to something like 25 per cent of the nation's requirements. There had been enthusiasts for the introduction of sugar beet into British rural economy for many years, and one or two factories had been built, none of which operated successfully, notwithstanding encouragement received from the Government through preference in the excise duties on sugar. In 1925 was passed the British Sugar (Subsidy) Act, under which a diminishing subsidy was guaranteed to manufacturers of sugar from home-grown beet for a period of ten years, during which it was expected that the industry would establish itself and thereafter be strong enough to stand alone. The expectations of the Act were realized to the extent that experience in growing the crop has enabled farmers to reduce their production costs to meet the periodic fall in the rate of subsidy. They were falsified in that reductions in costs have not sufficed to enable the industry to meet world competition at the prevailing price of sugar.

The sugar beet industry all over the Continent is a subsidized industry, and the conditions under which the crop has been established in this country are so artificial that it is difficult to trace much connection between it and the economic crisis. Through all the years since 1929 the crop has been a profitable one, and the area devoted to it has expanded steadily.

The Act of 1925 under which the subsidy is secured, expired at the close of 1934. Up to date it has cost the Treasury about £40,000,000. It was announced by the Minister of Agriculture in July, 1933, that it would be extended for a further period of one year, to give the industry an opportunity of formulating a scheme for its future.

from C. S. Orwin, 'Agriculture', in the British Association, *Britain in Depression* (Isaac Pitman and Sons, 1935)

B17 The Engineering Industry (1935)

Judged as an aggregate the engineering industry appears to have made ground. Comparing 1923 with 1929 the Ministry of Labour's statistics show that both the volume of insured and of employed persons has increased. Production indices show that production has expanded, and, as a publication of the Employers' Federation has remarked, 'on balance this country has, during the last four years, held its own against its chief foreign competitors so far as the export trade is concerned, the rate of decline in most cases being not so great in the case of the U.K. as it is in that of the other countries.' But it has been made plain that within the engineering industry as a whole are very divergent sectional tendencies. It is these which provide the clue to engineering's main problems, particularly that of decline in old-established centres. The post-war period, however, contains abundant evidence that in all sections technical development has occurred: technically, in old and new centres alike, much has been accomplished. Marine Engineering firms have taken up the production of various types of heavy oil engine and have thus shared in the orders which have been placed for the fitting of engines into motor ships. This has been a gain, for the proportion of motor ships to the total tonnage of vessels launched has steadily increased. Against this, however, must be set their financial weakness, the added complexity in technical competition which these developments mean, and the present shrunken nature of international trade and therefore of shipping work. In General Engineering contraction in armament work and general machine work, has been offset in part by attempts to produce heavy-oil engine vehicles for use on railways and on the roads: outstanding examples of developments in the production of such vehicles are to be found in developments at such widely separate places as Fodens in Cheshire and Armstrong Whitworths on Tyneside. In Electrical Engineering the last few years have seen considerable activity on work for the national grid system. This was an addition of work to an industry already expanding and it has resulted in giving this section a sound financial basis. Such work is not indefinite: replacement work is evidently remote, and while work of a similar nature on foreign account may be expected, manufacturers have been experimenting with and developing the production of power-using goods, such as wireless-sets, cleaners, and water-heaters, with a view to ensuring a maintenance of work. In the Motor Vehicles section, mass-production methods, illustrated clearly by Morris Motors of Cowley, have not ceased their quest for lower costs. Its continued expansion, in view of this, may perhaps be expected, though it is clear that the proportion of replacement-sales, as distinct from expansion-sales, will tend to increase. Its importance in the post-war period, apart from this, lies in the greater opportunity such methods afford for the use of semi-skilled and female labour, and in its concentration in the southerly parts of the United Kingdom.

Two main strands of the problem emerge therefore out of this consideration of British Engineering. The first comes from the older and contracting sections and is bred of trade difficulty and high unemployment partly long standing and partly cyclical in its character. The second comes from the newer and expanding sections and is derived from their increasing use of mass-production methods. The two converge and are focused in the discussions which have taken place between the Employers' Federation and various unions on the subject of wages, and, recently, the forty-hour week. For the unions the problem is summed up in persistent unemployment side by side with methods making for greater productivity which would seem to make their wish practicable. For the Federation the problem is summed up in keen trade competition with both foreign and home rivals and a level of 'pre-charges' to which a shorter day would be an impracticable addition. So, at the moment, the issue rests, but it is perhaps evident from the analysis which has been made that no answer to the problem can be satisfactory which fails to take into consideration the divergent post-war history of Engineering's different branches.

from E. Allen, 'Engineering', in the British Association, *Britain in Depression* (Isaac Pitman and Sons, 1935)

B18 Special Areas (1936)

Coal

81. The coalmining industry is of such importance to the Special Areas that it deserves particular notice. Mechanisation and rationalisation are constantly reducing the number of men required to raise a given quantity of coal. Thus, the output per man shift has risen from 21.69 cwts. in 1929 to 23 cwts. in 1935 and 24 cwts. in the first quarter of 1936. It is obvious that, if the present hours of employment are maintained, a constantly increasing output would be necessary to give employment to the same number of men.

82. In my First Report I referred to the large part played by the coalmining industry in the economy of the Areas and in particular to

the importance of the export trade. This has indeed been of special importance, both to the Durham and Tyneside Area and to the South Wales Area, but more particularly to the latter. The North East coast has its shipbuilding and allied industries, whereas these do not exist to any appreciable degree in South Wales and even the small amount of ship-repairing done in that area has been reduced by the fall in the trade of its ports. The loss of the coal trade, therefore, has been of particular disadvantage to South Wales and every possible effort should be made to improve its prospects.

83. The changes in the coalmining industry of recent years are illustrated in the following table:

Disposal of Coal in Special Areas and Great Britain. In million tons.

		1929.	1932.	1934.	1935.
Northumberland and Durham	Output	53.55	39.97	44.42	44.30
	Shipped abroad	23.99	15.66	16.39	15.28
	Available for Home Consumption	29.56	24.31	28.04	29.02
South Wales	Output	48.15	34.87	35.17	35.03
	Shipped abroad	28.80	19.72	18.86	18.39
	Available for Home Consumption	19.35	15.15	16.31	16.64
Great Britain	Output	257.91	208.73	220.73	222.25
	Shipped abroad	82.15	57.15	57.09	55.64
	Available for Home Consumption	173.50	149.50	161.48	164.47

It will be noted that, as compared with 1929, there has been a substantial fall in the general output and a still greater fall in the amount shipped abroad (which includes coal shipped as bunkers for ships in the foreign trade). It will, however, be observed from the table that whereas the amount shipped abroad in the North Eastern area and South Wales had decreased in about the same proportion, the amount available for home consumption in Northumberland and Durham had by 1935 almost reached the 1929 level, while for South Wales it was still substantially below the 1929 figure. Figures for the first six months in 1936 for the Country as a whole show that, while shipments abroad are still decreasing, the amount available for home consumption has now exceeded the amount for the first six months of 1929. Separate figures for the Areas are not at present available for 1936, but it seems apparent that not only has South Wales continued to lose in the export market but it has also failed to keep abreast of the rest of the country in the home market.

84. Special attention is frequently drawn to the export position and various suggestions have been made, including that of subsidies to endeavour to recover that market. It should be realised, however, that the question is not the comparatively simple one of regaining markets that have been temporarily lost. Quite apart from international complications, the demand in some markets has been lost partially or irretrievably owing to economic causes, such as the constant improvements in the efficient use of coal and the substitution of oil for coal. In the past the main use to which Welsh steam coal has been put has been either for ships or for steam raising on land. In the case of ships, the steadily increasing amount of tonnage driven by oil has permanently diminished the demand for steam coal. Since 1925 the tonnage of motor ships in the world has increased by over 9½ million tons and there are now over 12 million tons of such ships out of a total world tonnage of 64 million; in addition over 20 million tons are fitted for, and in all probability normally use, oil fuel. Further, the amount of fuel required by coal burning ships is being greatly reduced through increased efficiency. In other fields there have also been great economies in the use of coal for the raising of steam and other industrial purposes, while the development abroad of water power has still further reduced the demand for coal. The market which could be recovered, therefore, is now very much less than that which has been lost, and of the 26 million tons of trade lost since 1929 it might not be far out to say that about half is irrecoverable.

85. I have already dealt with the need for encouraging the development in the Special Areas of processes for the extraction of oil from coal. There is one further suggestion regarding the use of Welsh coal which in my view merits examination. It is pointed out above that South Wales has recently failed to keep abreast of other coal fields in the home market, and it seems worth considering how a greater share of this market could be obtained. One direction in which important results might be looked for was suggested by the authors of the 1931 Industrial Survey of South Wales, in which they state 'it would be foolish to ignore the fact that South Wales supplies admirable coals of the smokeless variety which might well be sold on the domestic market at a price with which low temperature coke will not be able to compete for some time. An expert on low temperature carbonisation has declared that he has never yet come across any manufactured smokeless fuel which is equal to the natural smokeless fuel which can be obained in South Wales and

which can be burned in the open grate.' A greater use of this coal domestically, and also for other purposes where possible, would not only be of considerable value in providing employment in the mining areas of South Wales, but would also have the advantage of making a real contribution to smoke abatement. The recent exhibition opened at South Kensington by the Minister of Health showed clearly the great damage to national health and property caused by the smoke which is created mainly by the domestic hearth.

86. Increasing pressure is being brought to bear upon manufacturers who have to comply with requirements imposed under the Public Health Acts to reduce the emission of smoke and dust, and plant has often to be installed which involves a considerable capital outlay. Is there not a case in the interests of the public for insisting on a similar abatement of smoke from open hearths which causes so much damage and is deleterious to health? I recommend that a start should be made by insisting that all houses over an agreed rateable value should not use in open hearths anything except Welsh or other smokeless coal or fuel.

87. The use of Welsh coal for domestic purposes is not suggested as an alternative to the production of smokeless fuels by low temperature carbonisation processes. It is frequently stated, however, that the demand for these fuels is much greater than the present available supply, and in the South Wales steam coal there exists a vast reserve of smokeless fuel stated to be better than any fuel manufactured by artificial processes, which is unduly high in price.

Iron and Steel

88. In my Second Report, I gave certain statistics of the iron and steel industry, indicating an increase in output without a corresponding increase in employment. The figures available for 1936 confirm the views there expressed that no likely expansion of the iron and steel producing industries would do more than provide employment for the present workers.

89. In 1935, the output of pig iron averaged 535,500 tons per month, as compared with 632,400 tons per month in 1929. For the first nine months of 1936, the monthly average was 633,400 tons, only slightly higher than the 1929 average, though the 1936 steel output, as shown below, was nearly 19 per cent. greater, showing that the demand for pig iron has not increased in proportion to the steel

output. The number of insured workers in the pig iron industry at July, 1936, is not yet available. The unemployment percentage had fallen to 13.5 at August, 1936, as compared with 20.0 in August, 1935, but a comparison may usefully be made with 1929, when with a slightly lower output, the number of insured workers was greater by nearly 6,000 and the unemployment percentage only 10.1.

90. The output of crude steel for 1935 was 9,842,400 tons and was the greatest since the War, the monthly average being 820,200 tons. The monthly average for the first nine months of 1936 is 957,500 tons, an increase of nearly 17 per cent. on the 1935 average, and of nearly 19 per cent. on 1929; while in September the output exceeded one million tons. The number of insured workers engaged in the production of steel at July, 1936, is not yet available, but the unemployment percentage of 16.2 in August last as compared with 21.1 in August, 1935, while showing a substantial decrease, suggests that the workers are not being absorbed as rapidly as the increased output might have led one to hope.

Shipbuilding

91. The improvement in shipbuilding referred to in my Second Report has continued. The amount of tonnage under construction in the United Kingdom, which on 31st December, 1935, was 743,086 tons, had risen by 30th September, 1936, to 928,571 tons. The proportion of this tonnage being built on the North East Coast (including the Tees) has increased from 24.5 per cent. at the end of last year to 26.2 per cent. on 30th September last, the amount having risen from 181,845 to 243,923 tons, which is rather more than twice the figure for 30th September, 1935. Account must be taken also of the substantial amount of naval work already placed, and still to be placed, in the Area, which will give a considerable amount of work not only to shipbuilding yards and marine engineering works in the North East, but to other industries there. The situation has, therefore, greatly improved since last year, and this is reflected in the fall in the unemployment percentage in the shipbuilding and ship repairing industry since August, 1935, from 46.3 to 31.4, an improvement in which Durham and Tyneside have evidently fully shared.

92. It seems desirable, however, to repeat the warning given in my Second Report against too sanguine expectations of a great revival in shipbuilding. The tonnage now under construction is still a long way below the average figure of the order of 1,500,000 tons

which obtained prior to the depression and which some have regarded as a normal figure. I have previously referred to the greatly increased efficiency of the more modern ships. While this may not at present be very clearly reflected in the movements of shipping, it must be remembered that the greatest improvements are of quite recent date and that only 9.5 per cent. of British tonnage and only 7.7 per cent. of the world's tonnage is less than five years old. As the proportion of up-to-date ships increases, their effect on the general carrying capacity will be more and more felt, and the demand for new tonnage is, therefore, likely to be stabilised at a lower figure than that which obtained up to 1930.

General Conclusions

93. From the foregoing short review of the position in the heavy industries of the Special Areas it will be seen that, while there has been a definite improvement during the present year in the shipbuilding and iron and steel industries, there is no prospect of the three basic industries absorbing any large proportion of those at present out of work in the Areas. It should be remembered that the great expansion of the iron and steel industry has little direct effect on the Special Areas, seeing that they contain only three iron and steel works of importance in actual operation, these being in Cumberland and Durham. There are no large units in operation at present in the South Wales Special Area, though when the Ebbw Vale works are in full operation they will, of course, make a substantial contribution towards the improvement of conditions in that part of the Area. Improvement in shipbuilding also has little or no effect in either South Wales or Cumberland.

94. The experience of the last 18 months confirms the view expressed in my First Report that, if the Areas are to attain the degree of prosperity prevailing in other parts of the country, it is essential that they should attract a variety of other industries, mainly of the lighter type. Trading Estates should help in this direction, but in my view further measures are necessary, as indicated in Part I of this Report.

from the Third Report of the Commissioner for Special Areas (October 1936): Cmd 5303

B19 Depression and Partial Recovery in Lancashire (1936)

In late 1929 conditions in Lancashire took a sudden turn for the worse with the beginning of the Great Depression. In a few months unemployment more than doubled. For every 100 cotton workers who had been employed in 1929 only sixty-six were employed in 1930. The depression ran its course through 1930 and the first part of 1931 but, at least so far as Lancashire was concerned, the worst was over by the autumn of 1931 when the abandonment of the gold standard produced a spurt in the exports of cotton goods. Not all the gain was maintained, but between 1932 and 1935 a gradual increase in employment continued.

The world depression had, as one of its outstanding features, a substantial reduction in the volume of world trade, which fell by 26 per cent. between 1929 and 1932. Lancashire's export industries were naturally affected. Exports of cotton piece-goods fell from 3,672 million square yards in 1929 to 2,407 million square yards in 1930 and to 1,716 million square yards in 1932. Exports of textile machinery fell by more than one-half in the same period. Lancashire trade suffered more severely than world trade.

The recovery in Lancashire since 1932 has been only partial. In 1929 the number of insured persons unemployed in the Lancashire Industrial Area was 180,000; in 1935 it was 47 per cent. greater than this, and in March, 1936, it was still 32 per cent. greater, in spite of a decline of 30,000 in the numbers insured between 1929 and 1935. Between 1932 and 1935 the quantum of world trade increased by 10 per cent., and British exports by 18.7 per cent. British exports of cotton piece goods in 1935 were the same as they were in 1932; exports of textile machinery (again a Lancashire product) increased by 6.3 per cent. It seems clear, therefore, that the improvement in Lancashire's foreign trade has lagged behind that of the rest of the country.

So the post-war history of Lancashire consists of two sharp collapses in 1921 and in 1930-31, and two periods of slow recovery. But in both cases the recovery was not complete; the previous high level of activity was not attained. And in that fact lies most that is disturbing for the future.

from the University of Manchester Economic Research Section, *Readjustment in Lancashire* (Manchester University Press, November 1936)

B20 The Coal Export Trade (1936)

Natural Advantages of British Coalfields for Export

The coalfields of Great Britain are situated to the best possible advantage for export trade. With the exception of a small part of the Midland districts, all British coalfields are within easy access of the sea, the average length of haul for export coal being no more than 25 miles. This compares with 50 miles in the case of the Belgian coalfields, 35 to 70 miles in France, 100 to 150 miles in the case of the Ruhr (though the development of internal water transport has minimised the effect of distance from the seaboard in Germany), and 400 miles in the case of Polish Upper Silesia. Polish Upper Silesia can, in fact, only sell abroad, owing to the preferential railway rates given for export coal and by subsidisation through a levy on inland trade. German coal exports are assisted in a similar manner and are subsidised by the industry itself.

The natural advantages of the British industry are such that under conditions of free competition it can land coal on the German North Sea Coast or the American North Atlantic ports rather more cheaply than it can be supplied at those places from the German or American mines.

The Post-War Decline in Export Trade

The history of British export trade since the War is easily told. Before the War cargo exports had averaged 65½ million tons in the five years 1909–13, the principal markets having been France (10.6 million tons), Germany (9.0 million tons), and Italy (9.2 million tons). The pre-war level of exports was exceeded in 1923 (79½ million tons) when, owing to the occupation of the Ruhr and to some extent the effects of hostilities on the productivity of the French coalfields, exports to both France and Germany were greatly inflated. About three times the pre-war quantities were exported to Holland and Belgium also, but the Italian market was already beginning to decline. By 1925 British exports had fallen back to 50.8 million tons. French demand had returned to the pre-war level; German demand, owing to the re-equipment of the Ruhr during the inflation, was at less than half the pre-war average; the competition of reparations coal was beginning to be felt, particularly in Italy, whose purchases from Great Britain were more than 2 million tons below the pre-war average; the seven-hour day had been abandoned by Germany in October 1923 and the export price of German coal was cut heavily at the end of 1924 in an attempt to recover trade; Polish competition was also beginning to be felt in the Baltic. The British export trade at this time probably suffered as much as anything from the reaction of consumers to the profiteering that had occurred in 1923 during the occupation of the Ruhr. The re-establishment of sterling on a gold basis also raised the price of British coal abroad.

The real turning-point of the export trade did not, however, occur until the stoppage of 1926. This inevitably encouraged the more rapid development of domestic production in Germany, Belgium, Holland, and Poland, and enabled the countries which were able to export, notably Germany and Poland, to gain a substantial foothold in markets which had formerly been mainly British. German exports increased from 22½ to over 38 million metric tons between 1925 and 1926 and Polish exports from 8¼ to nearly 14¾ million metric tons. Until August 1924 exports had been denied to Germany by the Reparations Agreement, except to the Netherlands. There has latterly been a considerable development of Turkish production.

Much of this trade was won back in 1927 and following years but not all of it, and while British exports returned to round about the same levels as before 1926, German and Polish exports showed a permanent increase. Competition from reparations coal continued, although it was to some extent held in check under the Dawes and Young Agreements. This was particularly the case in Italy to which Germany regularly exported more than 4 million tons between 1926 and 1929 compared with less than 1 million in 1913, and to which British shipments declined to between 6 and 7 million tons compared with over 9½ millions in 1913. Even after reparations deliveries ceased, German exporters continued to exploit the commercial connections which they had made on the strength of their reparations supplies.

Competitive Efficiency of Foreign Producers

The advance of foreign coal exporters in neutral markets and the decline of British exports to countries which had formerly been large importers of coal was assisted by the general improvement in the technical efficiency of the other European coal producers at a time when efficiency in Great Britain advanced hardly at all. The following figures of output per man-shift do not take account of changes or differences in hours of work, but they serve to show the magnitude of the advance in foreign countries compared with Great Britain.

Output per Man-shift (cwts.)

	Great Britain	Ruhr	Polish Upper Silesia	Pas de Calais	Belgium	Holland
1913	21.5	18.6	23.6	14.9	10.4	16.2
1924	17.6	16.9	14.3	11.4	9.1	14.6
1925	18.0	18.6	20.1	11.8	9.3	16.5
1926	18.5	21.9	23.7	12.9	10.1	19.5
1927	20.6	22.3	25.1	12.7	10.1	20.0
1928	21.3	23.4	26.9	13.4	10.9	22.9
1929	21.7	25.0	26.4	14.2	11.3	24.5
1930	21.6	26.6	26.5	14.2	11.3	24.5
1931	21.6	29.3	29.4	14.4	11.6	25.7
1932	22.0	32.1	31.2	15.4	12.0	28.4
1933	22.5	33.0	35.7	16.3	13.1	30.7
1934	22.9	33.0	38.5	16.6	14.4	33.2
Per cent increase 1913–1934	7	77	63	11	39	87

By 1934 output per man-shift in Germany had reached 33 cwts. compared with 18 ½ in 1913, and in Poland 38 ½ cwts. per man-shift compared with 23 ½ cwts. in 1913. In Great Britain the improvement has been only from 21.5 cwts. to 23 cwts., so that the pre-war advantage of nearly 3 cwts. over Germany has been transformed into a disadvantage of 10 cwts. while the superior productivity of Poland has been increased from 2 cwts. to 15 ½ cwts.

Mechanisation Abroad

The transformation has been due (a) to greater progress in mechanisation abroad and (b) to the greater concentration of production abroad in the larger and more efficient mines.

Output and Percentage of Coal won by Mechanical Means[a]

	Great Britain		Ruhr		Polish Upper Silesia		Pas de Calais		Belgium	
	Million Tons	Per Cent	Million Tons	Per Cent	Million Tons	Per Cent	Million Tons	Per Cent	Million Tons	Per Cent
1913	24.8	8.2	2.5	2	–	–	–	–	–	10
1926	28.2	22	73.6	66	5.8	22	13	53	18.0	71
1927	59.4	23	95.0	80	7.2	26	16	65	22.3	81
1928	62.4	26	98.9	86	8.4	28	17.9	68	23.7	86
1929	73.1	28	112.8	91	10.6	31	21.1	72	24.0	89
1930	77.0	31	100.5	94	9.0	32	–	–	25.1	91
1931	78.1	35	82.1	96	–	–	–	–	25.0	93
1932	81.6	38	70.4	96	–	–	–	–	20.3	95
1933	89.2	42	74.7	96	–	–	–	–	24.4	96
1934	105.4	47	87.6	97	–	–	–	–	–	–

[a]In making a comparison of the progress of mechanisation in Great Britain and abroad it should be remembered that Continental mines have been mechanised mainly with ripping picks and British mines with mechanical coal-cutters.

The output of coal won by machines increased in Germany from 2 per cent in 1913 to 66 per cent in 1926 and 97 per cent in 1934. Seventy-two per cent of the output in France was mechanically mined as early as 1929 and 91 per cent in 1931. Progress in Poland has been less rapid and only 32 per cent of the Polish output was won by machines in 1930. It should be mentioned that mechanisation abroad has involved almost entirely the adoption of pneumatic picks, while in Great Britain coal-cutting machines, usually of the chain type, predominate. In 1913 only 8 per cent of the total output was cut by machine in Great Britain and this figure had only increased to 35 per cent in 1931 and 47 per cent in 1934. The chief explanation of the advance of productive efficiency in foreign coalfields, however, probably lies in the concentration of production. There are still more than 2,000 mines in Great Britain raising an annual output of 220 million tons, though their potential capacity is more in the neighbourhood of 350 millions. The Dutch mines each have an annual output approaching 2 million tons. In France, two-thirds of the total output is controlled by about twelve groups. In Germany, by 1929, an annual output of 160 million tons was being raised by 170 mines,* while in Poland 95 per cent of the output is raised by 23 mines, each having an annual output of over half a million tons. Fifty per cent of the Polish mines are producing 1 million tons of coal or more per annum.

Wage Costs Abroad

It has frequently been stated in the past that the competition of foreign, and particularly Polish, coalfields has been subsidised by the employment of sweated labour. This has undoubtedly been a factor, but much less has been made of it in recent years and the gap is in fact being closed. The depreciation of sterling in 1931 has in fact put Continental wages, in terms of sterling, much more on a par with British wages. It is not often mentioned either that the incidence of labour costs per ton of coal raised is much less on the Continent than in Great Britain owing to the more intensive mechanisation abroad. Owing to mechanisation and concentration of output wage costs per ton on the Continent are generally as low as or lower than in Great Britain, and markedly so in Germany and Poland:

*In 1927 there were 20,211 separate workings in the Ruhr, by 1930 the number had been reduced to half. The output per man per working day rose from 20 to 35 tons in the same period.

Wage Costs per Ton of Coal Raised (shillings)

	Great Britain	Ruhr	German Upper Silesia	Polish Upper Silesia	Saar	France	Belgium	Holland[a]
1913	6.34	5.91	3.47		5.51	6.4	8.2	5.5
1924	12.10	–	4.81	–	7.74	9.6	12.4	11.5
1929	8.50	7.21	4.90	3.36	8.01	8.1	9.8	7.4
1933	8.12	6.35	4.65	3.48	8.90	9.4	9.3	–

[a] Estimated

Even prior to 1929, as the following figures show, there was a tendency for the gap between British and Continental earnings in terms of sterling to be closed. As a result of sterling depreciation the sterling equivalent of earnings per shift in some countries is now actually higher than earnings in Great Britain (though hours of work are sometimes somewhat longer). In terms of national currencies, miners' earnings abroad have declined substantially since 1929, but on the whole the cost of living has been similarly reduced and real earnings have been comparatively undisturbed as the table shows:

Average Earnings per Shift (shillings)
A. Money earnings. B. Earnings including allowances in kind.

	Great Britain		Ruhr		France	Belgium	Netherlands	Polish U.Sil.	Saar
	A	B	A	B	A	A (net)	B	B	A
1913	6.35[a]	–	5.43	5.53	4.28	4.10	4.66	–	4.70
1924	10.64	–	6.08	6.80	5.35	5.66	9.43	–	5.77
1929	9.22	9.61	8.36	8.85	5.53	5.63	8.69	4.58	6.58
1933	9.13	9.51	9.66	10.19	7.69	5.96	11.48	6.20	9.80

[a] Estimated.

from Political and Economic Planning (now Policy Studies Institute), *Report on the British Coal Industry* (1936)

B21 The Housebuilding Boom (1938)

It was with total output at this level of about 200,000 houses per annum that the economic blizzard of 1931 sprung up with full fury. Contrary to some expectations, the blizzard did not deal an immediate disabling blow at house-building. Actually output increased during the year ended 31st March, 1932, as compared with the preceding twelve months.

At this stage of the picture one must think more of the sitter and less of the background; for the way is now clear — using this word in a relative sense — for a discussion of housing output and the building industry at closer quarters.

The table given [below] summarizes housing output according to its source and circumstances since 1930.

Table I: Housing Output (England and Wales)

	Private Enterprise			Local Authorities			
Year ended 30th Sept.	With State Assistance	Without State Assistance	Total	With State Assistance	Without State Assistance	Total	Total Output
1930	2272	107,410	109,682	49,052	2,965	52,017	161,699
1931	1866	129,790	131,656	60,169	3,119	63,288	194,944
1932	2656	130,830	133,486	66,434	2,056	68,490	201,976
1933	2456	166,644	169,100	47,977	1,236	49,213	218,313
1934	2581	257,746	260,327	49,679	3,663	53,342	313,669
1935	230	275,069	275,299	32,685	10,660	43,345	318,644
1936	306	274,348	274,654	63,749	1,125	64,874	339,528

Three main facts emerge clearly: the boom started from a level of output which, in the light of immediately preceding experience, must be regarded as considerable — the industry was, in other words, very far from being demoralized by the crisis; the boom, as judged from the official *output* figures, was not decisively established as such until 1934, when output suddenly leapt forward by 50 per cent; and the increase in output which constituted the boom was due entirely to the activity of unassisted private enterprise.

It is, perhaps, remarkable that the erection of houses was so little affected by the crisis, even allowing for the fact that operations extend over a considerable period and are not easily susceptible to immediate adjustment. The sale of houses was no doubt less easy for an interval, but it remains true that output was not materially influenced.

. . . reference has been made to the combination of favouring economic breezes and developments in building society mortgage technique which have resulted, judged from the standpoint of monthly outgoings, in a material cheapening of a given amount of housing accommodation. The importance of these factors should not on any account be underrated: nor were these (shall we say regional?) favouring economic breezes alone; there were also more general favouring economic breezes. The most notable of these was, perhaps, the rising tendency of real wages over a period of years for those in full employment. As the *Economist* has put it, 'Wage and salary earners . . . after buying their food, drink, tobacco, and clothes had something like £250 millions a year more left over in 1932 than in 1924 – 7.' Moreover, these breezes were supplemented by various developments, some primary and some secondary. For, instance, improvements in transport, and especially in flexibility, made possible the estates on the fringes of the towns; the migration of industrial population and the changing location of industrial enterprise have called forth housing accommodation; the building societies and builders have both undertaken widespread publicity with a view to impressing the public with the merits of home ownership and the attractions of new houses. These factors, along with the rest (including normal need and any shortage remaining as a result of the war), must be given due weight. None the less, it appears doubtful whether they could, by themselves, have fanned housing output up to boom proportions unless some deep underlying force had been present. The presence of such a force, and especially in the more academic discussions of the boom, has passed almost unnoticed. It is this force, however, which, given the various favourable circumstances already enumerated, has transformed the boom from a potentiality to a reality. 'Nothing in economics,' says Professor Taussig, 'is automatic. Everything we have to deal with human beings.' In other words, the essential driving force behind the boom has been an almost revolutionary conception of what are tolerable housing standards among a vast section of the population. One may spread the feast and tempt the appetite, but it depends upon the public whether it is consumed. In the last analysis, therefore, much turns upon public appetite; and in the past decade public appetite has over large areas become omnivorous. Furthermore, it is an appetite which grows on what it feeds. The force of example — the fact that one's friends have moved into a new house, with all the modern amenities — is of enormous potency. The sudden emergence of this appetite must no doubt be interpreted against a historical background. For the mass of wage-earners and small salaried workers, housing has been one of the least progressive elements in social life throughout the Industrial Revolution. In industrial areas, for instance, many families are living in houses which several generations of their forbears have occupied, despite the rise in the standard of living that has occurred meantime.

It is undoubtedly the womenfolk who are the motive force behind this changed conception of housing standards. It will bring in its train a host of problems which are outside the scope of this review, but it will be a force to be reckoned with for a number of years to come. For very many of the families the new houses have represented simply a transfer from a poorer to a better standard of housing accommodation, with little or no increase in total outgoings, or where outgoings have increased the additional burden has no doubt been considered justifiable in view of the better standard of accommodation obtained; and the changes in the building society mortgage technique have simplified the process of transfer.

from Sir Harold Bellman, 'The Building Trades', in the British Association, *Britain in Recovery* (Isaac Pitman and Sons, 1938)

B22 The Motor Industry (1938)

From the facts available, it would appear as though the first stage of the depression was felt by the motor industry about September, 1929, and that recovery in production took place between 1931 and 1932. It is probable that June and July, 1932, were the real turning points, from which months the industry continued to expand right up to September, 1937.

. . . The production of vehicles by classes, compiled according to horse-power, unladen weight or seating capacity, is unknown, but as the United Kingdom producers to-day hold such a large share of the home market, at least 94 per cent, it can safely be assumed that home sales, or new registrations as they are generally called, will reflect fairly closely the proportion of each taxation class that is produced. In this connection, however, it must be borne in mind that the assessment of the higher horse-power categories of private cars presents a difficulty, as they are affected by the imports from U.S.A. and Canada, all of which are of 17 h.p. and over . . .

Imports

In the past, imported vehicles played an important part in the growth in motor vehicle usage, and it may be that the economic depression of 1930 was a blessing in disguise, as, in that year, total [vehicle] imports dropped from 37,784 to 11,278; by 1932 imports had further declined to only 3,072, of which 310 were commercial vehicles . . .

One of the significant features of imports is that whereas the average values of complete private cars have, with the exception of 1931 and 1937 (this latter year being affected by large numbers of low horse-power private cars from Germany and Italy) fluctuated only about £25 either side of £180, in the case of commercial vehicles the average values show quite violent fluctuations. It will also be appreciated that owing to the requirements of industry, in all its many spheres, the majority of goods vehicles, buses, and coaches imported are chassis, the purchasers having bodies built to their own particular requirements.

The motor industry receives protection from import duties. The first duty was imposed on all vehicles in September, 1915, at 33⅓ per cent *ad valorem*. This duty was repealed in August, 1924, but was re-established in July, 1925, for private cars and in March, 1936, for commercial vehicles.

Exports

There can be little doubt that the foregoing duties and the method of taxation have had some considerable effect in retaining their own domestic market for the United Kingdom producers. Taxation in particular, being very high, has brought about the production in the United Kingdom of a vehicle of a size and efficiency which is the most economical to run of any produced in the world. This typical British product undoubtedly shows great advantages for the home market, but is unfortunately not appreciated as so suitable for overseas conditions.

It cannot be denied that the motor industry has played a very large part in the economic recovery of Great Britain. In 1932 its exports of vehicles were only 1,843 below the previous peak year of 1929 . . .

The development of the small private car to suit the home taxation level does mean, however, that a very serious problem . . . presents itself. As readers will be aware, the U.S.A. producers dominate the world motor market and have established not only in their own domestic market, but in other countries, the demand for a large car of about 25 h.p. weighing in the neighbourhood of 25 to 35 cwt. The United Kingdom producers is therefore left with a domestic demand for a small car and an export demand for a large low priced car in many of the most important of the world's markets. There can be little doubt that if in 1932 and 1933 we could have met the general demand for a larger car, the United Kingdom producers would now predominate in the export market. With domestic taxation at so high a level, however, the problem could only be partially solved and no little credit can be given to the United Kingdom producers for the magnificent efforts they made, despite the almost insurmountable handicaps . . .

Sales

Sales of new private cars first showed signs of recovery in August, 1932. Goods vehicles were, however, several months later in showing definite signs of improvement, that is to say, not until May, 1933. Sales of new private cars have in the recovery period made vast strides and the classes of horse-power sold indicate a point that is often missed, viz. that the introduction of a popular 10 h.p. car which moved the 9 and 10 h.p. group from 14 per cent in 1931 to 32 per cent of the total market in 1937, still left the up to 8 h.p. group and the 11 and 12 h.p. group little changed in the share they held of total sales . . .

In January, 1935, there was a 25 per cent reduction in the horse-power tax, and it was hoped that this would give an impetus to the sales of cars of larger sizes, but actually there has been little change in the average horse-power of new cars. An important effect of this reduction was, however, the fact that fewer cars were laid up during the winter months. Thus the loss in revenue from direct taxation was made up not only from natural expansion but from increased usage. National revenue was also increased as more petrol was consumed.

The recovery period has seen two very important changes in the sales of goods vehicles, the first being the tremendous growth in the 2–2½ ton class from 5,055 in 1932 to 24,249 in 1937. The second important change was the introduction of an efficient heavy oil engine in 1932, at which date there were only 279 in use. By 1936 this total had grown to 6,149. It is probable, however, that for goods vehicles the growth in use and the new sales of heavy oil vehicles, which amounted to 1,660 in 1937, would have been considerably more if the heavy oil tax had not been raised in August, 1935, to 8d. per gallon for oil used for vehicle propulsion, even though the differential direct duty on heavy oil vehicles was at the same time abolished.

from F. Duval, 'The Motor Industry', in the British Association, *Britain in Recovery* (Isaac Pitman and Sons, 1938)

SECTION C: 1940 – 80

1940 saw a government approach to the economic demands of modern warfare which compared favourably with that of 1914 – 18. On the whole, the achievements of the wartime economy have been acknowledged as substantial. War eventually brought full employment and a commitment to economic management. It also brought a burden of debt and the liquidation of overseas assets that made improving the visible balance of trade a major postwar objective. However, postwar market conditions were, on balance, favourable.

The record of economic reconstruction and performance after 1945 was uneven. As the crises of 1947 and 1949 demonstrated, not all economic and financial goals were achieved. By the 1950s, it was apparent that many sectors of the British economy would have to improve their performance if the generally successful export growth of the postwar period were to be maintained in the more competitive conditions then emerging. With the development of the Common Market and of the European Free Trade Area, and with the increasingly evident strength of, in particular, the German economy, the capacity of British industries to prosper without protection became ever more of an important issue. In addition, by the mid-1950s Britain was into the 'stop-go' cycle of government policy which has been seen, through its effect on entrepreneurial initiative, as contributing to a poor overall growth record.

By the 1960s and 1970s, Britain's economic failings were indisputable. There was a reappearance of the interwar problems of high unemployment and acute regional economic difficulties. Economic growth, even in relatively successful industries like plastics, compared poorly with that of other major industrial nations. Not only was Britain unable to sustain her share of world manufactured exports but import penetration in manufactures grew rapidly. The quality and quantity of investment, the level of research commitment and the willingness to develop or adopt innovations all received considerable criticism. So, too, did Britain's industrial relations, her labour productivity and the increased unit cost of many of her products, when compared with the achievements of major competitors. Failings were most apparent in industries such as iron and steel manufacture, shipbuilding, vehicle production and textiles.

North Sea gas and oil did not provide the solution to Britain's problems, nor did membership of the EEC.

Successful mobilisation for war is the subject of *C2* and *C3*, although shopfloor opinion (*C1*) presents a rather different perspective. *C3* stresses the need to apply lessons learnt in wartime if full employment, particularly in the previously depressed regions, is to prevail. *C4* assesses achievement in converting to a peacetime economy and emphasises the need to increase coal output if progress is to be maintained. *C5* deals with trading expectations in the postwar world, arguing that export growth would have to be based on 'new' and higher quality export goods (e.g. artificial fibres, chemicals or drugs) and that no long-term expansion can be expected in traditional export industries such as cotton or coal. The importance of maintaining full employment, particularly in the United Kingdom and in the United States, is seen as a prerequisite of world prosperity and, therefore, of healthy demand. *C6* deals with the emergence, admittedly in a sellers' market, of the motor industry as a major exporter, especially to hard currency areas, but *C7* offers a warning that overseas markets can be expected to be more competitive in the future. This extract also indicates the unevenness of postwar increases in productivity, in which manufacturing industry had performed much better than the transport or distributive industries or agriculture. *C8* Also comments on poor productivity and on the dangers of inflation and of 'stop-go'. *C9* welcomes the diminishing trade barriers envisaged in a common market or a free trade area and indicates the potential strength of the highly-concentrated British chemical industries but points out the rapid pace of development in the equivalent industries of Germany and other European states.

The extracts from the 1960s reveal growing concern. Although the economic growth rate was, in historical terms, still high, it compared very poorly with that of other major industrial nations apart from the United States. *C14* indicates that the absence of the structural backwardness associated with a large agricultural sector was one explanation of the comparative growth rate but so too was a low investment level as a percentage of GNP. *C12* deals with the need to improve business education, in particular the need for high-level management schools. *C15* denies any lack of research investment but is critical of the reluctance to experiment. With regard to particular industries. *C10* suggests that the problems of the shipyards stem not from inefficiency but from the low replacement rate of vessels by British owners, whilst *C11* sees the apparently healthy position of the coal-mining industry as dependent on a combination of protection and relative pricing that is unlikely to continue. Against this pessimism, *C13* and *C14* emphasise the dynamism now evident in agriculture, with *C14* seeing atomic energy and pharmaceuticals as similarly progressive and expanding sectors.

By the 1970s, in the face of mounting unemployment, gloom was even more widespread. While the export performance of some sections of the engineering and chemical industries was good (*C20*), the general position was far from encouraging. Increased import penetration was noticeable in vehicles, iron and steel, and textiles (*C17* and *C20*). The shipbuilding industry was seen to have a poor record in productivity and in meeting delivery dates (*C18*). Even in plastics, performance and prospects compared badly with those in West Germany (*C16*). Poor productivity records and high unit costs, especially in relation to our new EEC partners, were seen as fairly general problems (*C19* and *C21*).

C22 reveals that 1980 found Britain in a deepening recession. Manufactured exports were falling, the only major exceptions being electrical and mechanical engineering goods. In spite of the recession, there was the rare phenomenon of a visible trade surplus (primarily the result of Britain having become a net oil exporter). Conversely (and again largely due to the North Sea oil operations), the IDP account (showing net interest, profits and dividends) was, for the first time, in deficit.

C1 'How Efficient is Industry?' (1942)

'I think the industrial situation is very good and if we can organize industry as well after the war, there'll not be very much wrong.' (Clerk, age 50.)

'Damned good — we're shifting some stuff now.' (Labourer, 30.)

'I know there's been a lot of criticism, but I think it (industry) is very good all the same.' (Housewife, 35.)

'To my mind, we're really beginning to buckle in.' (Plasterer, 50.)

'Although we are now at last approaching a war footing much remains to be done. The next important things immediately are the planning and co-ordination of all similar industries to a single plan and the allocation of new materials accordingly. The Lender system and cost plus system to be replaced by this means, by Government costing on basis of raw materials supplied.' (Research chemist, 27.)

'Things are as good as they can be with all the difficulties of world events.' (Managing director, concern employing 10,000 workers, 40.)

'Things are in a shocking mess, we're not doing 50 per cent of what we could and should and want to do.' (Managing director, concern employing 10,000 workers, 55.)

'I still think the whole industrial effort is too half-hearted, when one considers we are fighting for our very existence.' (Secretary, industrial concern, 35.)

'Not a hundred per cent war effort. Probably eighty per cent.' (Clerk, 40.)

'Our industrial war effort is barely satisfactory and highly precarious — capable of either greater improvement or rapid deterioration.' (Business manager, 50.)

'A glorious muddle.' (Machinist, 55.)

'The industrial situation is bloody lousy.' (Instrument maker, 20.)

'Production's practically at a standstill, isn't it?' (Firewatcher, 40.)

'We ought to have a general strike.' (Nursery hand, 25.)

People are very ready to voice strong and definite opinions on our present industrial efficiency. Experience or inexperience of industry is hardly a qualification or limitation in giving definite judgement on the subject. There are, of course, some who are more diffident:

'I don't know much about it, but it seems to me that even now the country's industries are not more than about half mobilized.' (Insurance broker, 20.)

'I haven't *thought* anything about war production — only what the propagandists give you.' (Able seaman, previously articled to Chartered Accountant.)

Many of those voicing the most definite opinions have themselves no direct contact with the efficiency or inefficiency of war production. Even schoolboys readily give their views, like this one:

'I think the industrial situation provides a great problem for us and we are not solving it — the trouble is manpower.'

In a case of this kind, it is important to analyse the basis upon which opinions are formed and given. The opinion is no less relevant whether formed on the basis of fact or of feeling. Indeed, there are many occasions on which opinion based on feelings (which may deviate from the facts) can be more important in producing public opinion pressure and consequent political effect, than where opinion is based solely on the logic of events. Anti-semitism, defence of the Sabbath, and people's behaviour in the battle of Britain, are three of many examples which reflect, in different ways, the strength, and persistence of opinions based very considerably on emotion and only to a lesser degree on a calculation of the facts and realities of the time. And . . . emotional feeling is at a premium in the industrial field. Indeed, in some sections of industry the things one group say about another are more belligerent than the things either of them say about the enemy, Germany, Italy, Japan. In an extreme case — a group of war industries studied in the North — the unit, after making a most careful study of the whole situation from all points of view, reported as follows (this is only one paragraph from a detailed local report):

> The most striking feature of the industrial situation here is the survival of strictly peacetime procedure in the conflict between employers and men, which is still today the predominant conflict here. One looked and listened in vain for any sign of a unity binding all parties in the fight against Germany. From the men, one got the fight against the management. From the management, one experienced hours of vituperation against the men. Both sides claim to be concerned only with improving the situation to increase the strength of the struggle against Fascism, but nevertheless, the real war which is being fought here today is still pre-war, private and economic. There are many reasons and excuses for this, and all parties readily offered them to the investigators.

The above is by no means typical, but the substance of the comment applies widely in war industry. A striking feature of war industry today is the amount of cross-accusation and counter-charge which is going on between different groups of people engaged in war production.

from Mass-Observation, *People in Production* (John Murray, 1942)

C2 Supply for War (1944)

Raw Materials

44. One of the important problems facing the Government during the war has been to meet the demand of the munitions and other indùstries for essential raw materials and, at the same time, to economize in the use of imported raw materials and semi-finished products. This has been particularly important in the case of the iron and steel industry which has previously relied on large imports of iron ore. To this end the home output of iron ore has been increased by more than one-half since before the war. In spite of the fact that this has meant using low-grade home ore instead of high-grade imported ore, the output of pig iron has been maintained at a high level. The total steel production has been consistently above the pre-war average (notwithstanding the need to increase greatly the proportion of alloy and high-grade steels produced), so limiting the increase in imports which the activity of the munitions industries would otherwise have made necessary. Another substantial contribution to the domestic supply of steel has been made by a severe curtailment of our exports of steel products.

45. In order to save shipping, salvage of many kinds of scrap and waste has been intensified and the collection of iron and steel scrap for steelmaking is one-third larger than before the war. Substantial savings in shipping space have also been obtained not only by severely restricting the consumption of timber but also by increasing home production until, in 1943, it was more than four times as great as the outbreak of war.

46. Some of the most outstanding increases in production have been made by the light metals industry to meet the requirements of aircraft and incendiary bomb production. Magnesium production is more than eleven times the pre-war rate — an achievement which has meant the creation of virtually a new industry.

47. In some industries output has been reduced in order to save labour or the shipping space required for the import of raw materials. Thus, in 1943 the output of newsprint was only 15 per cent. of what it was in 1935 and cotton yarn output was about 60 per cent. of its pre-war amount . . .

Agriculture

48. The dominant aim of agricultural production during the war has been to increase the domestic output of food and so save

shipping space. In the United Kingdom, unlike many other countries, there was very little scope for doing this by increasing the area of cultivated land, for almost, all . . . cultivable land was already in agricultural use. Reclamation of waste land has played, therefore, only a comparatively minor part in the drive to increase agricultural output, and the area of land reclaimed and brought into cultivation has, in fact, been more than offset by losses of farm land to military and other non-agricultural uses. The problem has, therefore, been to increase the output of human food on the existing land of a country where production was already of an intensive character. This has been done in two ways — by increasing the actual physical yield of the land (largely by ploughing up grassland) and by increasing the proportion of crops available for direct human consumption.

49. The production of wheat, potatoes, sugar beet and vegetables for human consumption have all been very substantially increased. In 1943 the quantity both of wheat and of potatoes harvested, for example, was more than double the pre-war average, while increases of more than 30 per cent. were achieved in the output of sugar beet and vegetables. To alleviate the shortage caused by the reduction in imports and animal feeding-stuffs, including the by-products of imported materials (which before the war amounted to about 8¾ million tons and in 1943 had fallen to less than 1 ¼ million tons), larger quantities of fodder crops have been grown at home, mainly to maintain the production of milk. The output of meat, poultry and eggs has, however, had to be curtailed considerably.

50. It has been estimated that the net output of human food from British agriculture has increased by at least 70 per cent. in terms both of calories and of protein. The outcome of this agricultural production programme, coupled with the control of food distribution was that, by 1943, it had become possible to maintain our total food supplies at an adequate level while at the same time reducing imports of food by 50 per cent., thus releasing an equivalent amount of shipping for other war purposes. This has been accomplished in spite of the loss of about 100,000 regular male workers. An extremely important part in the food production programme has been played by the Women's Land Army, the enrolled strength of which was over 80,000 at the middle of 1944. In addition, farmers have been assisted by schoolchildren and adult volunteers who have spent their holidays on the land . . .

51. An intensive drive has also been made to encourage produc-

tion in private gardens and allotments through the 'Dig for Victory' campaign. The number of allotments has increased from about 800,000 before the war to about 1½ millions in 1943 and there has been a large increase in the garden area devoted to vegetable production, with the result that private gardeners have themselves produced a substantial proportion of the vegetables essential for the maintenance of health and working efficiency.

52. The reduction in imports of animal feeding-stuffs and the diversion of cereals to human consumption has brought about an inevitable decline in the number of sheep, pigs and poultry. Efforts have been made to increase the number of dairy cows to offset the decline in milk yields per cow which has resulted from the lack of imported feeding-stuffs. The number of other kinds of cattle has been largely maintained . . .

Fisheries

53. During the war two-thirds of the deep-sea trawler fleet and nearly three-quarters of the steam-drifter fleet have been requisitioned for naval purposes, as well as many of the motor vessels engaged in inshore fishing. As a result, the average total landings of fish of British taking throughout the war have amounted to less than one-third of what they were in 1938.

Landings of Wet Fish of British Taking

Calendar years	Thousand cwts.
1938	20,907
1939	15,687
1940	6,268
1941	4,904
1942	6,091
1943	6,175

Section III — Shipping and Foreign Trade

54. The character of the war has made great demands on the use of our limited shipping resources. Since the close of the campaign in France in 1940 and the entry of Italy and later of Japan into the war, the British Commonwealth and Empire Forces have had to be supplied over very long shipping routes. The opportunities the enemy has had to attack our merchant shipping have been greater than in the last war and each successive campaign — Libya, Tunisia, Sicily,

Italy and France — has necessitated large demands for shipping for military purposes.

55. The size of the ocean-going merchant fleet, including tankers, under the British flag at the beginning of this war was 17½ million gross tons of vessels of 1,600 gross tons and over — about the same as at the beginning of the last war. The losses which occurred from the beginning of the war up to the end of December, 1943, were to a large extent met by the production of 4½ million gross tons of merchant ships in United Kingdom shipyards; by the production in Canadian shipyards; by the purchase and temporary acquisition of ships (existing and new) from the United States and other countries; and by captures. Nevertheless losses exceeded gains and the size of the ocean-going merchant fleet under the British flag at the end of 1943 was 15½ million gross tons. When, however, allowance is made for ships which in due course will be returnable to other flags, the total becomes 13½ million gross tons — a fall of 23 per cent. If the ocean-going merchant fleet on United Kingdom and Colonial Registers is taken alone the fall over the same period is about 29 per cent. Since the beginning of 1944 the situation has improved.

Shipping losses . . .

57. At the beginning of the war convoy and other defensive measures for the protection of shipping were introduced without delay. Losses of merchant ships from all causes were nevertheless severe from 1940 to the early months of 1943, rising to successively high levels during the different phases of the Battle of the Atlantic. Losses were also increased by our operations in the Mediterranean. Although losses in any month were never higher than in the worst periods of 1917–18 the attack on British shipping by U-boats, mines and aircraft has been maintained at a high level for a longer period than in the last war. Shipping has, in addition, been subjected to attack by weapons that did not then exist.

Merchant shipbuilding

58. The tonnage of merchant vessels constructed in the United Kingdom in the years 1940 to 1943 averaged nearly one-fifth more than in the years 1915 to 1918. Many of these vessels were of types specially designed to meet particular operational and other war needs, such as carrying and lifting very heavy and awkward cargoes, and were not adaptable to methods of mass construction. As in the

case of naval vessels, war experience called for an increasing complexity of armament and special equipment. This programme was carried out in spite of the heavy demands of essential naval shipbuilding, the difficulties of the blackout and the very large volume of repair work of all kinds. Repairs to merchant vessels absorbed more than half the manpower available for merchant work; this was due to damage caused not only by enemy action, but also by the abnormal weather met with in the high latitudes frequented by convoys to and from North America and Russia. At one period the amount of merchant shipping in hand for repair was over 2½ million gross tons.

New Merchant Vessels Completed in the United Kingdom
(Tankers and non-tankers of 100 gross tons and over)

	Thousand gross tons
1939 September to December	243
1940	810
1941	1,158
1942	1,302
1943	1,204

59. Out of the reduced total of British shipping available during 1942 and 1943, a considerable amount was allocated to the Fighting Services either as troopships, naval commissioned vessels or for carrying military stores. Moreover, a substantial proportion of the ships available are always temporarily idle because they are undergoing repairs as a result of damage due to enemy action or marine risk. Shipping has also had to be allocated to meet the essential needs of British Empire and Allied countries. The greatest economy has, therefore, been needed in every way, not only in speeding up the movements and turn-round times of the ships available, but in bringing into the United Kingdom only those foodstuffs and raw materials and manufactures which have been considered necessary for the war effort and for meeting essential civilian requirements.

from *Statistics Relating to the War Effort of the United Kingdom* (1944): Cmd 6564

C3 The Effects of War (1946)

What successive Conservative governments were unable to do, Hitler achieved within two years. The war solved the problem of the Special Areas — at least temporarily — and brought full employment not only for the workers in heavy industry, but for their wives and daughters. Unemployment was not immediately wiped out — as late as February 1940 there were still 40,000 out of work on Tyneside — but with the Dunkirk drive and later the invasion preparations, the numbers of unemployed fell to the 'irreducible minimum'. By the autumn of 1943, there were only 12,000 unemployed in the North-east area, and 16,000 in Scotland. By D Day, the number out of work in the whole of Wales was only 12,000.

Of the depressed areas, South Wales was the first to feel the economic impact of the war. Being regarded as relatively immune from air attack, it acquired shadow factories and evacuated firms, even before war actually broke out. Nearly a dozen Royal Ordnance Factories were built, for the manufacture of shells and explosives, guns, small arms and ammunition and for shell-filling. Whereas before the war there was no tradition of female employment, because of the absence of suitable industries, the number of women workers rose spectacularly. The Treforest Trading Estate which employed only 1,870 workers in May 1939, had increased to 15,000 by January 1944, most of whom were women. South Wales acquired new light engineering and electric factories; a metal works was opened by Imperial Chemical Industries in a town where nearly three quarters of the insured population were out of work before the war. These developments had a revolutionary effect on the character of employment and on the distribution of the employed population. Whereas before the war 65 out of every 100 workers were miners, dock workers and steel and tinplate workers (47 out of every 100 being miners) the proportion had been reduced by the end of the war to 32 out of every hundred.

The North-east coast was regarded as being exceptionally vulnerable to air attack and this attitude was maintained long after it became apparent that it was no more dangerous than any other area. The consequence was that the Tyneside and Durham area missed the wave of shadow factories and engineering ROF's which settled in Wales. It acquired virtually no aircraft production, apart from a few components, and comparatively little new war production was introduced, although existing firms on trading estates were switched over to war orders. Three ROF's, at Aycliffe, Spennymoor and Birtley, employed between them about 26,000–30,000 workers, mainly women, and the expansion of the chemical industry provided additional employment. In all, in the first three years of war, the number of women employed increased by about 100,000. At the same time, the North-east coast became an 'export' region and, much to the indignation of the local people, lost about 60,000 of its younger and most able-bodied workers to the munitions industries of the Midlands and South.

Scotland, like the North-east coast, was comparatively late in acquiring new war production, and did not immediately benefit by shadow factories. There were, however, Royal Ordnance explosives Factories, and Rolls-Royce decided to develop aero-engine production at Hillington at an early stage of the war. There was strong pressure from the Scottish Members of Parliament and from the newly-formed Scottish Council on Industry to bring new additional war industries to Scotland. The increasing pressure of labour shortage in other parts of the country was a more potent economic factor and although there was little new factory building, there was a considerable influx of war industry especially after the end of 1940. Most of the existing factories and mills were devoted to war work — linoleum, carpet and lace curtain factories started to manufacture shells, torpedoes and cartridges. Even Dundee acquired a share of war production, first with ball-bearings, batteries and machine tools, and later through the development of its 'jerrican' industry. The Scottish chemical industry was enormously expanded. Quite apart from explosives, which was carried on in scattered parts of the country, the production of fertilisers, and phosphates, dyestuffs and drugs was developed. The manufacture of aluminium expanded, and a new magnesium industry was introduced . . . They have increased the lopsidedness of their economic structure, by increasing their dependence on heavy industry, while much of the war employment was on shell-filling and explosives, which would not be maintained. As an article in *The Times* (23.11.43) pointed out:

> The Special Areas have not been disposed of by the war . . . Indeed it is likely that the unhappy potentialities of those Areas have been aggravated by many of the industrial developments imposed by the war.

At the same time, the war had two positive effects. In the first place, it showed industrialists that their fears and prejudices against the Special Areas were unfounded. Secondly, it increased the adaptability and mobility of productive resources, and especially that of labour, a most important factor for any post-war employment policy.

But of even greater importance for the formulation of any long-term policy is the fact that the war-time experience showed that under conditions of full employment it is economically necessary to push production into the Areas of under-employment. Reasons of security and reasons of sentiment may have played their part in effecting a redistribution of the industrial population to the advantage of the old Depressed Areas during the war, but the fundamental underlying motive, which is as compelling in peace as in war, was the economic pressure of labour shortage. It is indeed the only way by which the national income can be increased under conditions of full employment.

from Margaret Stewart, *Taking Work to the Workers*, Fabian Research Series (November 1946)

C4 Economic Survey for 1947 (1947)

Capital Equipment and Maintenance

42. Of great importance also was the restoration of the nation's capital equipment, which had worked at great pressure throughout the war, with entirely insufficient maintenance. Our houses and buildings had been heavily battered from the air. The need was great for re-equipment of mines, public utilities and transport, for housing and for the maintenance and replacement of industrial plant and buildings. The engineering industry had to get free of munitions contracts, and convert for civil work; the building and building material industries had been drastically scaled down and had to be expanded again.

43. Some expansion of the building and civil engineering industries had been achieved in 1944 – 45, in order to deal with the repair crisis caused by bombing and in order to make a start with site preparation for housing. In June 1945 there were 520,000 employed male operatives aged 16 years and over — probably not much more than half the pre-war labour force. The rate of intake through 1945 – 46 was very fast however, and by the end of the year the

labour force had risen to 943,000 — not far short of pre-war. The distribution of this force was as follows:

	June 1945 ('000)	December 1946 ('000)
New house construction and conversions	60	355
War damage repair	219	167
Industry, agriculture, commerce utilities	61	165[a]
Other (mainly maintenance and repair of houses)	180	25[a]
Total employed male operatives aged 16 and over	520	943

[a] Figures at end of October.

Virtually the entire increase in the building labour strength had been put into new housing and industrial building; the expansion in general maintenance and repair has been almost all offset by the tapering-off of war damage work. It is significant however, that it has been necessary continuously to use over half the building labour force on maintenance and war damage and other repair of houses.

44. The effect of the building activity during the period under review was that by the end of 1946 nearly 300,000 family units of accommodation had been made available: 58,000 permanent and 92,000 temporary houses had been completed and 200,000 permanent houses were under construction. Building work had been done for industry, agriculture, commerce, and public utilities to the value of around £100 millions. Factory building work to the value of £10 millions had been carried out in the Development Areas, excluding major iron and steel projects.

45. Industry's needs of plant, machinery and vehicles were also very pressing. The engineering industries were better able to make a quick start on civil production than the industries which had lost most of their workers during the war, they ended the war with good equipment and an expanded labour force. By the end of 1946 the labour force engaged in satisfying this type of need was well above the normal pre-war level, and, of course, was far above that of mid-1939 when much of the engineering industry was already making munitions.

46. It is too early yet to say how much capital equipment and maintenance work of this sort was done in 1946. It was probably

much the same as in a normal pre-war year. But this does not go far towards making up arrears from six years' deferred maintenance.

Consumption

47. The public's need for more goods and services was hardly less urgent. Food supplies had been maintained throughout the war at a level which was nutritionally adequate, but no better than that. In the six years of war the people had received less than four years' normal supply of clothing and less than three years' supply of household goods. Much more was required both for increasing consumption now and for making good accumulated shortages.

48. There has, in fact, been a considerable increase in supplies. This is shown by the level of retail sales, which at the end of 1946 were running at about 20 per cent by value above the figure of a year ago. Taking price changes into account, the amount of goods sold is probably not more than 10 – 15 per cent, below pre-war.

49. But the improvement has been limited throughout by the world shortage of food and by the slowness of recovery of the labour force in the consumer goods industries — especially textiles and clothing — which had been radically cut down during the war. There would have been far more goods in the shops if more workers had gone back to these industries. The volume of exports of the scarcest consumer goods has been small and a switch of these supplies from exports to the home market would have made little difference to home consumers but would have seriously jeopardised any hope of re-building the export markets in the future.

50. Food consumption has been dominated by the world supply situation. Compared with a year ago, much more fish and fruit are available to the public; much the same amount of sugar, milk, meat, eggs and tea, but less cheese, bacon and fats. In broad terms, the diet remains much the same as it was a year ago; increases in some of the supplies which provide more variety have been offset by a decline in certain basic foods.

51. There has been a very substantial increase in clothing and household supplies since the end of the war. In clothing and footwear there has been an increase of around 40 – 50 per cent; in furniture and furnishings of 150 per cent; supplies for the home market of hardware have doubled. The amount of footwear and clothing in the present ration period is about three-quarters of pre-war and in hardware and hollow-ware and other domestic supplies the pre-war level has now been reached. Supplies of manufactured goods for

consumers are still small in relation to the demand, but supplies of many products are now coming forward at a rate which allows a start to be made in making up war-time arrears. Throughout this field there has been a great improvement in the amounts which the public can buy.

52. There is much more purchasing power in people's pockets than ever bfore, and it is more evenly distributed. Full employment, the introduction of minimum standards of living supported by subsidies, higher rates of national insurance benefits and old age pensions, family allowances and redistribution of income through taxation all contribute to this fact. Subsidies and family allowances alone amounted to £450 millions in 1946, which meant a substantial increase in effective purchasing power.

53. The weight of purchasing power in relation to the supplies available is shown by the fact that nearly one-third of the total of people's incomes is either taken as direct taxes or is saved. Before the war, this proportion was about one-sixth. This shows how important a part has been played by the people's savings in 1946; if an attempt were made to use all this purchasing power, the goods would vanish even more rapidly from the shops.

54. It is clear that to overcome shortages in the shops, it would be necessary for far more plentiful supplies to be available than before the war. For a large section of the people, however, the present food and clothing rations are more than they could normally afford even in good pre-war years, and are much more than they could afford in years of depression.

55. The effect of this heavy purchasing power has been very apparent in the consumption of services. This is shown in the very high figures of passenger travel and in the level of expenditure on entertainments which, even adjusted for the increase in prices, is over 50 per cent above pre-war. In a similar category is the consumption of tobacco, now 30 to 35 per cent above pre-war.

56. On balance, although consumers' standards have not increased as fast as had been hoped, there has been considerable improvement. At least part of the shortage which now exists results from the unprecedentedly high level of purchasing power of the mass of the population.

Public Service

57. The public service has expanded slightly since the end of the war, and now employs 2,130,000 men and women, compared with

1,465,000 in June 1939. This covers a varied range of workers — teachers, policemen, street-cleaners, storekeepers, Post Office workers, firemen in addition to officials of all grades in national and local government. Of the present total, just over one-fifth are civil servants (excluding the Post Office). This is more than double the pre-war figure, but is the inevitable result of the expansion of the Government's responsibilities in the economic field — rationing systems must be maintained as long as severe shortages continue, and the winding-up of war-time activities takes time and manpower. Continuous efforts are made to reduce the claim which public administration makes upon the national resources, but a high level of employment in this field compared with pre-war is bound to continue.

The Eighteen Months' Results

58. On a broad view of the last eighteen months, the result has been that:

(i) The defence sector (armed forces and munitions) has been cut to a little over one-fifth of its size at the end of the war.
(ii) Exports have expanded to 110–113 per cent of 1938 volume, an amount still insufficient to pay for imports at 70–73 per cent of 1938 volume.
(iii) A normal pre-war year's work of industrial equipment and maintenance has been done in 1946.
(iv) Homes have been provided by new building and repair, for nearly 300,000 families, and the way has been cleared for as fast an expansion in home-building as the material supplies will permit.
(v) There has been little change on balance in food consumption, but a considerable expansion in supplies of manufactured goods to the home civilian market, to levels ranging from two-thirds to over 100 per cent of pre-war.

59. This is the way in which the national resources have been used in 1946. In certain respects, the general balance has not been unsatisfactory. A beginning has been made with each of the major objectives of reconstruction. By the end of the year the change-over to civil production was well on the way to completion. Aided by a favourable record of industrial peace, a high level of industrial activity had been achieved.

60. The expansion of production and consumption throughout 1946 put a heavy strain in particular upon coal and power supplies, but also upon steel, transport, and other basic industries and services. Coal production in the year as a whole exceeded the production of 1945 by 3.6 per cent. But it did not grow nearly fast enough to match the growing consumption as the conversion of industry and the restoration of the civil economy got under way. The by no means unfavourable industrial results for 1946 were achieved only by a draft of 5 million tons on coal stocks. In a sense, indeed, we have been living on a coal overdraft. The demand for power likewise exceeded the capacity of the power stations; the demand for transport was up to the limit of what could be carried by the railways' depleted rolling-stock; the demand for steel was more than could be produced or imported. Indeed, our basic industries and services were limiting the nation's productive effort. By the end of 1946 we had reached a stage at which further expansion of our productive effort was vitally necessary, but was extremely difficult unless industry could obtain more coal and power.

from *Economic Survey for 1947* (February, 1947): Cmd 7046. Reprinted by permission of the Controller of Her Majesty's Stationery Office

C5 The Export Trade (1947)

Export Trends

Between 1913 and 1929 our total exports fell in volume by about one-sixth, in spite of a concurrent increase in the volume of world trade. Between 1929 and 1937 they fell again by about one-sixth, while world trade also declined, but much less steeply. Our exports thus constituted a steadily declining proportion of a volume of world trade which itself declined after 1929.

. . . the war precipitated this decline. Exports in 1943 were only 29 per cent of their 1938 volume, although by the last quarter of 1946 they rose to 111 per cent of the 1938 quarterly average. Spectacular as these developments undoubtedly were, they represented a highly abnormal state of affairs. For this reason, what follows will be mainly concerned with the pre-war trends.

Table [1] shows our main visible exports in 1913, 1937, 1938, 1945 and 1946. In comparing the values shown, it should be noted that, between 1913 and 1937, average export prices increased by about 40 per cent, between 1937 and 1945 by about 85 per cent, and between 1945 and 1946 by about 5 per cent. Declines in value, therefore, indicate greater declines in volume, while increases in value indicate smaller increases or even reductions, in volume . . .

Table I: Principal United Kingdom Exports (£ million)

	1913	1937	1938	1945	1946
Spirits	4.2	12.7	11.4	9.5	11.8
Coal	50.7	37.6	37.4	6.6	9.1
Pottery, glass, abrasives, etc.	7.4	10.0	9.6	13.0	27.6
Iron and steel and manufactures thereof	55.4	48.4	41.7	20.9	80.0
Non-ferrous metals and manufactures thereof	12.0	15.7	12.3	12.1	37.7
Cutlery, hardware, implements, and instruments	7.1	9.7	9.0	10.0	27.0
Electrical goods and apparatus	5.4	12.5	13.4	13.8	37.4
Machinery	33.6	49.7	57.9	47.1	113.8
Cotton yarns and manufactures	126.5	68.5	49.7	42.6	63.2
Woollen and worsted yarns and manufactures	35.7	35.5	26.8	21.6	43.6
Artificial silk yarns and manufactures	—	5.7	4.2	17.1	23.8
Other textiles	18.3	16.1	10.7	7.1	21.8
Clothing and footwear	21.0	12.4	10.5	12.4	35.4
Chemicals, drugs, dyes and colours	19.5	24.7	22.3	38.2	66.1
Paper, cardboard, etc.	3.7	8.1	6.9	5.1	14.4
Vehicles	24.5	39.9	44.5	19.1	113.5
Miscellaneous manufactures	25.9	29.3	29.0	19.8	57.2
All other exports	74.4	84.9	73.5	83.3	128.3
Total	525.3	521.4	470.8	399.3	911.7

Among exports which declined in relative importance between 1913 and 1937 were coal, iron and steel, clothing and footwear, and, above all, cotton textiles. Exports which increased in relative importance in the same period included spirits, pottery, glass and abrasives, non-ferrous metals, cutlery, hardware, implements and instruments, machinery, artificial silk and mixtures, chemicals, drugs, dyes and colours, paper and cardboard, and vehicles. Between 1937 and 1938, textiles (including clothing) declined from 26 per cent to 21 per cent of total exports — they were 38 per cent in 1913 — while exports of vehicles and machinery increased from 17 to 22 per cent.

The most notable features of our export trade by the end of 1946 were the almost complete elimination of coal as a major export — it was only 13 per cent of its 1938 volume — and the really substantial increases in volume over 1938 levels which were obtained in pottery, glass, abrasives, non-ferrous metals, cutlery, hardware, electrical goods, artificial silk yarns and manufactures, clothing, chemicals, and vehicles. Some of these increases, however, were due to adventitious causes, such as the virtual absence of Germany as a competitor. Between 1938 and 1946 there was also a striking change in the composition of United Kingdom exports, raw materials declining from 12.1 per cent to 3.6 per cent of the total, and manufactured goods increasing from 77.6 to 86.3 per cent. Of the latter group, metals increased from 37.3 to 44.1 per cent, textiles declined from 21.5 to 20.5 per cent, and other manufactures increased from 18.8 to 21.7 per cent.

In examining the prospects for particular British exports, they will be divided rather arbitrarily into capital and consumption goods.

Capital goods

It has been argued above that the process of industrial development in countries less advanced industrially than ourselves is likely to increase the demand for our exports of capital goods. For instance, the pre-war expansion of demand for our exports of the more complicated or specialised forms of capital goods, such as machinery, vehicles, electrical goods, and non-ferrous metals, will probably continue, and as a proportion of our total exports they will tend to increase. Geographically, the scope for selling them is practically unlimited, although a great deal will depend on a wise policy of international investment to ensure that the most urgent world demands are made effective.

Exports of machinery and vehicles should be capable of considerable expansion. For all types of machinery, overseas demand is likely to be stepped up for many years beyond the transitional period by the accumulated needs arising from war-time deterioration and destruction. To satisfy this demand will call for a substantial increase over the pre-war size of the industries concerned — an increase which, to some extent, has been achieved during the war — as before the war we were already exporting 20-25 per cent of the total output of our general and electrical engineering industries. For processing machinery in particular, e.g. textile machinery, there is likely to be a continuing and expanding overseas demand, which would justify a substantial increase in our productive capacity.

For road vehicles there is every reason to expect increasing world demand, and in spite of strong competition particularly from the United States of America, prospects for British exports are not unfavourable. We can make these prospects more favourable by continuing the immediate post-war policy of concentrating on a smaller number of models, and by making adequate provision for servicing and the supply of spare parts. We should also pay much greater attention to the needs of specific markets in matters of design and finish. Increased exports of cars should encourage increased exports of tyres, particularly as we can supply certain sizes not made by other countries. In exports of motor cycles, to judge by the pre-war trends, we are less likely to enjoy expanding demand. Bicycles and parts, however, have been in steadily increasing demand — our main customers were India and South Africa — and, with rising standards of living, this should continue in spite of increased local competition. Exports of locomotives and rolling stock were declining before the war and this trend is likely to continue as soon as the abnormal post-war demands have been met. Exports of aircraft should continue to expand in spite of greatly increased world production. On the other hand, demand for British ships, which declined steeply before the war, is hardly likely to recover in the long run, particularly as world capacity has greatly increased.

Exports of non-ferrous metal manufactures should be capable of expansion. Our best prospect is to concentrate on high-quality alloys, the manufacture of which is highly specialised.

Exports of less specialised forms of capital products, such as iron and steel, are not likely to increase in the long run except in special lines, for in their simpler forms these are the kinds of capital goods which may be produced at a relatively early stage of a nation's industrial development. Indeed, the growth of an iron and steel industry is often a measure of such development. This tendency towards increased self-sufficiency among our large customers, such as South Africa, India, and Australia, was already causing a decline in our exports of iron and steel before the war. During the war these countries, as well as some in Latin America, further developed their iron and steel capacity, and the result is likely to be the gradual exclusion of imports of steel bars and sections with a low conversion value. A fair export market will probably remain for specialised British products, such as steel railway track material and also for sheet products, in the manufacture of which extremely expensive capital equipment is required. The bulk of the iron and steel industry's contribution to our export trade must, however, consist of providing the materials for highly manufactured exports — that is, products with a very high conversion value.

Consumption Goods

The trend towards 'new' and higher-quality consumption goods was already apparent in our export trade before the war, and to some extent was maintained during the war. Artificial silk and chemicals, medicines, drugs, dyes, etc., are clearly exports capable of continued expansion; so, too, are spirits, paper, cardboard, etc., pottery, glass and abrasives, cutlery, hardware and instruments, many items in the 'miscellaneous' group of manufactures, high-quality foodstuffs, such as biscuits and confectionery, and the best qualities of all groups of manufactured goods.

It is significant that, in the manufacture of many of these products, the Census of Production reveals a relatively high 'net output per person employed'. This would seem to imply either that labour is highly skilled in the industries concerned or that the latter are highly capitalised. Human skill and an accumulation of capital equipment are advantages which we should be able to maintain in relation to the majority of other countries, provided that by our efficiency and inventiveness we keep ahead of them in industrial development. It is also significant that for many of these products exports constituted only a small proportion of total output. For instance, in 1938, exports of rayon piece goods amounted only to 15 per cent of a total output of 426 million square yards, while the exports of cotton piece goods represented 51 per cent of a total output of 2,700 million square yards. This suggests that some of the industries to which we must look for the major increase in our exports have been less 'export-minded' than the older industries. It is true, of course, that they have never had quite the same inducements as the latter once had in the shape of rapidly expanding world markets.

Among exports of consumption goods, woollen and worsted yarns and manufactures formed a relatively steady proportion of British exports before the war, and constituted some 40 per cent of total world trade in these goods. This share was maintained, but since total trade contracted there was a corresponding contraction in the volume of British exports. Although local production by some of our best customers, including Australia, Canada, and Argentina, increased during the war, it should be possible to reverse the downward trend, particularly if we concentrate on higher qualities of wool textile manufactures. The same applies, although perhaps with less force, to our exports of linen goods, clothing, and footwear.

Two great industries stand out as almost certainly incapable of long-term export expansion. These are coal and cotton textiles. Our exports of coal fell steeply between 1913 and 1937, and, for the latter part of that period, were a declining proportion of a declining volume of world exports. Faced with the development of new forms of power throughout the world, and in spite of new uses for coal in the production of synthetic materials, both world exports and British exports of coal are likely to suffer a continuing long-term decline in demand. In addition, there is good reason to believe that our productive efficiency in relation to other countries has declined.

Exports of cotton textiles declined even more steeply than those of coal during the pre-war years. Piece goods, which constituted two-thirds of our cotton exports, formed a declining proportion of a declining volume of world trade, while world production of cotton goods increased. This trend in our exports was due 'almost equally to Japanese competition and to the increase in local production in the various markets'. During the war this local production has expanded very considerably in many countries, and there is little doubt that it will receive some form of protection. Moreover, recent information about the relative inefficiency of the British cotton textile industry as a whole suggests that, failing drastic technical improvements in the industry, our competitive power in world markets will be seriously affected, at least in cheaper-grade goods.

As regards market, our highest quality exports of consumption goods will probably tend to gravitate towards wealthy countries, such as the United States, Canada, Australia, and New Zealand; demand will not, however, be limited to these markets, for in any country which is developing industrially there will be a growing demand for high-quality imports. For the bulk of our consumption goods exports, namely, those of medium and low quality, increased demand is likely to centre mainly in the 'developing' countries, for example in South Africa and Latin America; to a rapidly growing extent also in India, China, and, possibly, the U.S.S.R. For some years the war-ravaged countries of Europe should also be included in this category.

. . . Shipping income, if it is assumed that world trade reaches the high level which is necessary for the achievement of our visible export objective, should at least be capable of restoration to its pre-war level (adjusted to current price-levels). Receipts from short interest, insurance, and commissions, the value of which in our export drive should not be overlooked, will also benefit from a healthy state of trade. Net income from overseas investments on the other hand — the reduction of which is the main single cause of the gap in our balance of payments — could not be restored except over a very long period. Of other invisible items, gross receipts from the expenditure of overseas tourists visiting Britain, from the export of industrial know-how and also from the exhibition of British films abroad, should, in due course, be capable of appreciable expansion.

Special attention should be drawn to the importance of restoring our re-export trade and with it the substantial invisible export to be derived from it in the shape of *entrepot* charges . . . In 1938 our main re-exports were raw wool, hides and skins, non-ferrous metals, and tea, while our main customers were the U.S.S.R., the United States of America, France, and Germany. In 1946, raw wool, hides and skins, and tea still ranked high, and rubber increased in importance; main destinations were Germany, Italy, the Netherlands, France and the United States of America. It may be added that, if for any reason the distinction between hard and soft currencies persists, and the International Monetary Fund's objective of free convertibility of all currencies not attained, Britain's re-exports are likely to acquire increased significance as a potential source of hard currencies.

To sum up: The bulk of our visible exports, and in particular capital goods and high quality consumption goods, should be capable of substantial long-term expansion. The principal exceptions are coal, iron and steel, and cotton textiles. If these are assumed to regain but not exceed their pre-war levels — and this is almost certainly an over-optimistic assumption — the increase of 100 per cent suggested as necessary on our total pre-war exports becomes an increase of about 140 per cent on those exports which are judged capable of expansion; and this percentage will rise in so far as the excluded items fall short of their pre-war levels. As regards invisible exports, the possibilities of increasing these are rather limited, but in so far as we *can* increase them, we shall alleviate our need for visible exports.

Our immediate problem is to produce enough for export in face of a high level of domestic demand. Thereafter, when conditions are less abnormal, the necessary expansion of British exports can only be achieved and maintained on two conditions. First, there must be a high and rising level of world prosperity and a steady expansion of effective demand, resulting in a substantial increase in the volume of world trade and a lowering of trade barriers. This means, above all, the maintenance of full employment, or at least the avoidance of slumps, by Britain and the United States. Second, British industry must achieve and maintain a high degree of efficiency, flexibility, and inventiveness to meet and foster existing export demands and create new demands.

The first condition calls for a policy of doing all in our power to raise world standards of living and to promote a high and stable level of world employment; the second, for an intensive stimulation of our industrial research and development, the practical application of the results of that work in the production of new and better goods, the establishment of regular and systematic surveys of world needs, and adequate methods of marketing and finance.

from Political and Economic Planning (now Policy Studies Institute), *Britain and World Trade* (June 1947)

C6 Motor Vehicle Exports (1950)

Growth and Constitution of Exports

Since the second World War British motor manufacture has been primarily an export industry; during 1948, indeed, Britain became the largest exporter of cars. Even before the war, however, Britain exported a larger proportion of its output than did the U.S.A. — for the period 1929 to 1938 17 per cent by numbers of total production compared with about 13 per cent for the American industry . . .

Although during the war shipments shrank almost to nothing, by 1946 they had already reached the unprecedented level of 134,000 new vehicles and chassis, nearly 40 per cent of production. For 1948 the number was over 300,000 (more than three times the 1937 level), the value over 7 per cent of total British exports, and more than three times as much as exports of textile machinery. This represented more than 60 per cent of total production by numbers, 69 per cent for cars and 44 per cent for commercial vehicles. In the middle of 1949 the export percentage was 70 for the industry as a whole and higher still for the Big Six.

Before the war more than half the value of motor vehicle exports was accounted for by new cars and car chassis, and about a quarter by new commercial vehicles and chassis. In 1946 commercial vehicles represented about 40 per cent, a much higher proportion than before the war and only a little less than 1946 exports of cars. By 1947, however, cars had recovered their former importance, though in 1947 and 1948 exports of new commercial vehicles and chassis remained proportionately greater than before the war; there was a relative decline in exports of parts and accessories. The proportion of spares may be expected to rise in future as demands on overseas service depots come increasingly to reflect the rise in exports of vehicles.

The export of commercial chassis, to which bodies can be fitted overseas, is more important than that of complete commercial vehicles, and in 1948 about 60 per cent by numbers of goods vehicle chassis exported were unassembled. Body-building and assembly have been encouraged in some importing countries by appropriate tariff protection, and this tendency is likely to continue. The greater majority of cars are exported complete and assembled, though shipments of chassis and 'knocked down' vehicles will no doubt increase in importance, particularly since British manufacturers are developing assembly plants overseas. About a sixth of the vehicles and chassis exported in 1948 were 'c.k.d.' (completely knocked down). Though it reduced the value of exports, the c.k.d. system can bring important price advantages.

Between 1947 and 1948 there was a decline of almost 50 per cent in exports of cars of not more than 8 h.p. In 1948 the 8 – 12 h.p. class accounted for over 70 per cent of car sales. [It is possible to analyse] exports in 1947 and 1948 with cars and goods vehicles classified, as far as official statistics allow, by cylinder capacity or unladen weight. Such an analysis is not possible for pre-war years. A striking feature of exports of complete commercial vehicles is the preponderance of light vans, which accounted in 1948 for three-quarters of the number of complete goods vehicles, though since they are generally despatched complete they must have been less important in the total of vehicles and chassis. Vans played a much smaller part in exports before the war . . .

The statistics for complete vehicles weighing over 3 tons and for chassis with diesel engines suggest that medium and heavy lorries accounted for at least a quarter of the value of 1948 exports of commercial vehicles. Another sixth represented coaches, omnibuses and trolleybuses. In 1946 only about 11 per cent of public service vehicle 'units' were complete; by 1948 the percentage had increased to 28, which no doubt largely reflects the inceasing availability of bodies.

Destination

Before the war British motor vehicle exports flourished mainly within the protection of Imperial Preference. The bulk of the shipments went to Commonwealth countries. Eire was first in importance among European markets. The second and third most important on the average of 1937 and 1938, Denmark and Sweden, granted preferential tariff rates to British vehicles under commercial treaties made in the early 'thirties. Even with tariff advantages Britain did not dominate any major market except Eire and New Zealand. Australia and India, two of Britain's main customers in 1937, both bought largely from the United States, and the same was true of Denmark and Sweden. South Africa, the largest world importer in 1937, did not grant preference to British vehicles, and purchases from the U.S.A. were worth . . . four and a half times as much as those from Britain. In the case of Sweden, imports from Britain in 1937 were also exceeded by imports from Germany. For Continental Europe as a whole, Germany was a far more important supplier than Britain in that year, and French exports to European countries appear to have been at least as large as Britain's. In 1929 and 1937 a considerably larger proportion of private cars than of commercial vehicles went to Commonwealth markets . . . In 1937 one of the principal reasons for this difference was the fact that New Zealand, which took nearly a quarter by value of Britain's exports of private cars, provided a market for only about 7 per cent by value of the commercial vehicles . . .

The post-war currency situation makes it desirable that manufacturers should make a special effort to increase exports to particular markets. Among these are countries whose currencies are 'hard', so that Britain has difficulty in paying for exports from them. The great contribution which the motor industry has made to supplies of hard currency by altering the relative importance of its export markets can be seen by considering five countries — the U.S.A., Canada, Argentina, Belgium and Switzerland. In 1937 all the five countries took a smaller proportion of British exports of motor vehicles than of total merchandise exports. British motor vehicle exports to the five countries together amounted to only about £750,000, even including spares. By 1948 exports of motor vehicle products to these five countries were perhaps thirty times as great by value, whereas total merchandise exports to them . . . were only about three times their 1937 value. In 1948 motor vehicles formed a somewhat larger proportion of British exports to the five countries than of exports to all markets. Thus the motor industry's achievement was not only to have furnished a proportion of Britain's expanded exports which was about two and a half times as great as in 1937, but also to have become much more important, relatively to the rest of British industry, as an exporter to what are now hard-currency markets.

The decline of Germany, which has favoured British exports to the hard-currency markets, has also helped to increase sales in various other European countries, such as the Netherlands; another factor has been the general scarcity of dollars. The proportion of exports going to foreign markets has therefore been much higher than before the war. Though in 1947 (as before the war) a larger proportion of cars than of commercial vehicles went to the Commonwealth, the bulk of the increase in commercial vehicle exports from 1947 to 1948 was taken by Australia and other Commonwealth countries (not including Canada), while the foreign market for British cars expanded much more nearly in proportion to the Commonwealth market. In 1948 about a quarter by value of British exports of cars went to the U.S.A., Canada, Argentina, Belgium and Switzerland, whereas the proportion for commercial vehicles was only about 10 per cent.

from Political and Economic Planning (now Policy Studies Institute), ***Engineering Report II: Motor Vehicles*** (January 1950)

C7 'How Much Better Off?' (1953)

The wide publicity given to the increase of industrial output since the war — according to the official index by almost one-third between 1946 and 1952 — has had a somewhat dazzling effect on the assessment of Britain's economic position since the war. It has been understood well enough in general terms that the need to increase exports has lessened the amount of this increase of output which could be used either for personal consumption or for investment or for defence and other Government services. But it is only gradually being realized to the full how very far the effort to correct the balance of payments and to begin to build up some reserve has absorbed the increased wealth produced in the country since the war. Personal experience in fact, has so far been a better guide than statistics. We are nothing like so much better off as the figures have been allowed to suggest.

Now the analysis of national output and expenditure made by the Central Statistical Office and a complementary study by the London and Cambridge Economic Service . . . , taken together, have given common experience a statistical backing. In the first place the index of industrial production, which is predominantly an index of manufacturing output, has given an exaggerated view of the increase of output in all activities. Output in agriculture, transport, the distributive industries, and other activities has risen much less. National production as a whole, in real terms, rose between 1941 and 1952 by roughly 12 per cent, according to one method and 15 per cent, by another. That is, it rose at less than half the rate at which manufacturing output grew. Of this increase in national productivity roughly two-thirds was absorbed in turning an excess of imports over exports, which (in 1948 prices) amounted to £667m. in 1946, into a favourable balance of £248m. in 1952. The volume of the goods and services available for use within the country, for all purposes, rose between 1946 and 1952 by less than 5 per cent.

Calculations such as these cannot be precisely accurate, but their significance is clear. The relatively small rise of under 5 per cent. in the aggregate of consumers' expenditure (Government expenditure was less, in real terms, in 1952 than in 1946, and 'capital formation' — the provision of houses, factories, machines, stocks, and so on — rose by a half) show how little scope for a general increase of real earnings there has been at any time since the war. In the past two years the aggregate volume of goods and services on which earnings could be spent has actually fallen. The proportions which different groups of income earners could take out of the pool could be varied but the pool was smaller. In one respect the future may now look a little brighter. The terms of trade are more favourable than they were a year ago. But sterner competition in the export trade has introduced a new cold wind. There is no reason to suppose that the trend which has reflected the country's difficulties since the war will quickly undergo any radical change for the better. There are no easy times ahead.

from *The Times*, (5 September 1953)

C8 'Fill Up with Anti-squeeze' (1956)

Mr. Macmillan says that 'we have the second highest standard of living in the world and have never been so prosperous,' and Lord Beveridge says that he is in danger of living longer than he can afford. Mr. Macmillan means that one large and vocal section of the community has never before won prosperity so quickly from smaller, less vocal groups, and Lord Beveridge means that people with the inclination and opportunity to save are discovering that they can't afford to do so.

Mr. Macmillan knows that we are steadily falling back in the league table of productive efficiency and industrial output, and that the United States has increased its lead very substantially during the last ten years; so by increasing prosperity (which must be assessed relatively) he can only mean the continuing advance of the British wage-earner, the successful outcome of repeated wage-claims, the rapid progress of the social revolution — or, as Lord Beveridge put it, 'the claim of each industry to fix its own wages.'

Whenever the Chancellor of the Exchequer is warmly optimistic (he blows hot and cold with disturbing regularity) there are appeals for some relaxation of the credit squeeze. The motives of the appellants are varied. Some of them, knowing that inflation makes lending a mug's game and borrowing a cinch, are anxious to operate on tick. Others want to replace the squeeze by more direct and positive systems of financial control. And others — of whom I am one — merely use the opportunity to repeat grave warnings about the damaging effects of the squeeze on the national economy and the future of private enterprise.

The chief objection to credit pegging is that it makes the pattern of industrial activity rigid when it should be fluid. When credit is scarce big business finds its own capital for new investment. It hangs on to its profits and becomes self-financing. Money that would have been distributed and then re-invested in a variety of enterprises (according to their prospects and profitability) is ploughed back, whether the soil is fertile or infertile, on the instructions of managerial juntas. New enterprises, therefore, are deprived of funds.

Western capitalism is a sham if it leaves the shape of industrial things to come in the hands of the managers rather than the owners of capital. The credit squeeze encourages the totalitarian planner and gambles with the country's very limited free capital resources.

To say this is not, alas, very helpful to the Chancellor. The anti-squeeze brigade — or rather the responsible element in it — has no substitute solution to offer. In economic policy there is nothing to distinguish Left from Right: both sides are afraid of inflation, both know that credit restriction is a dangerous and inadequate lid on a cauldron of boiling acid. And neither side has the courage to challenge 'the claim of each industry to fix its own wages.' Fifty years from now Lord Beveridge's warning will have been heeded, but the troubles on the way are going to be truly formidable.

from *Punch* (31 October 1956)

C9 The Chemical Industry in Britain and Europe (1957)

The chemical industry is one of the most highly protected of all British industries, and in many respects more highly protected than the chemical industries of the other members of the FTA.* Over a wide range of synthetic organic chemicals a punitive duty of 33⅓ per cent *ad valorem* is levied on imports; imports of dyestuffs, if they compete with products made in Britain, have been effectively prohibited for thirty-five years. Can an industry that has grown up behind such protection hope to continue to provide the essential stimulus to the development and growth of other industries once it is exposed to the full force of Continental competition? The industry is in no two minds about it — it thinks it can. Over 80 per cent of the chemical industry, measured in terms of capital employed, has gone on record that, provided it was able to compete on fair terms, it would favour negotiations for an FTA.

The reason for this confidence in its own strength lies in the remarkable changes that have taken place in the structure of the British chemical industry in the thirty-five years since it was last openly exposed to Continental competition, and particularly in the changes that have occurred in the last decade. The industry that sought protection after the First World War was dwarfed, in capital resources, scale of production, and expenditure on research, by its German, Swiss and American competitors. By these same criteria it is now on an equal, or better than equal, footing, at least in Europe. The objectives sought in the formation of Imperial Chemical Indus-

*FTA — free trade area.

tries by merger of a large part of the industry — co-ordination of research, pooling of resources for development and . . . rationalization of production to reduce costs — have been achieved. Of even greater significance is the more recent growth of the petroleum chemicals industry; and as the British and British-Dutch oil companies are second only to the Americans in the petroleum industry, so in petroleum chemicals Britain has started with a commanding lead over its European rivals in capital resources, speed of development and capacity for research. In a space of less than ten years, the share of petroleum chemicals in the total output of organic chemicals in Britain grew from almost nothing to well over a third. This phenomenal expansion, which completely changed the structure and competitive position of the British chemical industry, was achieved in a period much shorter than the transition period during which the CM* and FTA are scheduled to come into effect. And the drive of the petroleum chemicals industry into aromatics, for example, or acetylene-based chemicals or other fields that it has so far barely touched in Europe is far from spent. Hard upon the heels of the petroleum chemicals comes another possible source of radical changes in the industry: radiation chemistry. Fast chemical reactions through radiation without the need for high temperatures and pressures, perhaps lessening the need for today's huge capital expenditure, or, alternatively, making automatic processing and quality control much more of a reality — these might provide opportunities which, if grasped first by the British chemical industry, could greatly increase its competitive power . . .

In 1955 Britain was the leading chemical producer in Europe; employment in the industry was estimated at 357,000, turnover at £1,240 million†. Germany came second in turnover — £1,105 million, and employment — 338,000, according to OEEC estimates, but its net output exceeded that of the UK. France and Italy were the next largest producers . . . The remaining European chemical industries are very much smaller, the largest of them in Belgium, the Netherlands and Switzerland each accounting for less than 5 per cent of European turnover. The Swiss industry, which sells over 90 per cent of output abroad, has, however, an importance as a competitor in export markets out of all proportion to its size. The

*CM — common market.

†These figures cover a slightly wider range of products than those included under the heading of chemicals in the Standard International Trade Classification; no direct comparison should be made between output value and trade figures.

difference in size of the four major European chemical industries has been considerably reduced since 1950. Output in Germany has grown roughly twice as fast as in the UK; the German index of chemical production (1950 = 100) reached 184 in 1955, 201 in 1956, while the British index rose only to 141 and 146. The rate of growth of French output was midway between the two, the index touching 161 in 1955 and 176 in 1956, but Italian growth exceeded even that of Germany, the index rising to 201 and 221. The disparity in growth rates should be less marked in future now that the German and Italian industries have largely completed their post-war reconstruction; but it suggests that Germany, rather than Britain, will be the leading European producers in an FTA, the more so since German recovery has been achieved in spite of the handicap imposed by the surrender of its chemical patents after the war.

Because the chemical industry can achieve substantial economies of scale, and because it costs so much to discover and develop a new product or process, the large firm in every European country usually has a distinct advantage over the small. The strength of the British chemical industry is, therefore, best measured by comparing, not the relative size of the entire industry, but the relative size and rates of growth of the largest chemical producers. In the countries that compete most closely with Britain in chemicals — in Germany, France, Italy and Switzerland — large firms predominate. All Britain's chief competitors, that is to say, can obtain similar economies of scale and have roughly the same capacity for research as the British chemical industry. But in none of them is the large firm quite as dominant as it is in Britain. The three largest German chemical firms, Bayer, BASF and Hoechst, which succeeded the IG Farben combine, account together for barely a third of the turnover of the German chemical industry — about the same proportion as that held by one firm, ICI, in Britain. No German firm can muster capital resources comparable to those of the Royal Dutch – Shell group and other major producers of petroleum chemicals in Britain. The share of output in the hands of the large firms in France and Italy is also less than it is in Britain, and the share of the more vulnerable smaller firms correspondingly greater.

In other respects the record is not so favourable to Britain. Although ICI's sales in 1956 were slightly greater than those of the three largest German chemical producers combined, the German companies' sales were increasing more than twice as fast as ICI's. While ICI exported from Britain chemicals to the value of over £73 million, accounting for between a quarter and a third of British chemical exports, the three German firms sold nearly £140 million abroad and accounted for over 40 per cent of Germany's chemical exports. This exceptional emphasis on export markets, especially in Europe, puts the German firms in a strong position to penetrate further into the vulnerable French and Italian markets when they lose their high tariff protection. In the petroleum chemicals field, however, in which ICI is well represented, the long lead established by the British and British-Dutch oil companies puts Britain in a position to share with America most of the advantages from the expected growth in European demand. The production of petroleum chemicals on the Continent is rising fast, but much of it is partly controlled by British and American capital.

The predominance of big firms both in Britain and on the Continent reflects the huge capital requirements of the chemical industry; with its close associate, oil refining, it is by a long way the most heavily capitalized of all manufacturing industries. Even setting aside the oil companies and the production of petroleum chemicals, most of the industry's activities require exceptionally heavy investment in plant and equipment. By the same token labour costs per unit of output are generally small, and the difference in labour costs between the British and Continental chemical industries probably has little effect on prices. There are parts of the chemical industry, it is true, where it is not feasible to use continuous process equipment, and batch processing is still the rule. The production of dyestuffs, which are made to exacting specification but in relatively small quantities, is essentially a batch process, involving many separate consecutive steps, although dyestuffs intermediates can be mass produced. Batch processing is also employed in the production of antibiotics, but in this case as volume increases it is possible to devise more continuous production methods with lower labour costs per unit. Where batch processes are commonly used, British production costs may be slightly higher than those of Continental producers. The levelling up of Continental wage costs should do something to minimize this disadvantage if Britain enters an FTA and, moreover, the importance of those sectors of the industry using batch processes is decreasing.

Labour costs may also be significant in packaging, particularly in the case of pharmaceuticals. In some cases it may be possible to overcome this disadvantage — at least as far as exports are concerned — by shipping in bulk and packaging nearer to the point of sale, where the local authorities permit this (though the tariff advantage often gained at present by shipping in bulk will disappear with the tariffs). The alternative is to make greater use of automatic packaging machinery. So far as many packaged products are concerned, however, the failure of British producers to design attractive wrappings may often be a more serious weakness than the slightly higher level of their labour costs.

For most of the basic raw materials it needs — coal, salt, limestone and water — which account for a far higher proportion of final costs than does labour, the British chemical industry is as well placed as its Continental rivals, in some cases better placed, for the juxtaposition of raw material sources relieves it of the burden of heavy transport costs. Where it is dependent on imported raw materials its competitors are for the most part equally dependent. There are a few exceptions: both the Italian and the French chemical industries have ready access to large reserves of natural gas, yielding sulphur and a useful range of cheap chemical feedstocks. For France this must be counted as a future gain, for the largest natural gas reserves were discovered only recently, and the development of a chemical industry based on them has barely begun. But recent discoveries of new sources of sulphur, in Mexico for instance, have wiped out sulphur shortages so that, although British producers may have to pay more than the French, expansion is no longer hindered by a shortage of supply. Britain's ability to compete in this respect is greater than it was a few years ago. One important fertilizer raw material, potash, is produced in excess of home requirements in Germany and France, but the only potash so far discovered in Britain has proved uneconomic to work. In electro-chemical production some Continental concerns have the advantage, denied to Britain, of low cost hydro-electric power. This is particularly important in the production of calcium carbide, for making acetylene; calcium carbide imported from Norway (where the main producer is British-controlled) is cheaper than that made locally in Britain. Because of this disparity in power costs, acetylene chemistry is more highly developed in Germany and France than it is in Britain. Copper sulphate producers have expressed fears that the removal of restrictions on the export of scrap copper might leave them short of supplies; but restrictions on German exports would also be removed.

On the other hand, Britain not only has abundant coal, but cheaper coal than its European competitors, although part, at least, of this advantage may be lost in an FTA. In the longer run, however, the British chemical industry may improve its competitive position more if it becomes less reliant on coal and more reliant on petroleum than its Continental rivals. For while the price of coal, both in Britain and on the Continent, seems likely to rise steadily over the next decade, the oil industry appears to be entering a phase in which the potential output of crude oil will be greatly in excess of demand, thus keeping oil prices low. Through its intimate association with the oil industry, in which British companies play a leading role, the British chemical industry has a guaranteed oil supply. And the highly integrated complex of oil refineries and chemical plants in Britain offers British chemical manufacturers an unsurpassed range of petroleum feedstocks on favourable terms. On balance, therefore, the British chemical industry should be at no disadvantage in an FTA on the score of raw material supplies and costs.

The question of relative production costs in an FTA comes back, then, to the cost of investment. Like most highly capitalized industries, the chemical industry, both in Britain and on the Continent, provides a large part of its capital needs from its own earnings. And although increased sales in an FTA should enable the cost of some plant to be recovered more quickly, it is at least as likely that keener competition in the home market will force a reduction in profit margins. There is no reason to fear that British chemical firms will be forced to operate on lower gross profit margins than will their Continental competitors; but there is some doubt whether the British tax structure will enable them to retain as high a proportion of earnings to help finance new plant. Allowances for depreciation, in particular, are more liberal in Germany than they are in Britain; and it is significant that while the British industry is stressing the need for equal tax treatment in an FTA, the German chemical industry is already seeking additional concessions in order to find more money for expansion. Even with more favourable tax treatment, however, it seems likely that all chemical firms, both in Britain and on the Continent, will become more dependent on outside sources of capital than they are now. In this industry, more than in any other, it is therefore of vital consequence that Britain should so order its affairs as to raise the level of net investment, and that it should make itself as attractive as possible to American capital which it can only do by joining an FTA.

from the Economist Intelligence Unit, ***Britain and Europe*** **(1957)**

C10 Shipbuilding Prospects (1962)

The Sixty-third Ordinary Annual General Meeting of Smith's Dock Company Limited was held on January 9th at North Shields. Colonel T. Eustace Smith, CBE, TD, DL, Chairman and Managing Director, in the course of his speech, said:

We are satisfied that we have obtained a reasonable proportion of the work available in shiprepairing and we are well placed to ensure that this state of affairs continues. Since the end of the year under review, we have been able to secure in competition with foreign yards, a contract for the repairs to the Norwegian tanker 'Fernmount.' This contract involves the construction of a new centre section at South Bank which when launched will be towed to North Shields for fitting in place, and it is gratifying to consider how well the Company is placed to undertake such contracts.

In the current year the shipbuilding department will be reasonably employed but thereafter we have gaps in our programme. We have so far not been successful in obtaining further orders in spite of having submitted very competitive quotations.

During the first nine months of 1961, some 6½ million gross tons of shipping were ordered in the world, yet only 500,000 gross tons were ordered in this country, 430,000 gross of which were for British Owners. British Owners have been ordering at the rate of 2½ per cent of their fleet whilst other countries have been ordering at a much larger rate, with Norway at over 9 per cent. Exports are vital to this country but so are the invisible exports which are provided by a large British Mercantile Fleet. To compete in the difficult conditions of today this fleet must be modern but 2½ per cent of new ships is not even normal replacement. British Shipyards are just as up to date as the yards abroad and have shown in recent months that they can compete with foreign yards, on equal terms, that is with those countries who do not grant direct subsidies.

Surely the time has come when we should give some encouragement to our British Shipowners to at least maintain a highly efficient Merchant Fleet of the same magnitude as at present. Failure to do so will mean further loss of invisible exports, serious curtailments of insurance and the many ancillary trades connected with the world of Shipping, and a cutting down of the capacity of British Shipyards which are geared to the requirements of British Shipowners. The Government, through their Export Credits Guarantee Department, provide credit guarantees for foreign owners, and in the last few months the City has made great strides in providing the necessary finance against these guarantees. Should there not be similar organisation for British Shipowners who wish to build in this country, a Home Market Credit Guarantee Department? Surely the City would make great efforts to find the finance necessary. Whilst this would not solve all the problems of the shipowners, it might well provide that extra encouragement which is so necessary. The report and accounts were adopted.

from Company Report, Smiths Dock Company (January 1962)

C11 Developments in the Coal Industry (1962)

An industry in which output comes from more than two thousand workplaces within several hundred production units, varying widely in efficiency, should obviously be able to increase its average productivity during any period when it is reducing production. But the increases in output per manshift that have now enabled Lord Robens to proclaim that British coalmining is now a high-productivity industry have not all come about simply by retreating from the most unrewarding corners of it. This strategic retreat is continuing to a greater extent than is now obvious: the process of concentrating output into faces that fulfil at least certain minimal criteria in terms of capacity is not as visible from outside the industry as was the closing of 163 mines between 1957 and 1961, but it could be of much greater, continuing importance. It is now beginning to have visible results in quickening the advance of labour productivity, which is the index to which the board is now anxious to draw — and pay — greater attention.

Concentration into the less inefficient pits and coalfaces is a matter of reorganisation that is accepted more easily at a time when output is being run down. The introduction of more and more mechanised equipment into the mines, which is one measurable positive development that the board can cite, might not necessarily be accepted as easily, particularly since powerloading equipment tends to upset the whole work cycle of mining, requiring reorganisation of jobs underground and some re-training of the miners to do them. But Lord Robens said this week that the board had never had less than full co-operation in the introduction of powerloading equipment; and whether or not this is also true of getting reasonable

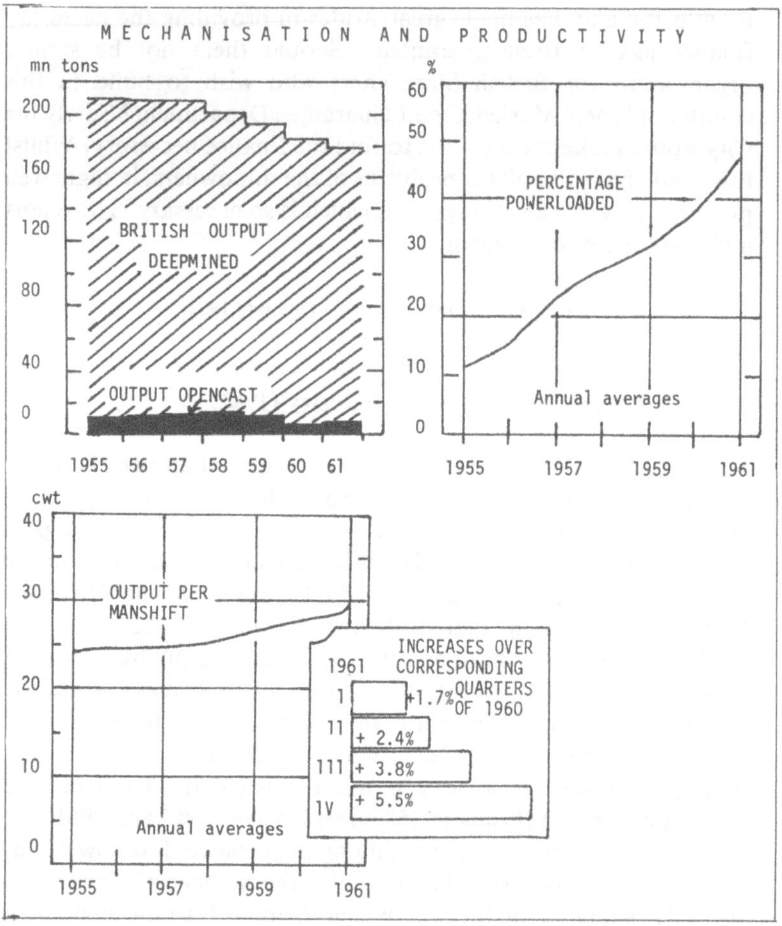

utilisation of all the equipment put in, he was able to record quite an impressive increase in the machines now working double-shift.

These machines, and the reorganisation of mining to make use of them, are now beginning to reap quite impressive rewards in terms of productivity. Last year deepmined output reached, at its peak, 30-31 hundredweight per manshift, which is the level that the board's last long-term investment plan reckoned might be reached by 1965. (It is only fair to note that it then expected to be mining 200–215 million tons a year at that level of productivity, not 190 million tons.) The advance mounted steadily throughout the year: in the first quarter productivity was up by 1.7 per cent compared with a year earlier, and in the last it was up by 5.5 per cent. Roughly speaking, labour productivity on the faces using powerloading is about twice as high as on those where coal is loaded (and in some cases cut) by hand. At the beginning of last year, the proportion of output powerloaded was about 40 per cent; by the end of the year it had reached 55 per cent. Once the 'rich' ingredient in a mixture begins to predominate, its effect upon the average quality of the mixture builds up. This now seems to be happening with powerloading, backed up by the first results of concentration at the more productive coalfaces — and presumably, some results at least from the extensive reorganisation and major re-equipment of many mines on which several hundred million pounds have been spent in the last decade . . .

Lord Robens said that the board has not finally agreed with the Ministry of Power and the Treasury on the 'target' rate of return it ought to be able to earn over the present five-year term of trial for nationalised industries. His own aims for the industry, in non-quantitative terms, were to make coal 'commercially viable'; to maintain the industry at its present size; to provide fair rewards for the manpower it needed; and to maintain 'relative price stability' (which, sensibly enough, does not rule out selective increases for coal on which loses are made, like that mined in Scotland or sold to consumers). One economic aim of which he has spoken in recent years is that by the end of 1964 the board should be self-financing in capital investment. He said this week that this was not part of the task set him by the ministries; and indeed it ought not to be a very exacting requirement. The coal industry's period of peak investment

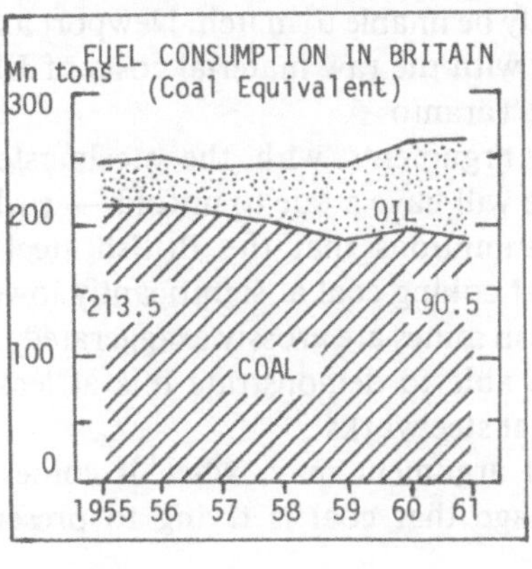

in real terms must already be past. By the mid-sixties, with a capacity of 200 million tons a year (which ought to be qualitatively somewhat better than the capacity of 240 million tons a year for which it first designed its long-term reconstruction plan) the Coal Board might well expect to be able to keep its capacity stable out of proper provisions for depreciation.

Within the framework of his own agreement, therefore, Lord Robens can call 1961 'a vintage year for coal'; he can record genuine progress towards the goals that he has proclaimed. The trouble is that this framework leaves out too many uncomfortable facts.

The most important thing that happened to the coal industry in 1961 was that Mr Selwyn Lloyd put a sizeable excise duty on fuel oil. Other facts of note were that Mr Richard Wood continued to refuse private consumers licences to import coal from America, but approved the Gas Council's scheme for the importation of methane and for the building of a diagonal pipeline across England that could potentially supply several of the country's gas boards with much larger volumes of petroleum hydrocarbons than are originally planned. This may not denote ministerial single-mindedness in fuel policy; but it did emphasise the extent to which Lord Robens's marketing hopes depend on factors beyond his control. Another external factor, plus or minus, was the Government's decision to seek entry to the common market. That may or may not be to British coal's political advantage; liberalism and protectionism are at least as oddly mingled in Brussels as in Whitehall, when it comes to energy policy. But in spite of protective policies in most of the Six, coastal steelworks around Europe are getting sizeable imports of American coking coal on long-term contracts that the Coal Board would frequently be unable to match: Newport and Ravenscraig will have to reckon with the raw material costs of Klöckner at Bremen and Finsider at Taranto.

On detailed arguments with the steelmasters, Lord Robens declares that he will have a tale to unfold — early in February. He insists that assumptions that the British steel companies could generally import coking coal at significantly lower prices than they get it from British mines are grossly exaggerated. It is not easy to see how he will be able to demonstrate this at least for most of the country's coastal steelworks.

This detailed argument may, when it comes, accord with the competitive image that coal is trying to present to the market;

maintaining what it has decided is 'the right' capacity, and within that capacity producing as much as it can sell. The board's idea of 'the right' capacity has been set largely by the weight of its mounting overheads. Once deepmined output falls much below, say, 190 million tons, capital charges per ton would start pressing on the prices the board needs broadly to maintain to have a chance of competing. Postulate that sales can be kept up to a level roughly in the region of that capacity, and all the arguments and efforts of the board make sense. Remove that assumption and one would need completely to reshuffle the pack.

To the outsider, the only circumstance in which the Coal Board could be really confident of maintaining such a level of sales are either a much higher rate of general economic growth within Britain, and hence of total fuel consumption or the continuance of as high a degree of protection of the British fuel market as exists now — perhaps both. Neither, cold-bloodedly, seems very likely. Since this year's duty was put on oil, sales of the black oils have no longer been growing at their earlier rate, they went up perhaps 10 per cent in 1961 against more than 25 per cent the year before, and the Coal Board reckons that oil simply captured the growth in the general fuel market, without encroaching further upon the board's own sales. It could be that the Chancellor last spring chose precisely the right level of excise duty to choke off the competitive advance of oil; but with newcomers edging their way into the oil market here, one would expect yet deeper discounting in black oil prices, and further inroads on coal's market, to ensue. Nor is it easy to believe that in two to three years' time, in the common market, coal can maintain quite as protected a position as it has here today.

The radical alternative to the Coal Board's present policies might have been retreat to a smaller core of its most efficient capacity, assisted by some writing down of capital, if the fixed-interest pattern has to be maintained, or by the introduction of some equity element so that the industry would not need to pay the same on its capital in good as in bad years. Fuel imports could have been allowed more freely, perhaps with a time-limited levy directed specifically to the retirement of uneconomic capacity and the retraining and re-location of redundant miners. Lord Robens has almost certainly considered those possibilities — which could not have depended on his initiative alone — and rejected them. They might not easily have fitted in with his hope of restoring this industry's morale; but they might have suited the British economy — and the developing pressures on the coal industry — better. As it is, one can only watch his and this industry's efforts with sympathy, but also with uneasiness.

from *The Economist* (20 January 1962)

C12 Management Education (1963)

20. *Facilities for education.* — Many management training courses are being provided under the aegis of the education departments, by the universities, the specialised management bodies, management consultants, independent colleges and other organisations, by industries and large companies. The United Kingdom Advisory Council on Education for Management is comprised of representatives from both educational and industrial organisations and has just submitted its first report to the education ministers, recommending a number of ways in which education for management might be further developed. The Foundation for Management Education has been helping to promote more management teaching in the universities with finance from industry and the support of the University Grants Committee. The Robbins Committee on Higher Education is considering whether the various roles of the universities, colleges of advanced technology, and technical colleges need developing, whether new institutions are necessary and whether present arrangements for planning and co-ordinating the various types of institutions need modifying.

21. In the past, with some notable exceptions, there has been too wide a separation between further education and the practical life of industry. Teachers with academic and industrial experience, available to teach management subjects are rare. There is also a shortage of case material for teaching and of fundamental research into the organisation and management of people in groups and the problems of relations and communications between them. Since the universities have, in the past, played only a small part in management education, this has been developed chiefly in the Technical Colleges, and Colleges of Advanced Technology. There is difficulty in finding qualified teachers, and the education authorities have recently announced plans for dealing with this problem; practical experience in industry is, however, an essential requirement which firms could help to provide. In some areas there is not yet a close

enough link between industry and the Technical Colleges although in others they work very closely together.

22. In the United States, there are a number of business schools, providing undergraduate and graduate courses, the latter usually lasting for two years. Their aim is not only to provide students with knowledge of the functions and principles of management, and the tools and techniques (business accountancy and law, statistics, financial and budgetary controls, operational research, marketing, method study, etc.) but also to develop certain qualities of character and personality; a capacity for exact analysis, the ability to work with people, some experience in decision making. They also aim to give an understanding of the problems of communications, and of the relations between industry, the Government and the general public. Graduates from these schools have a much more professional attitude to management than many of our managers and are much sought after by business in the U.S.A.

23. In the U.S.S.R. both future directors of industry and civil servants frequently take undergraduate courses in engineering combined with economics and sometimes other subjects such as, accountancy, and about a third of the student's time is spent in practical work in industry. He usually has had a year of practical work before entering the University.

24. In the United Kingdom it is generally accepted that academic education in management as such should come after the undergraduate stage. The new diploma in management studies which was started in 1961 by the Education Departments and the British Institute of Management is for graduate level students, and so are most of the university courses in management. These courses should preferably be taken after some practical experience in industry.

25. It is necessary that there should be adequate consultation at national, local and industrial level between those who provide management courses and potential users to ensure that the views of both are taken fully into account. Hitherto the initiative has come largely from the educationists; industry is beginning to make its needs felt but is not yet sufficiently agreed about them. At present, in spite of the growing interest in management training, some of the existing facilities are not fully used, but this may be because industry's real requirements are not always catered for and perhaps because some of the best courses are not widely enough known.

26. There is a need in this country for at least one very high level

new school or institute somewhat on the lines of the Harvard Business School or the School of Industrial Management at the Massachusetts Institute of Technology, either as an independent institution or as part of some existing University or College of Advanced Technology. This should help to provide better trained managers for industry, more trained teachers for the technical colleges, and a much needed national centre for research into problems of management and administration. More immediately, the development and co-ordination of the work already proceeding in the Technical Colleges, Colleges of Advanced Technology, and Universities would help to meet the urgent problem of providing better and much more widely-used educational facilities for management.

from the National Economic Development Council, *Conditions Favourable to Faster Growth* (1963). Reprinted by permission of the Controller of Her Majesty's Stationery Office

C13 Agriculture (1965)

Place in the National Economy

4. At present agriculture produces about 3.5 per cent of the gross domestic product and employs a similar percentage of the working population. Its products are worth about £1,800 million a year at farm gate prices (including subsidies) and it purchases about £1,000 million of goods and services from other industries.

5. About half our requirements of food and feeding-stuffs, however, are still imported at a net foreign exchange cost in 1964 of about £1,530 million. Much imported food could not of course be grown here. Excluding such produce, the import bill was £983 million (including £73 million for hard wheat, for which substitutes cannot be readily produced in this country). The main items are shown in Table [1].

Progress in Recent Years

6. On the basis of the support system and the stability this has given to the industry, agriculture has in recent years made a substantial contribution to the national economy. During the last decade the volume of net output has increased by rather more than one-third. This has been achieved largely through widespread improvements in technology resulting in marked increases of

Table 1: Imported Food and Feedingstuffs, 1964

	£ million[a]	Percentage of total supplies
Beef and veal	92	30
Mutton and lamb	75	58
Bacon	111	62
Wheat	107	53
Coarse grains (almost all maize)	86	31
Sugar[b]	86	68
Butter	152	94
Cheese	36	58

[a] Net foreign exchange cost, i.e. excluding that part of freight and insurance costs which is payable to British carriers and insurers.

[b] Net of raw sugar subsequently re-exported as refined.

efficiency in crop and animal production. Cereal yields, for example, have increased by one-third as a result of better varieties, the development of chemical control of pests, diseases and weeds and improved husbandry. Milk yields have been increased by about 15 per cent by rearing better types of dairy cows and by improving their feeding and management. Egg yields have increased by one-quarter as a result of the introduction of higher yielding strains of birds and improvements in the conditions under which birds are housed. Feed conversion rates, particularly for pigs and poultry, have improved substantially.

7. At the same time, the mechanisation of agriculture has been proceeding apace, with material reductions in the amount of labour required for crop and livestock production. The number of agricultural workers has fallen by some 25 per cent, *i.e.*, by over 200,000 workers or 20,000 workers a year. Over the same period there has been an annual release, mainly for building development, of some 50,000 to 60,000 acres of land, or in total about half a million acres.

8. These developments have resulted in an annual growth in labour productivity of about 4 per cent in 1954 – 60 and about 6 per cent in 1960 – 64.* Rather more than half of the increase is due to rising output and the remainder to the release of manpower. The rate of increase in labour productivity in agriculture is much higher than the average improvement in manufacturing industries and double the rate of improvement in the economy as a whole. Average

* If measured on the usual basis adopted for agriculture the annual growth in labour productivity was about 5 per cent in 1954 – 60 and 7 per cent in 1960 – 64.

output per man in agriculture is, however, lower than in industry generally.

9. The increase in agricultural output during the past 10 years has led to substantial economies in expenditure on food imports. The saving is estimated at about £250 million a year at 1964 import prices, after allowing for the additional feed and other imports required to produce the higher output. Had output not increased to this extent, not only would we have needed to buy more imports, but import prices might have been higher.

from the National Economic Development Council, *The National Plan* (1965): Cmnd 2764. Reprinted by permission of the Controller of Her Majesty's Stationery Office

C14 'How Fast Can Britain Grow?' (1966)

It seems safe to assume that the specifically post-war recovery elements were eliminated from the growth of all countries except Japan by 1955. We shall therefore concentrate our comparative analysis on the nine years 1955–64. The years 1955 and 1964 both exhibited well-nigh full use of capacity, and the period is long enough to avoid the intrusion of purely short-term influences.

From 1955 to 1964 all the major industrial countries, except the U.S., greatly exceeded their long-term historical growth-rates, in terms of both production and productivity (see Tables 1 and 2).

Table 1: Growth of Gross Domestic Product. Annual average compound growth-rate

	1955–64 %	1870–1955 %	1870–1913 %	1913–38 %	1938–55 %
Denmark	5.0	2.6	3.2	1.9	2.4
France	5.0	1.4	1.6	0.4	2.3
Germany	5.6	2.3[b]	2.9[b]	1.6	3.0
Italy	5.7	1.6	1.4	1.7	2.0
Japan	10.4	3.1[c]	3.3[c]	4.4	0.6
Norway	4.2	2.5[b]	2.2[b]	2.9	2.6
Sweden	4.3	2.6	3.0	1.8	3.2
U.K.	3.1	1.8	2.1	1.1	1.9
U.S.A.	3.1	3.7[b]	4.3[b]	2.0	4.8
U.S.S.R	6.1[a]	2.6	2.5	n.a.	n.a.

[a] 1955–63 [b] Earliest figure 1871. [c] Earliest figure 1879.

Table 2: Growth of Output per Man Employed. Annual average compound growth-rate

	1955–64 %	1870–1955 %	1870–1913 %	1913–38 %	1938–55 %
Denmark	3.8	1.6	2.1	0.7	1.6
France	4.7	1.4	1.4	0.9	2.1
Germany	4.4	1.5[a]	1.6[a]	0.8	1.9
Italy	5.7	1.2	0.8	1.5	1.6
Japan	8.8	2.2[b]	2.4[b]	3.7	0.5
Norway	3.9	1.6[a]	1.4[a]	1.9	2.0
U.K.	2.6	1.0	1.0	0.7	1.2
U.S.A.	1.9	1.8[a]	1.9[a]	1.2	2.4

[a]Earliest figure 1871. [b] Earliest figure 1879.

Moreover, several countries, including the U.K., had a better performance from 1955 to 1964 than from 1950 to 1960.

I have attempted elsewhere to explain in detail the reasons for this acceleration beyond historical experience, but our problem here is to analyse the reasons for differences between countries during 1955–64. What is striking is the fact that the U.K.'s performance from 1955 to 1964 was well below that of all the other countries except the U.S. The gap is narrower in terms of productivity than of production, because of the slower growth of the British labour force, but it is nevertheless very marked.

Factors Affecting Supply Potential

There are three major factors which have affected the supply potential of various countries in different ways.

Changes in Farm Population In the Continental countries and in Japan there were elements of structural backwardness not present in the U.K., and the elimination of these was an added source of growth. There was a considerable drop in agricultural population everywhere, but the impact on growth was larger in the Continental countries and in Japan, which had a bigger and more backward agricultural sector than the U.K. The extreme cases were Japan and Italy, where four million and three million people respectively left agriculture. As a result, non-agricultural employment expanded very rapidly indeed, as can be seen from Table 3.

Table 3: Change in Employment 1955–64

	Agricultural employment	Non-agricultural employment	Total employment	Total employment assuming agricultural workers moving to other industries to have been in disguised unemployment
	%	%	%	%
Denmark	-21.4	22.0	11.2	17.5
France	-27.5	13.3	2.6	10.6
Germany	-28.0	21.2	11.6	17.7
Italy	-37.6	26.2	0.4	18.4
Japan	-24.4	38.9	13.5	25.8
Norway	-19.7	7.7	2.2	6.3
U.K.	-17.6	5.9	4.7	5.6
U.S.A.	-29.1	11.5	10.8	15.2

If we make the extreme assumption that all the labour leaving agriculture had been effectively in 'disguised unemployment' in 1955, we get a downward adjustment to the productivity growth of all countries (see Table 4). Even this extreme assumption leaves Britain's performance substantially behind that of the Continental countries and of Japan.

Table 4: Output per Man Employed Adjusted for Removal of Disguised Unemployment 1955–64. Annual average compound growth-rate

	%		%
Denmark	3.2	Japan	7.6
France	3.9	Norway	3.5
Germany	3.7	U.K.	2.5
Italy	3.8	U.S.A.	1.6

Level of Productivity A country's productivity growth-potential will be inversely related to its *level* of productivity. The higher the level the more difficult further progress will be, and the lower the level the easier it will be to catch up. In 1955, the British productivity level was substantially higher than that of Japan and Italy, and these countries grew faster partly because they had elements of backwardness to remove in addition to the agricultural factor mentioned above. Similarly, slower growth in the U.S. can be partly explained in terms of its much higher actual level of productivity. However, the British productivity level was not too different from that of the other Continental countries.

In the future, it is Britain which should be able to exploit some of the opportunities of backwardness, for its over-all productivity level now is below that of France and Germany. The backwardness of the U.K. is most marked in the industrial sector.

Table 5: Level of Employment, Real Output and Output per Head 1964

	Employment millions	Real G.N.P. at U.S. relative prices	Output per man employed in the economy as a whole
		U.K. = 100	
France	19.9	88	112
Germany	25.9	112	110
Italy	19.8	65	83
Japan	46.7	141	77
U.K.	25.4	100	100
U.S.A.	73.1	506	176
U.S.S.R.	105.7	342	82

We can make only a very crude estimate of productivity levels by sector, but it seems likely that British industrial productivity is now below that of all West European countries north of the Alps, and probably not very much different from the levels in the U.S.S.R., Italy and Japan. Just as the other countries have exploited and, to some extent, can still exploit backward agriculture as a source of growth, so the U.K. has a good deal of backwardness to remove in industry.

Investment The third factor affecting supply potential was the higher average rate of investment in Continental countries and in Japan. Although the rate of investment has risen substantially in the U.K., it was still lower than elsewhere in 1964. For 1955–63 gross investment varied from 20 per cent. in France to 33 per cent. in Japan. In the U.K., the rate was only 16.6 per cent. It has been argued that higher investment would not have helped British growth, and that the U.K. was simply inefficient in the allocation of investment. However, there is good reason to believe that the higher capital-output ratio of the U.K. was due to inadequate investment, rather than to inefficiency in its use, and that more investment would have lowered the capital-output ratio.

There are several factors which explain variations in capital-output ratios between countries. One of these is inter-country variations in degree of capacity use, but this was probably not important from 1955 to 1964. Another is variations in the share of housing investment, which contributes little to growth and is very capital-intensive. In Table 6 we have, therefore, excluded residential construction from investment and from the capital-output ratios (the last two columns). Other sectoral variations in the composition of investment were not important.

Table 6

	Gross capital formation as a share of G.N.P at current market prices 1955–63	Gross non-residential capital formation as share of G.N.P. at current market prices 1955–63	Gross non-residential fixed capital formation as share of G.N.P. at current market prices 1955–63	Gross incremental non-residential investment output ratio	Gross incremental fixed non-residential investment output ratio
	%	%	%		
France	20.4	15.7	14.2	3.1	2.8
Germany	25.3	20.1	18.2	3.6	3.3
Italy	22.7	16.9	15.9	3.0	2.8
Japan	33.2	30.2	25.9	2.9	2.5
U.K.	16.6	13.7	12.7	4.4	4.1
U.S.A.	18.4[a]	13.9[a]	13.0[a]	4.5	4.2

[a] U.S. investment figures adjusted upwards by $5 billions a year to include government investment in machinery and equipment.

A factor which reduces the gross capital-output ratio in fast-growing countries is their smaller burden of replacement. In a country where the capital stock has been growing rapidly, its average age will be lower than in a slow-growing country, and the proportion of G.N.P. needed for replacement is smaller. As the share of G.N.P. going to net investment is higher, the share of replacement in total investment is smaller for two reasons. Replacement of non-residential fixed capital in an economy with a 3 per cent. growth-rate is likely to be 5.3 per cent. of G.N.P., compared with 3.3 per cent. for a 6 per cent. rate, and 1.5 per cent. for a 10 per cent. G.N.P. growth-rate (assuming that non-residential capital has a 30-year life, that the capital-output ratio is 2.5 and that growth has been steady). As inventories are measured net of replacement we should exclude them from our illustration. On these assumptions, the U.K. replacement burden from 1955 to 1964 would have been 5.3 per cent. of G.N.P., its net non-residential fixed investment rate 7.4 per cent. and its net capital-output ratio 2.4. Similarly, the Japanese net non-residential fixed investment rate would have become 24.4 per cent. and its net capital-output ratio 2.3. Our example is a highly simplified statement of a complicated problem,* but it is obvious that allowances for differences in the replacement burden is enough in itself to produce much closer convergence of the ratios of different countries.

The faster growth of employment has also reduced the capital-output ratio in several Continental countries and in Japan. More output can be obtained from a given investment in plant and equipment if more workers are available, than if they are not. 'Capital-widening' is cheaper than 'capital-deepening' (productivity-raising) investment.

The returns on capital-deepening investment will be affected by the *level* of productivity. In European countries the level of productivity in the mid-1950s was around half of that in the United States. In Japan it was about a quarter. Therefore, Europe and Japan could exploit their lower productivity position to get cheaper growth in terms of investment. These different opportunities might be reflected *ex post* in a lower capital-output ratio, but not necessarily so. Investment in the more backward countries may be pushed to the stage where the marginal returns are similar to those in the advanced countries. In this case, the capital-output ratio may not be different, but growth will be faster and investment higher. Thus it was possible to push investment up to 25 per cent. of G.N.P. in Germany and 33 per cent. in Japan. It seems quite likely that the U.K. can push productivity-raising investment further than it has done, particularly as its productivity level is now lower than elsewhere in Western Europe.

from A. Maddison, 'How Fast Can Britain Grow?', in *Lloyds Bank Review* (January 1966)

* ***Inter alia***, **it ignores the fact that replacement investment has a productivity bonus, and assumes that growth has been steady for a long period, cf. *Economic Growth in the West* for a more detailed statement of the problem.**

C15 'Technology: the Revolution that Wasn't' (1966)

Successive governments have so far failed to get to the bottom of British industry's disastrous reluctance to innovate. Industry re-equips, sometimes at a high rate of investment, but it does not experiment, and the fault does not lie — this is now quite clear — either in lack of research or shortage of the money with which to do it. In the eight years since Mr Hogg became Britain's first science minister, spending on research and development has probably come close to trebling itself. One can only guess, because no estimates have been made since 1961, when spending on all forms of research was then running at £634 million a year, 60 per cent of it being paid for by the government. On previous form, and assuming some slackening in the rate of growth, current research spending might now be around £1,000 million a year. In terms of the percentage of national resources allocated to science, we do nearly as well as the Americans and a very great deal better than any other country in Western Europe. No, money is not really the problem.

And if shortage of money is not the difficulty, then it follows that the easiest option open to any government, of pump-priming with more cash into more laboratories, is not going to be the cure. What we are up against is a peculiar form of English sickness that shows itself in a blank refusal to exploit new developments, and which does not appear responsive to the normal financial incentives. It used to be said that the British were good at basic research but poor at engineering development, in contrast to the Americans whose talents were the other way round. And this led successive postwar governments to put ever-increasing sums into development in order to right the balance. The list of new developments pioneered in Britain to the point of demonstrating working prototypes, i.e. to the stage just short of full commercial production, is one that a country this size can feel proud of. But pick at random some of the best known and see what has happened to them:

Vertical take-off aircraft, now flying for 14 years, not in use.

Blind landing for civil aircraft, first demonstrated 19 years ago, not in use until 1968.

Integrated microcircuits for electronic wiring, invented in government laboratories here 9 years ago, developed in the United States.

Variable geometry (pivoting wing) aircraft, patents taken out in

Britain more than 20 years ago, models flying since mid-1950s, developed in United States.

Communication satellites, first published references in Britain in 1946, developed in the United States.

Hovercraft, first commercial versions bought by Sweden.

Computer controlled machine tools, on the market for years, virtually unsaleable.

and there are others.

It is outrageous to think that an aircraft can fly for 14 years before the Air Force gets down to discussing a production order. Either vertical take-off has some value, in which case the Hawker fighter should have been put into production six or seven years ago (the version the RAF is now contemplating has been flying since 1960), or it has no value and £150 million? £200 million? more? has been frittered worthlessly away when the project ought to have been cancelled years back. And if the Ministry of Defence is so dilatory — remember that it turned down variable geometry aircraft, and hovercraft, and a British equivalent to the Phantom fighter, and wire-guided anti-tank missiles, and the Stalwart cross-country army lorry, until it saw other countries buying them or their foreign-built equivalent — British industry can hardly be blamed if it takes its tone from Whitehall.

This is the Ministry of Technology's brief, to break down this autistic attitude to innovation. And it has been the Ministry's failing since it was formed to have given no signs of any constructive thinking about how to cope with it. And yet it had certain guide-lines. There are three widely contrasted industries in this country where new developments are taken up with alacrity. One is atomic energy, where a consistent programme of research, followed by the construction of prototypes, followed by commercial application has been carried through with a steady nerve and to a successful outcome, although at times it seemed otherwise. Here, development is in the hands of an independent public corporation, the Atomic Energy Authority, with its own annual budget allocated among projects on the basis of scientific judgment and without, in the early stages at least, over-much heed to what the customer may be saying. If the AEA cancels projects, it does so sooner rather than later and without excessive fuss. It is not blamed or publicly pilloried for reporting at the end of the year 'we tried X, and it won't work.' The country builds, on average, better nuclear plants than it does aircraft, we don't ask often enough why this should be.

The second industry that responds to change is, improbably, farming. Even miserably small farmers are willing to experiment with new methods, new machines and the sort of new chemicals that would stop the average factory inspector in his tracks. Some people think that they rush almost too precipitously into new techniques before these have been properly worked out or they properly understand them. But the fact is that men labelled by tradition as ultra conservatives are highly receptive to new ideas. And for this there are two explanations. One is the high cost and rising shortage of farm labour, which gives farmers the incentive to try anything that looks as if it might reduce labour costs and increase labour productivity. It is a classic economist's situation from which manufacturing industry is protected by what are still relatively low wages and relatively high prices. Industry can hoard labour and indulge in a good deal of concealed under-employment like the British Motor Corporation's £30 for 30 hours. Farmers cannot.

So farmers have the incentive to innovate. And they are helped to do it by the outstandingly good advisory service run by the Ministry of Agriculture, whose men go out to the farmer rather than waiting for him to come to them. The Ministry's expertise takes two important forms, scientific and cost-control, so that it makes up to the most backward farmer for his own lack of technical and commercial nous. The chemical companies do much the same, and have become expert at thinking up the kind of schemes that will qualify for the maximum farm subsidy. Farmers have been forced into the sort of predicament where they must modernise or go under, government departments and their suppliers are at hand to show them the way to do it. Put like that, it sounds obvious, but apply it to manufacturing industry, and it proves to be the exception. The Treasury should have squeezed labour-hoarding industries in the way that the drift from the land has squeezed farmers; the Board of Trade and the Ministry of Technology should have been offering the same sort of skilled advice as the Ministry of Agriculture but at the factory bench. But they have not.

The third obvious innovators are the much abused makers of drugs. Their experience is important because it highlights the importance of marketing when it comes to selling new ideas. The way the drug companies go about this is open to criticism on the grounds that it is leading to exaggeratedly high profits, but it cannot be faulted on grounds of effectiveness. And if one wants a short explanation of why computers were slow to catch on in this country, or why computer controlled machine tools lag even now, it is because these industries failed to study their customers. It is wasting time to attempt selling a computer to a brewery without knowing in detail how a brewery works. The computer companies have learnt the hard way that selling requires learning more about the customer's business than he knows himself. Their selling staff has increased proportionately. But the machine tool manufacturers have not learnt this lesson yet, and their sales of computer-controlled tools lag.

from *The Economist* (19 March 1966)

C16 'How the UK and West German Plastics Industries Compare' (1972)

West Germany is similar to the UK in size, population and pattern of industry. Whilst part of the differences in plastics consumption is due to West Germany's higher rate of GDP growth and membership of the EEC and the UK's tariff disadvantage, this is not a complete answer. The next step therefore is to examine the user industries and markets in each country.

Plastics Materials

By type of material, production is similar in each country, with thermoplastics accounting for 72 per cent of total output in 1968. PVC* represented 19 per cent and LDPE† 18 per cent of West German output compared with 23 per cent and 20 per cent respectively of UK output. Net output per head in the UK plastics materials producing industry was £3,557 in 1968, based on the Census of Production, £200 higher than the average for the chemical industry as a whole. No comparable figures are available for West Germany, but in the chemical industry as a whole productivity is higher in West Germany than in the UK and this is probably true for plastics materials.

One of the features of the UK plastics materials producing industry is concentration of production, with three companies making 70

*PVC — polyvinylchloride.
† LDPE—low density polyethylene.

per cent of output in 1968. Similarly, in West Germany the bulk of production is concentrated in three companies, all of which are large producers of petrochemicals. The dominant companies in both the UK and West Germany operate on a world basis, use similar technologies, and sell largely to the same markets. Published comparisons of the total R&D expenditure by the three largest West German and two largest UK based chemical firms show a somewhat larger share of turnover allocated to R&D in West Germany. This probably holds true for the plastics materials sector but no breakdown by products is available.

Plastics Processing

West German plastics processing output in 1968, at manufacturers' prices, is estimated to have been £1,300 – 1,400 million, slightly more than twice the UK output of some £600 million.

Table 1: Productivity and Earnings in Plastics Processing, West Germany and the UK 1968

	Index 1963 – 100	
	West Germany	UK
Output per employee	157	149
Output per employee hour	164	153
Earnings per production worker	128	144
Earnings per non-production employee	141	144

Sources: West Germany—*Report of the Association for plastics processing industries* (GKV) *1968;* UK—*1968 census of production* (provisional) *DE gazette.*

Productivity increased slightly faster and earnings more slowly in West Germany than in the UK between 1963 and 1968 (Table [1]).

Estimates of total assets per employee in 1968 indicate a slightly higher average capital intensity of £2,540 in West Germany compared with £2,245 in the UK. West German demand for plastics processing machinery in 1968 was almost three times UK demand although the level of plastics consumption in West Germany was only about 2½ times as great as the UK's. A better West German use of assets in 1968 is also suggested by a higher ratio of sales to assets than in the UK — 1.9 compared with 1.5.

Markets

Many of the main markets for plastics products have accounted for a greater share of the West German economy than the UK's. In both countries building was the largest market for plastics in 1968, accounting for 26 per cent of plastics consumption in West Germany and 25 per cent in the UK. Because of post-war reconstruction, housing accounted for a much higher proportion of West German than UK GDP in the 1950s and 1960s. By 1968, West German consumption of plastics in building totalled 650,000 tonnes compared with 272,000 tonnes in the UK. Building output in West Germany was more than 1½ times as great as in the UK, with higher spending per dwelling. But this is not the whole explanation: there has also been higher penetration of plastics in the West German building industry.

In 1968, automotive products and land transport used 65,000 tonnes of plastics in the UK and 150,000 tonnes in West Germany. The difference was partly due to higher vehicle output, 2.8 million units compared with 1.8 million in the UK. There was also higher usage of plastics per vehicle in West Germany; the average weight of plastics per car was 34 kg compared with 22.3 kg in the UK.

According to the *Reader's Digest* survey, ownership of the principal consumer goods has increased much faster in West Germany than in the UK. Furthermore, the West German plastic industry has the advantage of an electrical engineering industry with an output just over three times that of the UK industry in 1968. Sales of domestic appliances in the 1960s grew much faster in West Germany and output of refrigerators and washing machines was double that of the UK.

These comparisons have been based largely on data for 1968, and in fact the UK has dropped even further back since then. The difference in the rate of growth of consumption of plastics in the two countries widened in both 1969 and 1970; growth over the two years was 24 per cent in the UK and 40 per cent in West Germany.

This is still not a complete explanation of the different levels of plastics consumption in the two countries. Other factors, not so readily quantifiable, are: different patterns of comparative prices of materials, with the UK believed to have the cheapest tinplate in Western Europe; a greater reliance on statutory regulations in West Germany as opposed to voluntary codes of practice in the UK; and, lastly, West Germany's enforced use of synthetic materials during and immediately after the Second World War contributing to a greater willingness to use new materials.

from the National Economic Development Office, *The Plastics Industry and Its Prospects* (1972). Reprinted by permission of the Controller of Her Majesty's Stationery Office

C17 Car Imports (1973)

Lost Output at Home is a Major Reason for the Rising Sales of Foreign Cars in Britain, but it is not the Whole Story

Imports took more than 27 per cent of the British car market in March; in the same month, thanks to strikes, weekly car production was 5,000 cars down on the year before. When all British factories were working smoothly towards the end of last year, imports fell to 24 per cent, and the industry points out that the 225,000 cars that strikes cost it in 1972 correspond roughly to the numbers by which British exports fell and imports rose. This suspicion that strikes are at the root of it is borne out by individual sales. British Leyland's Marina, which has been strike-free for the past three months, has for the first time reached third place in the pop charts, close behind the Ford Escort. And, as far as the foreigners go, Fiat is the only importer not to have improved its sales significantly in Britain this year — and attributes that to its own dreadful labour problems in Turin. Renault has just had to close a strike-hit factory at Flins, which could cost it its crown as the top British import, while the Rubery Owen strike is beginning to be felt on British assembly lines.

It is also fair to point out that what is happening in Britain happened before to all the common market countries as tariffs came down and the feeling of common membership made companies less inhibited about allowing staff to buy foreign-built cars on the firm. Foreign manufacturers themselves saw the growth potential in the British market last year, and made the most of it while many of their other markets were lagging.

The biggest success story so far this year has been Datsun, suddenly in second place among importers, just ahead of Volkswagen. Datsun's first job was to get its dealer network right before it started selling in a big way (Volkswagen policy, too); it was helped by the fact that all the British manufacturers were having a shake-up in dealerships and their computers were slinging out some good dealers with the bad. In the 1200 Datsun has a straightforward car which is easy to understand, and is popular with driving schools. Like Volvo, Volkswagen and BMW before it, Datsun also put a lot of emphasis on reliability. Warranty costs work out at 65p per car.

Renault has still kept the first place from which it toppled Volkswagen last year. Its cars are now designed for an international market and it tends to build-in as standard such accessories as heated rear windows and anti-theft locks that other manufacturers charge as extras. The Renaults capture a good share everywhere of the market they are designed for. The R12, the top-selling model in Britain, came to within 8,000 of the sales of the Cortina 1300 last year, and many of the Cortinas were largely for fleets, a market Renault has not tapped yet.

The latest Renault, the R5, is an up-market Mini-equivalent, showered with car-of-the-year-awards, and is typical of the compactness of modern continental design. It had a third door, a large boot and a folding back seat, so that it can be used as a van. All this is winning sales from the larger cars. Herr Rudolf Leiding, the chairman of Volkswagen, has said: 'The modern customer wants a small car with three times as much room inside as outside.' Fiat is a master of this theory. Its 127 has a transverse, front-wheel-drive engine which enables it to provide much the same room inside as a Ford Escort or Vauxhall Viva, although outside it is more than a foot shorter. The 903cc engine achieves the same top speed, faster acceleration and better fuel consumption than British cars of 1300cc.

Top of the pops
January – March, 1973, 000s

Top selling models:		Top imports:	
1 Cortina	57	Renault	19
2 Escort	35	Datsun	14
3 Marina	34	VW	13.7
4 Viva	31	Fiat	11.4
5 Mini	26	Chrysler (France)	8.4
6 – 13 other British cars		Volvo	6.2
Top selling foreigners:		Citroen	5.2
14 VW Beetle	9.5	Audi/NSU	5.0
16 Datsun 1200	7.6	Peugeot	4.2
19 Renault 12	5.6	Toyota	4.2
21 Volvo 144	5.2		

Among the bigger cars, Ford's Consul/Granada and the Triumph Dolomite have been moving up the charts, but BMW's larger models and the Mercedes are together now within 20 per cent of the total of Jaguar/Daimler's sales. The south of France, always a good test of trends in expensive cars, is flooded with BMWs. Apart from reliability, the BMW 3.0Si seems to have established a reputation for pleasant driving. The suspension is built for faster speeds than the engine, with racing car struts. The wheels dig into the ground as they corner. The company aims at 95 per cent availability of spares, and flies out parts that are not stocked in Britain. But, at approaching £5,000, it is more than £1,000 dearer than the Jaguar XJ12, which has been acclaimed as possibly the finest car-for-money on the road. It is lack of production that hits Jaguar, and its price tag of nearly £6,000 in Germany reflects its true value.

from *The Economist* (21 April 1973)

C18 Should Shipbuilding be Subsidised? (1973)

To prevent at least one major yard closing the British taxpayer will have to be tapped for another £250m in capital grants to shipbuilding, plus £20m a year in revenue subsidies. Even then employment in the industry will fall by nearly a third. This is one of several options put to the Government in a report by the consultants, Booz-Allen and Hamilton, published on Wednesday. The findings are bleak enough. But, on the basis of the facts presented, Booz-Allen may have underestimated the improvement in productivity needed, and therefore also the cost to the taxpayer. If so, the subsidy could go as high as £700m.

The object of subsidising the shipyards on even the Booz-Allen scale is the expectation that, by achieving a 15 per cent cut in costs, it will bring Britain up to the current standards of the Japanese. But that is going to work only if foreign shipyards conveniently do not continue to improve their own productivity in the meanwhile. Japan has thousands of naval architects engaged constantly on rationalisation, while Kockums of Sweden believes in re-building itself from the ground up every few years; a recent German report has advocated a major modernisation programme.

World over-capacity is likely to keep ship prices falling. By Booz-Allen's own pessimistic reckoning, capacity will be twice the demand for new ships in 1980, at 58m gross registered tons. The chances of it being cut substantially are small, both because shipbuilding is supported for political reasons and because a large increase in output is needed to produce a small cut in costs. The reason for this is largely that more than half shipbuilding costs are in materials, outside the yard's control. This gearing is reflected in the fact that output per employee in the six modern European yards studied by Booz-Allen is four times that in Britain. A 15 per cent cut in British costs would itself need a doubling of British shipbuilding capacity, adding to the world surplus. If Europe were to become as efficient as Japan, world capacity would double.

Productivity Gap

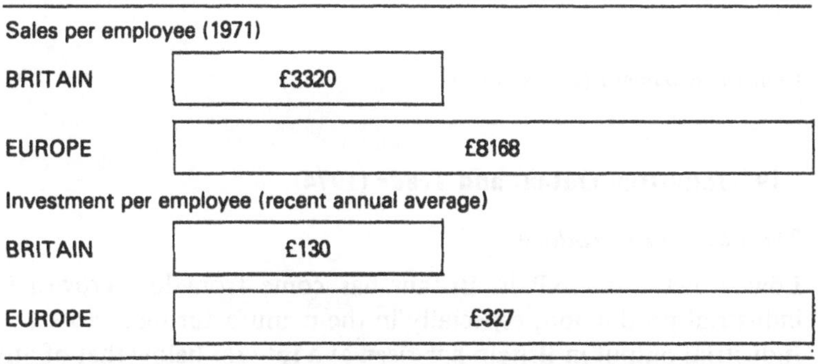

The spate of orders for British yards this year, largely from one company, Maritime Fruit Carriers, should not be allowed to disguise the underlying sickness, as a previous recovery in orders did in 1968, after the Geddes report. Assuming a 5 per cent drop in world prices, and a 10 per cent improvement in foreign productivity, the cost of putting the British industry on its feet could reach £700m, equivalent to the industry's total revenue in the past five years. That is on the optimistic assumption that the second tranche of cost-cutting could be achieved with less subsidy. An even bigger drop in employment would be needed, too. Is it worth spending £700m to save at most 25,000 jobs, at £28,000 a job, in an industry whose labour force even now is less than half that of Imperial Chemical Industries, and which has already extracted £160m from the taxpayer?

As it is, the idea that there is a bottomless purse in the Treasury just for shipbuilding has long weakened the industry. This is reflected in days lost through stoppages, three times the national average in 1967 and five times in 1971. Significantly, the main reason for disputes has turned from demarcation arguments to pay. This must partly be responsible for the fact that two-fifths of ships are delivered over a month late, though management incompetence emerges as the main reason for that. The current dispute which is nearly bringing to a halt Harland and Wolff, the showpiece of British shipbuilding — since it has the most modern facilities — is the kind of strangulation that unlimited subsidies encourage.

Booz-Allen presented a series of options, covering different scales of subsidy, without making a recommendation between them. But it assumed a favourable relationship between the level of subsidy and productivity, although past experience suggests the reverse may be true.

from *The Economist* (19 May 1973)

C19 Industrial Output and Trade (1974)

The Failure to Produce

Low growth of GNP in Britain has come from low growth in industrial production, especially in the manufacturing sectors . . . Industrial output in Britain has risen at a rate far below that of any of the other main industrialised countries. In general, industrial output in the developed countries tends to rise on an average of 1 per cent faster than GNP. In Britain, over the 1960-70 period, it grew at a rate slightly less than that of GNP. The only sectors in Britain to have experienced significant growth were the chemical industry (including petroleum and coal) and utilities (gas and electricity) — a trend which can be observed in the other countries too. The textiles, food, and clothing sectors, as well as the basic metals sector, traditional low-growth industries, did worst. But the manufacturing sector as a whole did not do much better . . .

The main reason for the low increase in industrial output has been the very low rate of investment within Britain over recent years. Compared to other countries, British investment as a percentage of gross domestic product . . . has been far below that in all other developed countries except the United States. It has also increased more slowly . . . , at a 6.1 per cent average from 1960 to 1965, at 3.2 per cent from 1965 to 1970, and 1.8 per cent from 1970 to 1973. The United Kingdom has now the lowest rate of capital investment per employee of any major industrial country. Of the six largest industrial countries, the UK is the sixth in consumption of machine tools per employee.* As regards the age of machine tools, in Japan 62 per cent of all machine tools are less than ten years old. In Germany the figure is 56 per cent. In the UK only 38 per cent of the machine tools are less than a decade old. If this age profile is turned into relative

*Consumption of machine tools means home output plus imports, minus exports.

manufacturing advantage (lower direct labour costs, reduction in setting-up time, reduced scrap, etc), then, it can be calculated that the industrial users of machine tools in Germany and Japan have an advantage of roughly 15 per cent to 20 per cent over British manufacturers.*

Low investment has been the result of the stop-go policies of the various British governments. The 'stop' phase of the cycle, marked by restrictive monetary policy, wage freeze, credit squeezes etc. has served to curtail investment and production; the 'go' phase has unfortunately been focused on consumer-led expansion rather than a selective promotion of productive investment. Deflation has damaged the British economy in three major ways:

(1) By repressing home demand, deflationary measures have dampened business expectations and confidence. As investment seemed less profitable the expansion of productive capacity has fallen.
(2) By monetary restraint making it more difficult for business to raise money on the stock market, more costly to get funds from banks, and less profitable to borrow.
(3) By creating a general climate of uncertainty, deflationary action has made it difficult for business to visualise future demand and sales and hence to commit the necessary funds to avoid investment slumps.

Not only has investment been low over past years in Britain, but the quality of the investment has been poorer than in other industrialised countries. As a general result, productivity (output per man-hour) in the manufacturing industries has risen very slowly — far more slowly than in any other country of Europe . . . The absolute value of productivity (output per man-hour in the economy as a whole) was already lower in Britain in 1969 than in other countries. From 1969 on, the gap has been widening . . .

Britain's Foreign Trade Performance

Britain is foremost a trader nation, and the international market has provided invaluable benefits to the country. Traditionally, this role in world commerce has brought not only profits for traders buying cheap in one market and selling dear in another, but it has given the

**The Times*, 21.12.1973.

country much of its economic vigour as well as certain of its political characteristics.

In centuries past Britain seldom lacked competitors, but in the twentieth century competition for world markets has become much more intensive as well as extensive. Strong new trader nations entered the field. In theory, more competition is supposed to invigorate an economy, with inefficiency penalised and the rewards of excellence enlarged. Unprofitable firms become competitive or go out of business, and the national economy therefore benefits.

Moving from theory to reality, and looking at the last 15 years, we find that in Britain what was supposed to happen did not happen. Increased competition brought no significant increases in competitiveness. In fact, during these fifteen years Britain's position in the international economy eroded significantly. This pronounced deterioration in competitiveness must be seen as one major cause for the decline of British economic strength. This conclusion emerges strongly from a comparison of Britain's recent experience with that of other industrialised and industrialising countries.

During the 1960's and early 1970's wage increases have been a major component in the rising costs of the manufacturing process in industrialised countries. Wage rises, as such, do not seriously affect a country's competitive position if they are accompanied by corresponding rises in productivity. This has not been the case in Great Britain in recent years.

Wage increases in Great Britain during the 1960's were sizeable, but still smaller than in some of Britain's main competitor countries. So far in the 1970's wage increases in the UK have been larger but not significantly more sizeable than elsewhere. In absolute terms, wages remain low in Britain.

Table 1: Hourly Wages in Manufacturing (average annual increase in percentage)

	1962–65	1965–69	1970–73
United Kingdom	4.2	6.0	11.7
France	7.4	8.9	11.4
Germany	7.8	5.9	11.3
Italy	12.0	5.0	17.3
United States	3.1	5.2	6.2
Japan[a]	9.7	14.0	17.6

[a] Monthly earnings.
Source: OECD Main Economic Indicators.

But as we have seen earlier, productivity increases consistently have been low. It is these two factors taken together — higher wage costs and low productivity increases — that have brought about a damaging change in unit labour costs. Table [2] measures the relative movement of productivity and wages: a rise in unit labour costs indicates that wage increases are outpacing productivity, and it is therefore the best indicator of comparable production cost trends in manufacturing. From this table it is clear that in the late 1960's and especially in the early 1970's unit labour costs increased greatly. Of our sample countries only Italy shows a worse performance.

Table 2 : Unit Labour Cost in Manufacturing[a] (average annual increase in percentages)

	1962–65	1965–69	1970–73
United Kingdom	2.1	2.7	8.1
France	3.4	2.2	6.3
Germany	2.6	1.4	7.5
Italy	5.7	1.9	11.4[b]
United States	–0.8	3.6	2.4
Japan	5.0	0.8	6.0

[a] Expressed in national currency. 1970–72
Source: International Economic Report of the President, Washington 1974.

Certainly the productivity of labour is strongly influenced by capital investment. More modern technology helps labour to produce more during a given period of time and dampens the labour cost of a unit of output. We have already seen that investment has lagged in the United Kingdom. Nevertheless, labour's relatively poor performance cannot be entirely blamed on the slow introduction (or the absence) of improved technology. The productivity of labour has also been strongly and negatively influenced by the high number of working days lost due to employment disputes.

from the Hudson Institute, *The United Kingdom in 1980* (Associated Business Press, 1974)

C20 UK Industrial Performance (1977)

Market Shares

Between the years 1968 and 1976 . . . Britain's share of main manufacturing countries' exports of manufactured goods ('world trade') fell from 11.3 per cent to 8.8 per cent, the equivalent figure in 1963 being 15.3 per cent. In fact, over the last two decades there have been only two years in which this trend has been reversed — 1971, when our share of world trade rose to 10.9 per cent compared with 10.6 per cent in 1970; and 1975, when the figure was 9.3 per cent compared with 8.8 per cent in the previous year.

Meanwhile, imports of manufactured goods have made increasing inroads into our domestic market. As a proportion of total final expenditure in this country, imports of manufactured goods were 6.8 per cent in 1968, rising to just under 10 per cent in 1976, which was about double the figure ten years earlier.

Measuring Performance

To look in detail at the home and export performance of individual manufacturing sectors and industries, [we draw] on the results of a number of different ratios calculated from the extensive data available on manufacturers' sales and overseas trade.

The first ratio relates imports to home demand (= manufacturers' sales *plus* imports *less* exports): this is the ratio commonly used to describe import penetration, measuring the share of the home market for a product group captured by imports. However, the aim is to measure overall performance, and this ratio takes no account of the extent of an industry's exports, a high level of which might be considered to compensate for a high level of imports. Allowance for this is made in the second ratio, relating imports to home demand plus exports (= manufacturers' sales *plus* imports): this ratio, of course, reduces as exports increase. The third ratio relates exports to manufacturers' sales: while this is the most commonly used 'export sales ratio', it ignores the extent to which the same products are being imported. This factor is included in the fourth ratio examined — exports in relation to manufacturers' sales *plus* imports. Since the second and fourth ratios have effectively the same denominator (manufactures' sales plus imports) the difference between them can also be used as an indicator of the trade gap in a particular sector in relation to the size of that sector.

There are a number of methodological and measurement problems in calculating these ratios and, therefore, while they provide indications in general terms of industrial performance, they need to be interpreted with care. It is valid to use them for measuring the direction and magnitude of change for an individual industry, but the absolute values of the ratios are of only limited use for making inter-industry comparisons. Moreover, the ratios are based on current price data, and the trends might appear different if the ratios were to be calculated in volume terms.

Successful Sectors

Nevertheless, a number of interesting points emerge. Over manufacturing industry as a whole in the period 1968 to 1976 import penetration for manufactured goods rose from 17 per cent to 25 per cent, but the proportion of home-produced goods going for export grew at a similar rate. This follows the trend in world trade, one feature of which has been increasing national specialisation.

Within this overall picture, there have been marked successes in a number of UK manufacturing sectors and industries. *Food manufacturing* is one example: a number of industries in this sector have pushed down import penetration levels and at the same time increased the proportion of their products exported. So although the sector as a whole inevitably remains a substantial net importer, considerable inroads have been made into its deficit in recent years. In *chemicals* also the picture is encouraging, with exports growing much more rapidly than imports: the *soap and detergent* industry has achieved a particularly high level of export growth in recent years. With a few exceptions, both the *mechanical and electrical* engineering sectors have more than matched increased import penetration by higher export sales ratios, with the most marked improvements in industries like *industrial plant and steelwork* and *electronic computers*. In the latter case, the export sales ratio has grown substantially, whilst import penetration has fallen below its 1970 level. All in all, exports of Britain's engineering industries are generally higher than their imports: maintenance and improvement of their competitive position is an important part of the industrial strategy programme.

Higher Imports

The less successful sectors are generally predictable. One such is *metal manufacturing*, where for example, *ferrous metal* import penetration doubled between 1970 and 1975 while export proportions rose hardly at all. In the *vehicles* sector import penetration has also risen steeply, with the exception of *tractor manufacturing*. Between 1970 and 1976 import penetration for *motor vehicles* increased four-fold, and doubled for *motor cycles*. Although the motor vehicles industry still shows a strong surplus when the export sales ratio is taken into account, this declined substantially over the period, while the previous surplus for motor cycles has been turned into a deficit. On the other hand, the figures for the *aerospace* industry show a much healthier picture, the export share having increased faster than import penetration. In the *textile* sector most industries have experienced a marked upward trend in import penetration since 1970: the weaving of *cotton, linen and man-made fibres* and *hosiery and knitted goods* are notable examples. Only in the *carpets* industry has the increase in the export sales ratio exceeded the rise in import penetration. But although both *clothing* and *footwear* have experienced steadily rising import penetration, there was a marked recovery in the export performance of the clothing industry last year.

from *Economic Progress Report*, no. 91 (October 1977)

C21 Productivity (1977)

Productivity and Prices

Over the period 1955 to 1973 output per head in UK manufacturing industry grew at an average annual rate of 3.2 per cent, significantly

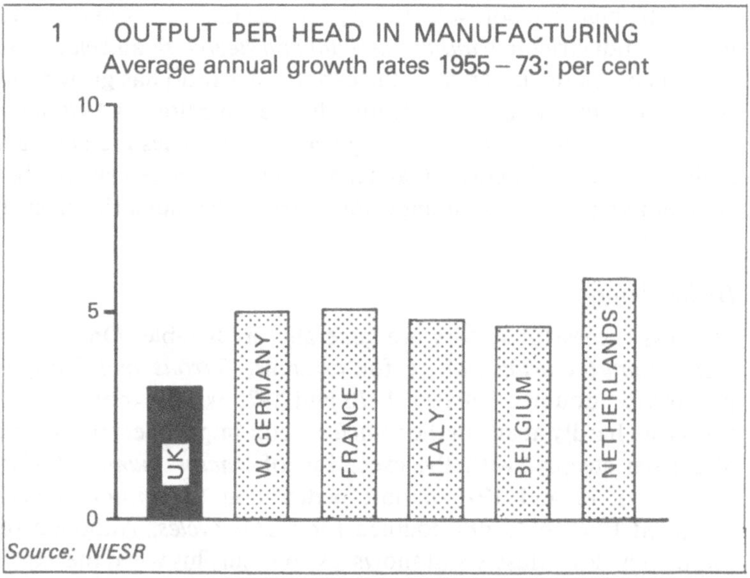

below rates in other major European countries. As can be seen in Chart 1, manufacturing productivity increased at an average annual rate of about 5 per cent over the period in West Germany, France, Italy, Belgium and the Netherlands. As a result manufacturing output per worker in the UK increased by just over three-quarters in the 18-year period, while average productivity in the other five EEC countries shown increased by nearly one and a half times.

At first sight there may not look to be a great deal of difference between the UK's average annual rate and those in the other European countries — for instance, between the UK's 3.2 per cent and West Germany's 5 per cent. But these are annual averages over almost two decades, so that the cumulative effect of the differences is very substantial. This can be seen in Chart 2, which shows the level of manufacturing productivity in each country in 1970 measured against the level of manufacturing productivity in the UK, using real purchasing power equivalents rather than exchange rates.

2 OUTPUT PER HEAD IN MANUFACTURING IN 1970 AS A RATIO OF UK LEVEL: UK = 100

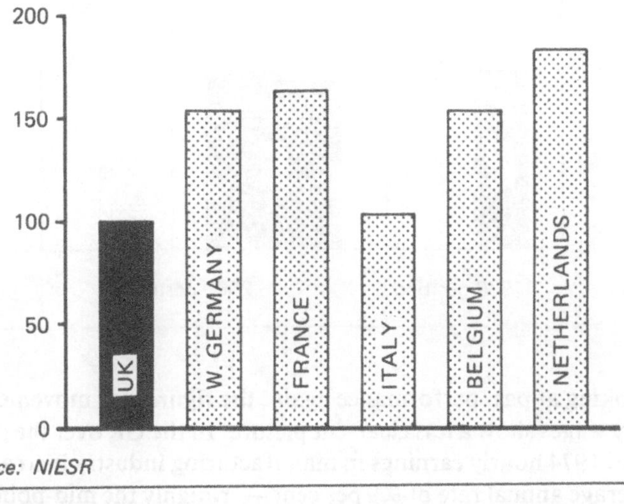

Source: NIESR

These differences were almost constant as between 1970 and 1973, which was the period when the growth of UK manufacturing productivity about equalled that in other European countries. Following the oil price rise and the deep world recession of 1974 – 75, output per person employed actually fell in most countries, including the UK. In 1976 and 1977 output per head began to rise again, if not as fast as previously: but ominously it is again rising faster in competitor countries than in the UK. Chart 3 shows the differences in levels of output per head that might occur by the end of this century, if we do not improve our relative performance.

3 OUTPUT PER HEAD IN MANUFACTURING IN 1970 AND IN 2000 ON TREND GROWTH AS A RATIO OF UK LEVEL: UK = 100
(width x height of 2000 bars gives hypothetical overall improvement over 1970 output per head)

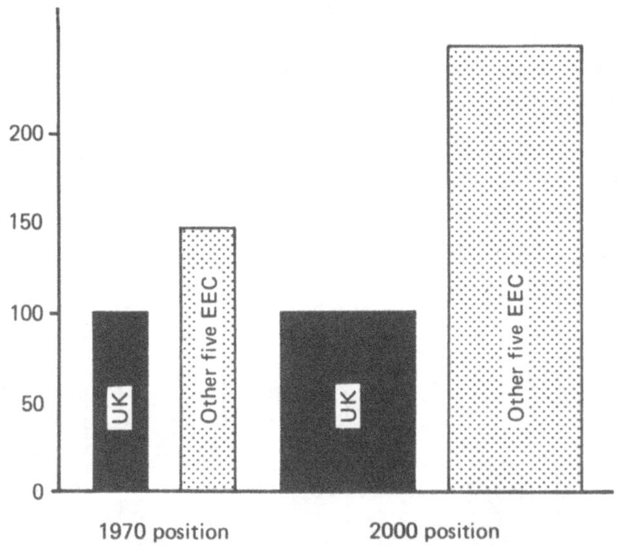

Looking at past performance again, the figures for movements in money wages show a less clear-cut picture. In the UK over the period 1964 to 1974 hourly earnings in manufacturing industry increased at an average annual rate of 9.9 per cent — roughly the mid-point of a range set by the low United States figure of 5.7 per cent and the high Japanese figure of 16 per cent. The equivalent figure for France was 10.8 per cent, Italy 11.8 per cent and West Germany 8.8 per cent. However, as regards the growth of unit labour costs (the product of the growth of money wages divided by the growth of output) the

United Kingdom was entirely out of the range of these other countries. Over the period 1964 to 1974, unit labour costs in UK manufacturing industry grew at an average annual rate of 7.1 per cent — a higher figure than in any other major industrial country. In Italy, for example, unit labour costs increased at an average annual rate of 6.2 per cent over this period; in Japan 5.8 per cent, in West Germany 5.5 per cent and in France 4.7 per cent. Similarly in the United States unit labour costs increased at an annual rate of 2.7 per cent — about a third of the rate of increase in the UK. For the other five major industrial countries taken together, the average annual increase in unit labour costs over the 1964–74 period was about 5 per cent — roughly two-thirds the UK figure.

It is self-evident that unit labour costs have a direct effect on prices of goods in the shops, though of course other important factors are involved in determining the overall rate of inflation. Over the period 1963–73 consumer prices in Britain increased at an average annual rate of 5.6 per cent. This was below the Japanese figure of 6 per cent: but it was significantly above the rate of increase in every other major industrial country. Over the ten years to 1973 consumer prices rose at an average annual rate of 4.6 per cent in France and Italy, 3.8 per cent in the United States and 3.6 per cent in West Germany.

Markets and Jobs

For a country like Britain, unit labour costs are a crucially important factor because, with relatively few natural resources, we depend on importing raw materials and turning them into manufactured products for sale at home and overseas in competition with other manufacturing countries. If the UK's unit labour costs are out of line with those in these other countries we are likely to be less competitive and therefore to lose markets. In fact, over the period 1963 to 1973 the UK share of the main manufacturing countries' exports of manufactured goods — the most appropriate definition of world trade for the UK — fell from 15.3 per cent to 9.4 per cent. The United States' share also fell, but those of West Germany, France and Italy — Britain's main European competitors — all rose, while Japan's share almost doubled, rising from 7.5 per cent to 12.7 per cent.

Of course, other factors than price are involved in competitiveness. But the evidence from studies of individual industries is that productivity — the efficiency with which resources of capital and labour are used — affects not only price competitiveness but also such important aspects of non-price competitiveness as delivery dates.

One result of this declining share of world markets can be seen in the figures for employment in the manufacturing sector, where there is a complete contrast between the experience of the UK and that of the other major industrial countries. Over the period 1955 – 73 employment in manufacturing industry *declined* by 13 per cent in the UK, compared with an *increase* of 11 per cent in France, 18 per cent in the United States, 31 per cent in West Germany, 57 per cent in Italy and a massive 155 per cent in Japan. Again the contrast between Britain and broadly equivalent European economies is particularly marked. In West Germany for example, employment in manufacturing industry grew at an average annual rate of 1.5 per cent over the 1955 – 73 period, whereas in Britain manufacturing employment declined at an average annual rate of 0.8 per cent. It fell further until 1976, but since then has shown a slight rise.

from *Economic Progress Report*, no. 93 (December 1977)

C22 The Balance of Payments in 1980 (1981)

Balance of Payments

For the fourth time in the post-war period, the trade balance was in surplus in 1980; and in the six months to February 1981 it was running at an historically high annual rate of $12¾ billion. The trade surplus more than offset the slight decline in invisibles receipts to give a record current account surplus which emerged after mid-year and continued to increase up to early 1981. The reasons behind the dramatic turnaround from a current account deficit in 1979 to a surplus in 1980 were first, a continuing amelioration in the non-oil terms of trade due to the effective appreciation of sterling; secondly, a significant improvement in the real foreign balance mainly due to the deep recession and the . . . associated substantial fall in import volumes; and thirdly, the United Kingdom became a net oil exporter in the second half of 1980. The overall balance benefited importantly from the deeper recession in the United Kingdom than in the rest of the OECD area, which helped to cut back imports and provide a stimulus to export. The improvement in the current account broadly offset a large rise in net long-term capital outflows and the decline in non-monetary short-term capital inflow with the result that the deficit in non-monetary transactions remained roughly unchanged (at about $7½ billion). Sterling holdings by overseas monetary authorities increased and there was again a small rise in official reserves which stood at $27½ billion at the end of 1980 (compared . . . with $22½ billion a year earlier) and £26½ billion at the end of May 1981. Official debt repayments amounted to £2½ billion in 1980 compared with $1¾ billion in 1979.

After being broadly stable for about two years, the volume of non-oil merchandise exports started to decline in mid-1980, their level by early 1981 had fallen 7 per cent below the 1980 average. The most notable feature of export developments was the continued deterioration in export performance of manufactures which began in 1978. The growth of the volume of manufactured exports was relatively buoyant in the seven years to 1977, the average annual loss of market shares being 11 per cent compared with the longer-run annual loss of around 2½ per cent. Since then, the loss of market shares has averaged 6 per cent. This is clearly related to the sharp swing in external competitiveness induced by the appreciation of sterling and steeply rising labour costs. Following a moderate improvement prior to 1977 relative export prices of manufactures rose by 27 per cent in the three years to 1980; the rise in relative unit labour costs was more pronounced — 67 per cent over the latter period. The important decline in profitability of exports is also evident from the falling trend in the ratio of export prices of manufactures to domestic producer prices (home sales) . . . In addition, the United Kingdom's manufactured exports suffered from increasingly severe foreign competition in areas other than prices, which in time of slack, as during 1980, tend to affect even more the less efficient exporters.

The volume of manufactured exports fell sharply after the first quarter of 1980 to reach a level in early 1981 of 12 per cent lower than a year earlier. Within the total, semi-manufactures declined substantially as did other consumer goods, chemicals and metals, particularly iron and steel. Export volumes of passenger cars also dropped markedly (8 per cent); the decline gathered pace in the fourth quarter so that the level at the beginning of this year was one-third below the 1980 average. The only sector which experienced continuing rapid export growth was intermediate manufactures and capital goods. After five years of stagnation, machinery exports reached an all-time high in 1980. Whereas electrical engineering exports had been on a steep upward trend during the 1970s, mechanical engineering exports steadily declined in the five years to 1979, but picked up in 1980 despite the slack in investment trends in the United Kingdom's main export markets. The electrical engineering and instrument engineering sectors were the only ones to experience a relatively fast growth of productivity between 1974 and 1980; annual rates of growth of 4 per cent and 3½ per cent respectively, compared with a broadly flat trend in the rest of manufacturing. Accordingly, these two sectors managed to absorb the increase in labour costs and continued to improve their profit margins on exports up to 1977 as indicated . . . by the rising ratio of export prices to domestic producer prices. However, after 1978 they also suffered from the strong appreciation of sterling, entailing a reduction in profit margins on exports in order to remain competitive. Exports in value to OPEC countries recorded the highest increase — 33 per cent in 1980 as a whole. To a large extent this reflected the recovery from an artificially depressed level of exports to Iran and Nigeria in 1979. Excluding this special factor, export growth in value to OPEC countries (12½ per cent) was the same as that to the other areas (excluding oil exports), implying a substantial loss of . . . market shares in this group of countries. The above-average growth of exports to OECD Europe was exclusively due to oil exports.

Reflecting the downturn in demand and notably the rundown of stocks which have a high import content, the volume of non-oil merchandise imports declined by 16 per cent between the cyclical high in the second half of 1979 and early-1981. This fall was much sharper than during the previous downturn in the three half-years to the first half of 1975, but the difference is almost fully explained by the much stronger fall in total demand (5½ per cent) in the recent period than in the earlier period (4 per cent). In view of the loss of competitiveness it might have been expected that imports would have been higher in 1980 than they were, but it seems that this effect was outweighed by the fall in demand. As in the mid-1970s, almost all categories of imports recorded large declines in real terms, the falls being most marked for basic materials and semi-manufactures. The only exception was imports of consumption goods (excluding passenger cars) which continued to rise substantially in real terms reflecting the high, though stagnating level of private consumption (again other than passenger cars). As a consequence, the longer-run import penetration of the United Kingdom consumer goods market, particularly in consumer durables, appears to have continued unabated last year.

The longer-run upward trend in the invisibles surplus came to an end in 1977, since when it has fluctuated at around \$3¾ billion each year. A steady rise in the service surplus was roughly offset by a deterioration in the surplus on net interest, profits and dividends (IDP) and by significant steep increases in net government transfers up to 1978. Because of the substantial rise in interest, profits and dividend payments, associated with North Sea oil operations from \$3 billion in 1979 to \$5¼ billion in 1980, the IDP account moved into deficit in 1980 for the first time on record. Net government transfer payments were about \$4 billion per year in the three years to 1980 compared with \$¾ billion during the first half of the 1970s. Nearly two-thirds of this increase reflects the net contributions to the European Communities, which have averaged about \$2 billion over the least three years. On the services account, the most notable feature is the substantial decline in net tourist receipts from the peak of \$2 billion in 1977 to \$600 million in 1980, reflecting partly the loss of competitiveness causing a reduction in foreign tourists into Britain and partly the substantial rise in real disposable income in foreign currencies (due also to the appreciation of sterling) boosting the number of British tourists abroad. The downward trend in travel receipts was, however, more than offset by rising transport revenues and receipts from other services . . .

Capital movements in 1980 were influenced by exchange rate uncertainties, interest rate differentials and institutional changes. The importance increase in the private long-term capital outflow over the last two years was made possible by the abolition of exchange controls on capital movements in 1979, which entailed a big surge in United Kingdom portfolio investment overseas to \$6½ billion in 1980 compared with some \$2 billion on average over the previous two years and cumulative net investment of less than \$100 million in the ten years to 1977 . . . The desire of both financial institutions and of individuals to diversify their assets may partly explain this development as may higher rates of returns abroad related to the faster growth of activity than in the United Kingdom. In addition, there was a sharp swing in the balancing item (errors and omissions) from an average inflow of about \$4½ billion over the three . . . years to 1979 to an outflow of \$100 million in 1980. The balancing item in the three years to 1979 was unusually high and probably reflects non-identified non-monetary and monetary capital inflows associated with the upward pressure on sterling. In order to by-pass the 'corset', trade credits from abroad (including those from British banks abroad) may also have remained at a high level during this period and after the lifting of the 'corset' in mid-1980 these credits were probably reversed. In the second half of 1980, a reversal of leads and lags seems to have also taken place. Possibly because of the narrowing in the interest rate differentials after mid-1980, net private monetary short-term capital inflows — though positive — were considerably reduced in the second half of 1980. In total, the balance of official settlements recorded a small deficit, which was more than offset by an increase in sterling holdings of overseas monetary authorities with the result that official reserves as noted earlier increased again in 1980.

Source: From the Organisation for Economic Co-operation and Development, *Economic Surveys: The United Kingdom* (July 1981)

SECTION D: STATISTICS

D1 Balance of Payments (Current Account), 1880–1913, (in £ millions)

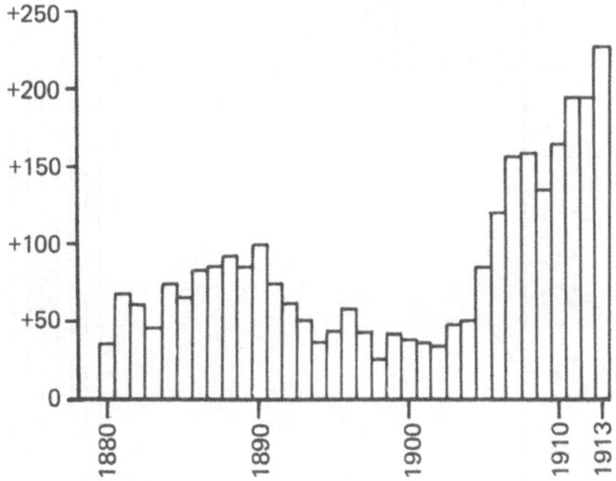

Source: Based on figures from B. R. Mitchell and P. Deane, *An Abstract of British Historical Statistics* (Cambridge University Press, 1971)

D2 Balance of Payments (Current Account), 1920 – 38 and 1938 – 45 (in £ millions)

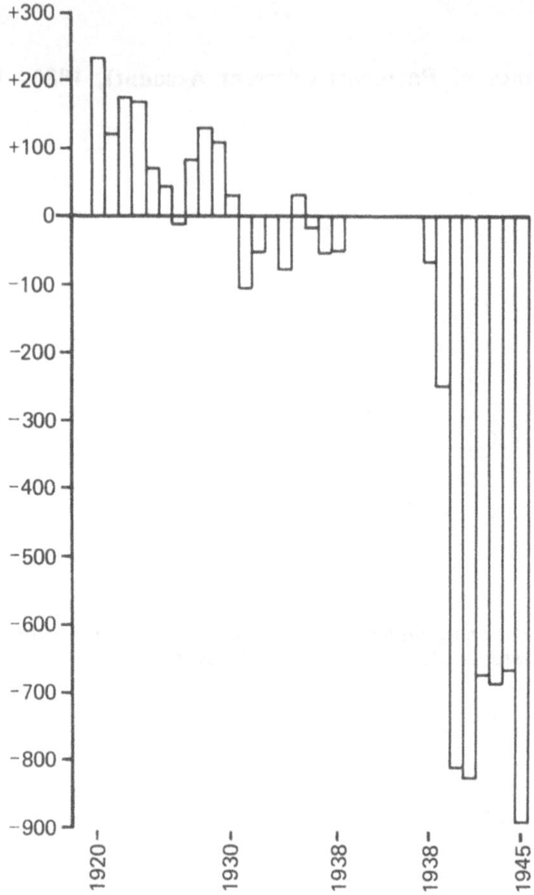

Note: Estimates for the period 1938 – 45 are not comparable to figures for the period 1920 – 38.

Source: Based on figures from the London and Cambridge Economic Service, *British Economy: Key Statistics 1900 – 1970* (Times Newspapers, 1975)

D3 Balance of Payment (Current Account), 1946 – 80 (in £ millions)

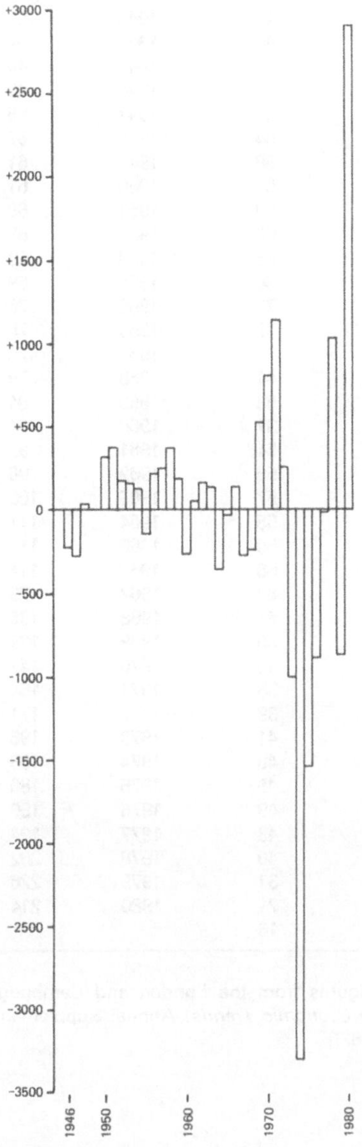

Source: Based on figures from *Economic Trends*, Annual Supplement, 1983 (HMSO, 1983)

D4 Visible Trade (Volume), 1900 – 80 (1963 = 100)

	Total Imports	UK Exports		Total Imports	UK Exports
1900	48	44	1943	50	12
1901	49	44	1944	54	13
1902	51	47	1945	44	20
1903	51	48	1946	49	43
1904	52	49	1947	55	47
1905	53	54	1948	57	60
1906	54	58	1949	61	66
1907	55	63	1950	61	75
1908	53	58	1951	69	74
1909	54	60	1952	63	69
1910	56	65	1953	68	71
1911	57	68	1954	69	74
1912	61	72	1955	76	80
1913	64	75	1956	75	84
			1957	78	86
1919	56	41	1958	79	83
1920	56	53	1959	84	86
1921	47	37	1960	94	90
1922	54	51	1961	93	93
1923	59	56	1962	96	95
1924	66	57	1963	100	100
1925	69	56	1964	111	103
1926	70	50	1965	112	108
1927	72	58	1966	114	112
1928	69	60	1967	123	111
1929	73	61	1968	136	126
1930	71	50	1969	139	140
1931	72	38	1970	147	146
1932	63	38	1971	154	154
1933	63	39	1972	171	154
1934	66	41	1973	195	175
1935	67	45	1974	196	187
1936	72	45	1975	180	180
1937	76	49	1976	190	197
1938	72	43	1977	194	213
1939	69	40	1978	202	218
1940	61	31	1979	226	226
1941	50	21	1980	214	230
1942	47	16			

Source: Based on figures from the London and Cambridge Economic Service, *British Economy* and *Economic Trends*, Annual Supplement 1981 and May 1982 (HMSO, 1981 and 1982)

D5 Acreage Devoted to Particular Crops, 1870 – 1980

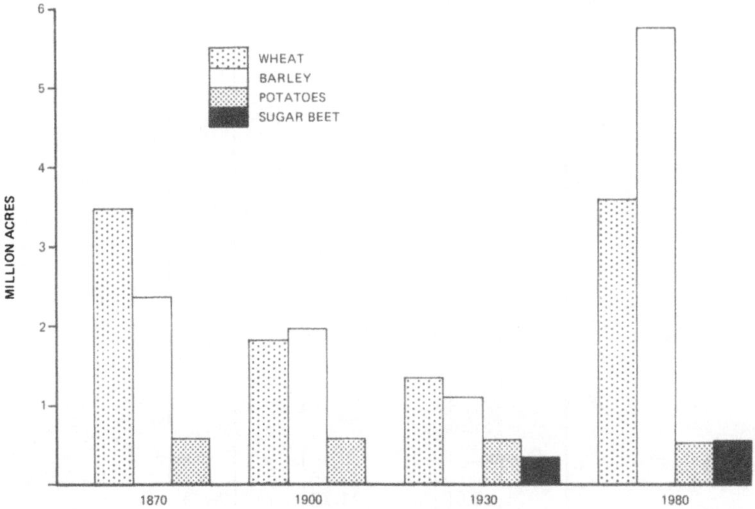

Source: Based on figures from Mitchell and Deane, *British Historical Statistics*; B. R. Mitchell and H. G. Jones, *A Second Abstract of British Historical Statistics* (Cambridge University Press, 1971); *Monthly Digest of Statistics* (HMSO, July 1981)

D6 Wheat Yields per Acre, 1938 – 62

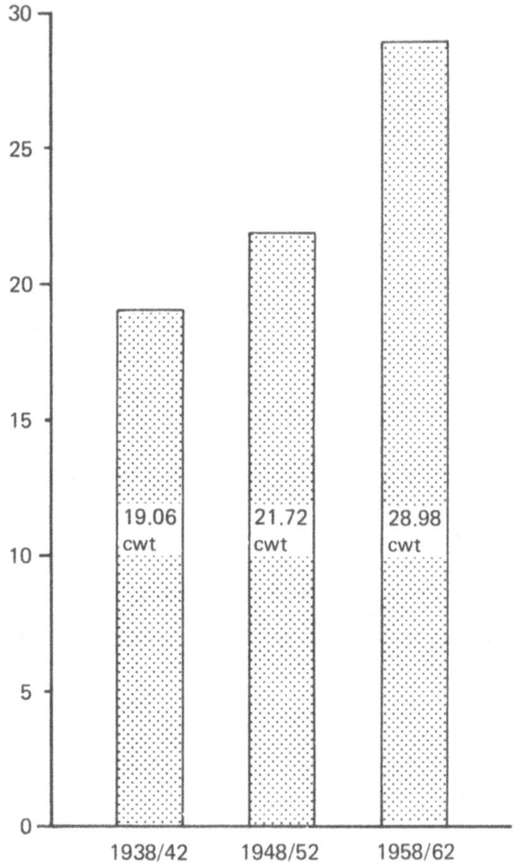

Source: Based on figures from Mitchell and Jones, *Second Abstract*

D7 United Kingdom Coal Output, 1880 – 1980 (in million tons, 1880 – 1970; million tonnes, 1970 – 80)

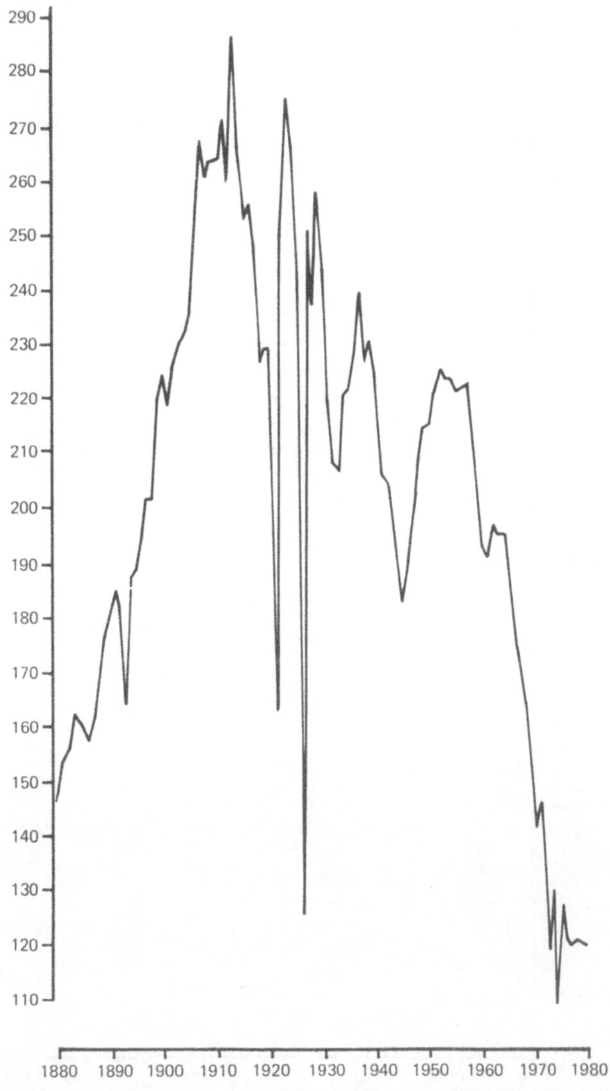

Source: Based on figures from Mitchell and Deane, *British Historical Statistics*; Mitchell and Jones, *Second Abstract*; *Annual Abstract of Statistics* (HMSO, 1972 and 1981); *United Kingdom in Figures, 1982* (HMSO, 1982)

D8 Electricity Generated in Great Britain, 1920 – 80 (in millions of kilowatthows)

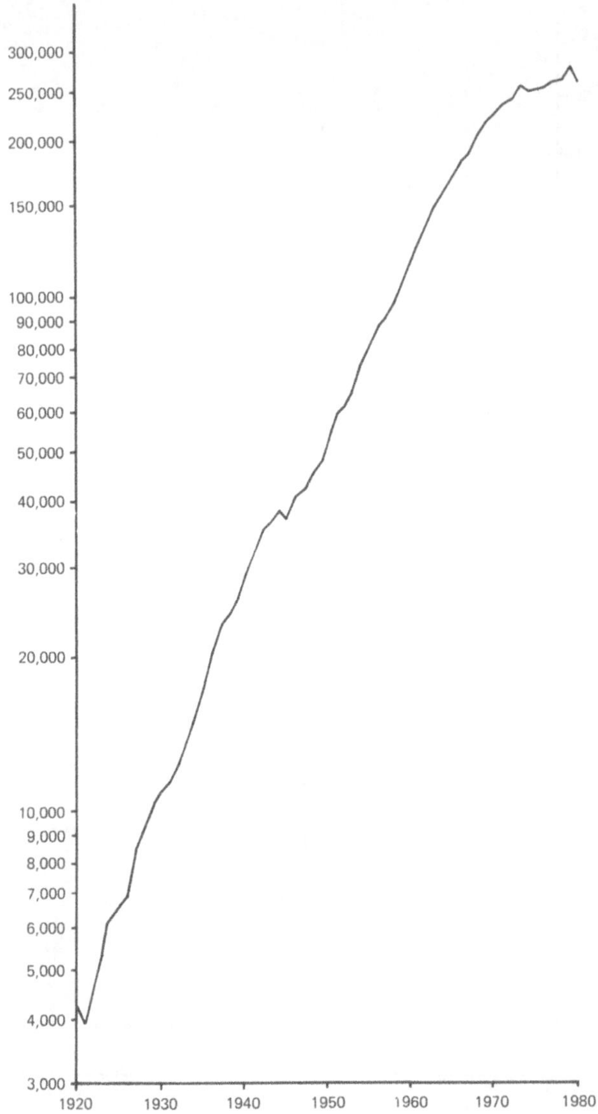

Source: Based on figures from Mitchell and Jones, *Second Abstract*; *Annual Abstract of Statistics* (HMSO, 1972 and 1981); *Monthly Digest of Statistics* (HMSO, July 1981)

D9 Crude Steel Production, 1880 – 1979

Annual averages	Thousand tons
1880/84	1793
1885/89	2814
1890/94	3143
1895/99	4260
1900/04	4955
1905/09	5995
1910/14	7026
1915/19	8938
1920/24	7067
1925/29	7647
1930/34	6733
1935/39	11649
1940/44	12680
1945/49	13535
1950/54	16896
1955/59	20380
1960/64	23126
1965/69	25580
1970/74	25331
1975/79	20912

Source: Based on figures from Mitchell and Deane, *British Historical Statistics*; Mitchell and Jones, *Second Abstract*; *Annual Abstract of Statistics* (HMSO, 1972 and 1981)

D10 Acid and Basic Steel Made by the Bessemer and Open Hearth Processes: 1889, 1913, 1938.

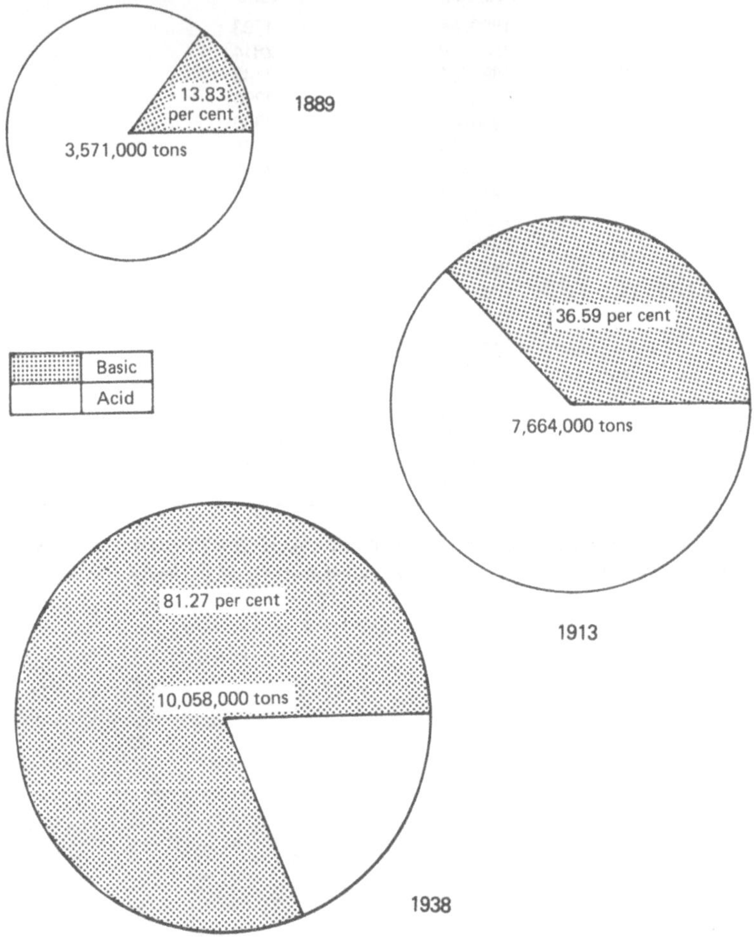

Source: Based on figures from Mitchell and Deane, *British Historical Statistics*

D11 Shipbuilding, 1880 – 1980 (million gross tons completed per annum).

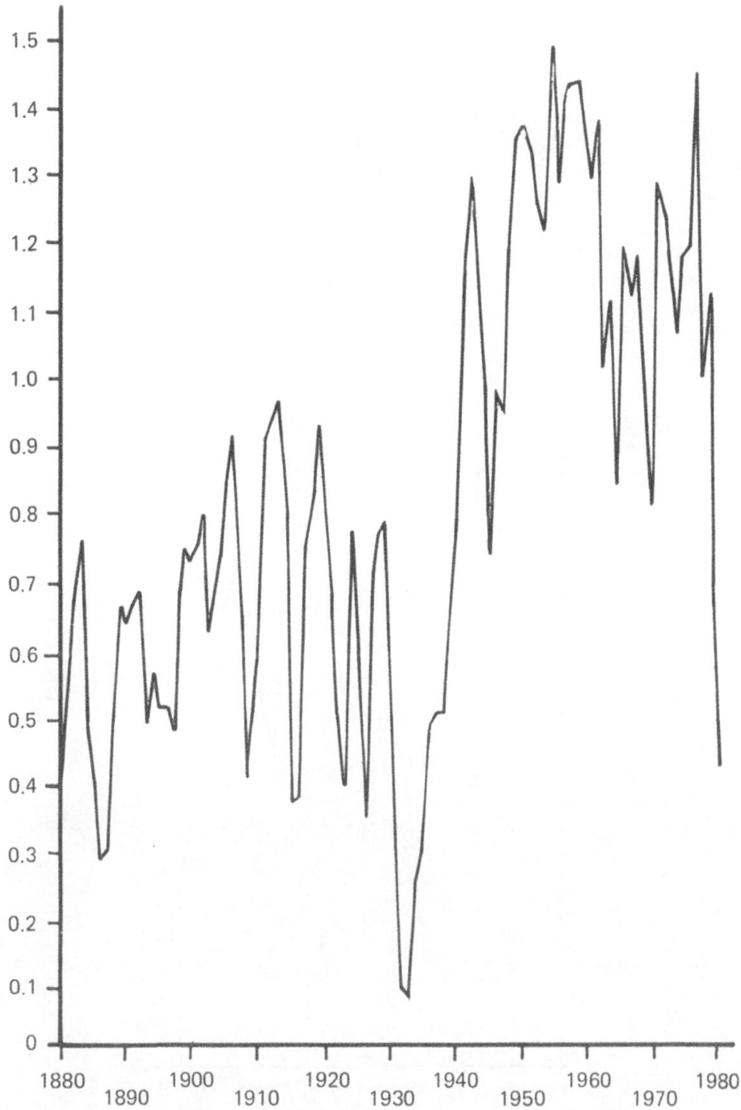

Source: Based on figures from Mitchell and Deane, *British Historical Statistics*; Mitchell and Jones, *Second Abstract*; *Annual Abstract of Statistics* (HMSO, 1972 and 1981)

D12 Exports of Cotton Manufactures, 1880 – 1971 (in millions of linear yards, 1880 – 1939; millions of square yards, 1938 – 71)

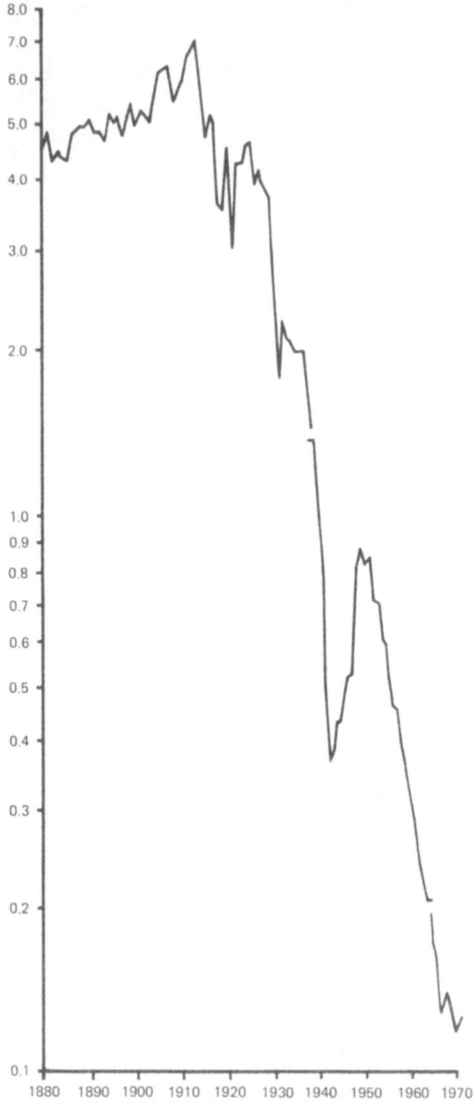

Source: Based on figures from Mitchell and Deane, *British Historical Statistics*; Mitchell and Jones, *Second Abstract*; *Annual Abstract of Statistics* (HMSO, 1972)

D13 Housing Completions in Great Britain, 1880 – 1980
(thousands)

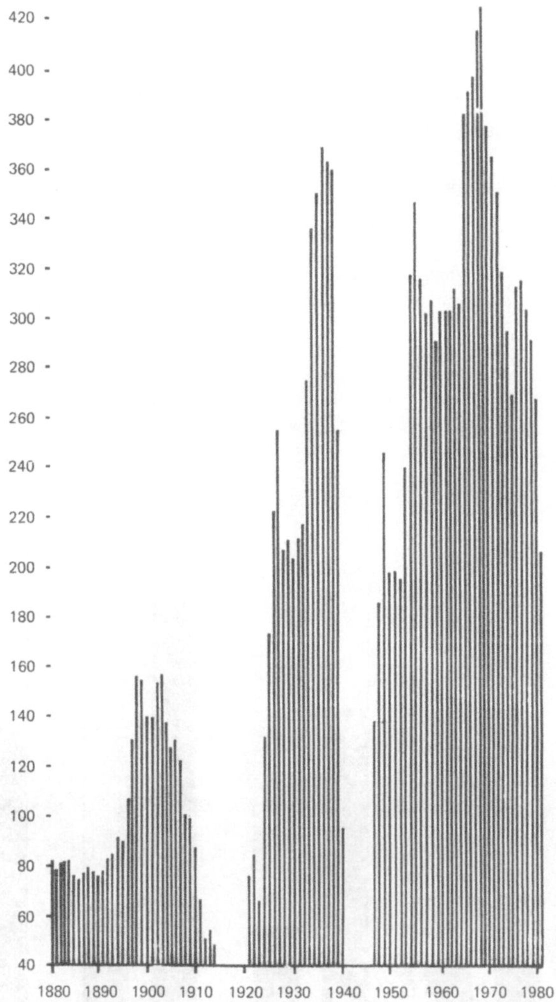

Source: Based on figures from Mitchell and Deane, *British Historical Statistics*; the London and Cambridge Economic Service, *British Economy*; the Central Statistical Office; *Economic Trends*, December 1980 (HMSO, 1980); United Kingdom in Figures, 1982 (HMSO, 1982)

D14 Motor Vehicle Production and Exports, 1946/50 – 1976/80
(average per annum in selected five-year periods)

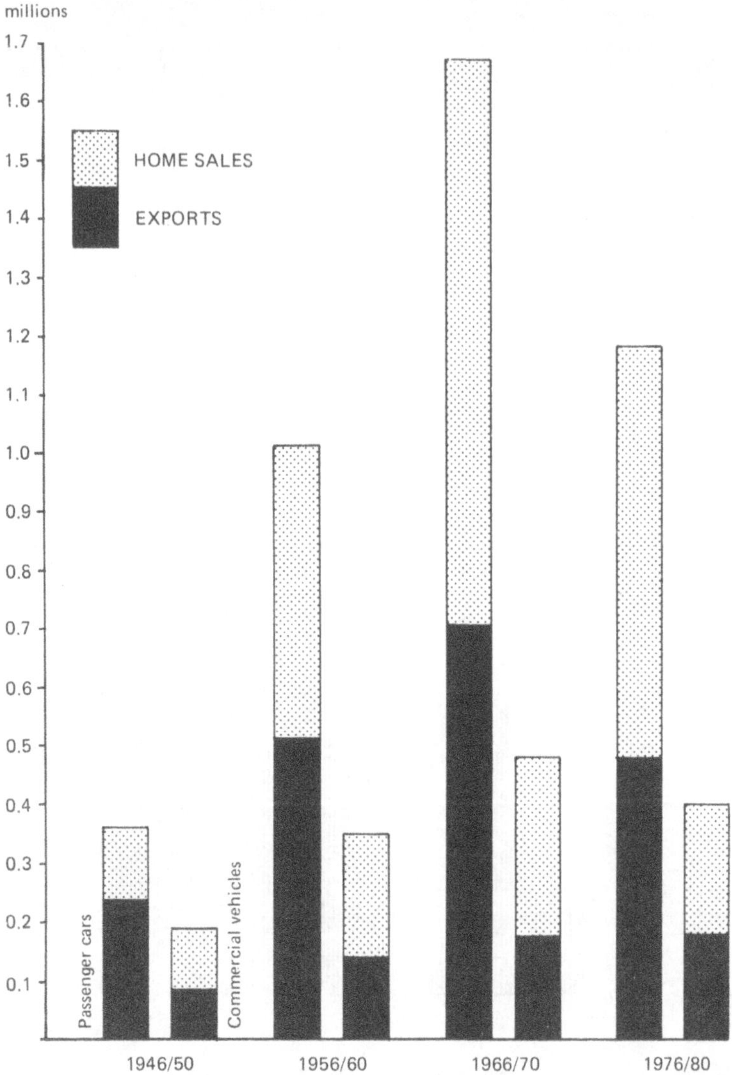

Source: Based on figures from *Economic Trends*, Annual Supplement 1981 and May 1982 (HMSO 1981 and 1982)

SOME FURTHER READING

Books Relevant to All Sections

T. C. Barker and C. Savage, *An Economic History of Transport in Britain* (1974)
N. Buxton, *The Economic Development of the British Coal Industry* (1978)
P. Deane and W. A. Cole, *British Economic Growth, 1688–1959* (1969)
R. Floud and D. McCloskey (eds.), *The Economic History of Britain since 1700*, Vol. II, *1860 to the 1970s* (1981)
E. J. Hobsbawm, *Industry and Empire* (1968)
M. W. Kirby, *The Decline of British Economic Power since 1870* (1981)
C. H. Lee, *Regional Economic Growth in the United Kingdom since the 1880s* (1971)
R. C. O. Matthews, C. H. Feinstein and J. C. Odling Smee, *British Economic Growth, 1856–1973* (1982)
A. E. Musson, *The Growth of British Industry* (1978)
M. J. Wiener, *English Culture and the Decline of the Industrial Spirit, 1850–1980* (1981)

Books Relevant to Section A

D. H. Aldcroft (ed.), *The Development of British Industry and Foreign Competition, 1875–1914* (1968)
F. Crouzet, *The Victorian Economy* (1982)
R. Floud, *The British Machine Tool Industry, 1850–1914* (1976)
A. R. Hall (ed.), *The Export of Capital from Great Britain, 1870–1914* (1968)
D. N. M. Closkey, *Economic Maturity and Economic Decline: British Iron and Steel, 1870–1913* (1973)
D. N. McCloskey (ed.), *Enterprise and Trade in Victorian Britain* (1981)
D. N. McCloskey (ed.), *Essays on a Mature Economy: Britain after 1840* (1971)

P. L. Perry, *British Farming in the Great Depression, 1870–1914* (1974)
G. Roderick and M. Stephens, *Education and Industry in the Nineteenth Century: the English Disease?* (1978)
L. Sandberg, *Lancashire in Decline* (1974)
S. B. Saul, *Studies in British Overseas Trade, 1870–1914* (1960)
S. B. Saul, *The Myth of the Great Depression, 1873–1896* (1969)

Books Relevant to Sections A and B

D. H. Aldcroft and H. Richardson, *The British Economy, 1870–1939* (1969)
W. Ashworth, *An Economic History of England, 1870–1939* (1960)
G. M. Holmes, *Britain and America: a Comparative Economic History, 1850–1939* (1976)
P. Mathias, *The First Industrial Nation* (1969)
B. R. Mitchell and P. Deane, *An Abstract of British Historical Statistics* (1962)
R. Sayers, *A History of Economic Change in England, 1880–1939* (1967)
J. Tomlinson, *Problems of British Economic Policy, 1870–1945* (1981)

Books Relevant to Section B

D. H. Aldcroft, *The Inter-war Economy: Britain, 1919–1939* (1970)
D. H. Aldcroft and H. W. Richardson, *Building in the British Economy Between the Wars* (1968)
B. W. E. Alford, *Depression and Recovery? British Economic Growth, 1918–1939* (1972)
N. Buxton and D. H. Aldcroft (eds.), *British Industry Between the Wars* (1979)
S. Glynn and J. Oxborrow, *Inter-war Britain: a Social and Economic History* (1976)
S. Pollard (ed.), *The Gold Standard and Employment Policies Between the Wars* (1970)
H. W. Richardson, *Economic Recovery in Britain, 1932–39* (1967)

Books Relevant to Sections B and C

D. H. Aldcroft, *Britain's Railways in Transition: The Economic Problems of Britain's Railways since 1914* (1968)

D. H. Aldcroft, *The European Economy, 1914 – 1970* (1977)

C. M. Law, *British Regional Development since World War I* (1980)

A. S. Milward, *The Economic Effects of the World Wars on Britain* (1970)

B. R. Mitchell and H. G. Jones, *A Second Abstract of British Historical Statistics* (1971)

G. A. Phillips and R. T. Maddock, *The Growth of the British Economy, 1918 – 1968* (1973)

S. Pollard, *The Development of the British Economy, 1914 – 1980* (1983)

A. Youngson, *British Economic Growth, 1920 – 1966* (1968)

Books Relevant to Section C

W. Hancock and M. Gowing, *The British War Economy* (1949)

P. Maunder (ed.), *The British Economy in the 1970s* (1980)

M. M. Postan, *British War Production* (1952)

G. Roderick and M. Stephens (eds.), *The British Malaise: Industrial Performance, Education and Training in Britain Today* (1982)

G. D. N. Worswick and P. H. Ady (eds.), *The British Economy, 1945 – 1950* (1952)

G. D. N. Worswick and P. H. Ady (eds.), *The British Economy in the 1950s* (1962)

J. F. Wright, *Britain in the Age of Economic Management* (1979)

INDEX

For Product Safety Concerns and Information please contact our EU representative GPSR@taylorandfrancis.com Taylor & Francis Verlag GmbH, Kaufingerstraße 24, 80331 München, Germany